Automotive MACHINING

A GUIDE TO BORING, DECKING, HONING AND MORE

Mike Mavrigian

CarTech®

CarTech®

CarTech®, Inc.
838 Lake Street South
Forest Lake, MN 55025
Phone: 651-277-1200 or 800-551-4754
Fax: 651-277-1203
www.cartechbooks.com

© 2017 by Mike Mavrigian

All rights reserved. No part of this publication may be reproduced or utilized in any form or by any means, electronic or mechanical, including photocopying, recording, or by any information storage and retrieval system, without prior permission from the Publisher. All text, photographs, and artwork are the property of the Author unless otherwise noted or credited.

The information in this work is true and complete to the best of the knowledge. However, all information is presented without any guarantee on the part of the Author or Publisher, who also disclaim any liability incurred in connection with the use of the information and any implied warranties of merchantability or fitness for a particular purpose. Readers are responsible for taking suitable and appropriate safety measures when performing any of the operations or activities described in this work.

All trademarks, trade names, model names and numbers, and other product designations referred to herein are the property of their respective owners and are used solely for identification purposes. This work is a publication of CarTech, Inc., and has not been licensed, approved, sponsored, or endorsed by any other person or entity. The Publisher is not associated with any product, service, or vendor mentioned in this book, and does not endorse the products or services of any vendor mentioned in this book.

Edit by Paul Johnson
Layout by Monica Seiberlich

ISBN 978-1-61325-717-3
Item No. SA378P

Library of Congress Cataloging-in-Publication Data

Names: Mavrigian, Mike, author.
Title: Automotive machining / Mike Mavrigian.
Description: Forest Lake, MN : Cartech, [2017]
Identifiers: LCCN 2016040480 | ISBN 9781613252833
Subjects: LCSH: Automobiles--Motors--Maintenance and repair. | Automobiles--Motors--Modification.
Classification: LCC TL210 .M3448 2017 | DDC 629.25/040288--dc23
LC record available at https://lccn.loc.gov/2016040480

Written, edited, and designed in the U.S.A.
Printed in the U.S.A.

Title Page:
Valveseats may be ground with an abrasive stone or cut with seat cutters. Cutters provide a more precise finish.

Back Cover Photos

Top:
With a deck plate installed and torqued, honing with the appropriate grade of stones begins. To reduce the effect of heat transfer between cylinders, bores are honed in an alternating manner. Cooling liquid is constantly applied during all stages of honing. This transfers heat from the block and aids in keeping the honing stones clean.

Middle Left:
After a bore gauge has been set up to match the crank main journal diameter, the gauge is inserted into the installed main bearing to determine the bearing ID relative to the crank main journal.

Middle Right:
The piston dome is receiving a custom dome profile on a CNC lathe.

Bottom:
This example shows a 4-barrel single plane intake manifold is mounted via a fixture plate, ready to be custom ported. Machining at a variety of angles is possible, since both the head and base move in various axes, achieving intricate cuts at varying angles. (Photo Courtesy Centroid)

CONTENTS

Acknowledgments 4
Introduction 4

Chapter 1: Engine Component Cleaning 6
Airless Shot Blasters 6
Hot Tank Cleaning 6
Jet Spray Cabinets 7
Cold Solvent Wash 7
Ovens 8
Soap and Water 8
Media Blasting 9
Soda Cabinet Blasting 12
Blasting Media 12
Tumbling and Vibratory Cleaning ...13
Ultrasonic Cleaning 14
Cleaning with Hand and
  Power Tools 14

Chapter 2: Precision Measurement Tools 15
Micrometer 15
Dial Indicator 18
Dial Bore Gauge 20
Mounting a Bore Gauge
  with a Setting Fixture 21
Depth Gauge 22
Internal Caliper Gauge 23
Measuring Pushrod Length 23
Valvespring Height Gauge 24
Valveseat Runout Gauge 24
Precision Straightedge 24
Rod Bolt Stretch Gauge 25
Torque-Plus-Angle 27
Ultrasonic Thickness Gauge 27
Torque Wrenches 28
Cam Lobe Checker 31

Chapter 3: Cylinder Block Disassembly and Inspection 32
Step by Step 32
Block Inspection 35
Crankshaft Inspection 38
Rod Inspection 39
Cam Inspection 39
Pushrod Inspection 40
Rocker Arm Inspection 40
Cylinder Head Inspection 40

Chapter 4: Cylinder Block Machining 45
Rough Edge and Obstruction
  Deburring 45
Main Bore Align Honing 45
Cylinder Boring and Honing 50
Cylinder Sleeving 54
Lifter Bore Honing and Bushings ...56
Block Deck Resurfacing 56
Threaded Hole Preparation 61
Block Blueprinting 61

Chapter 5: Crankshaft Measurement, Grinding and Preparation 64
Measuring the Crankshaft 64
Selecting the Grinding Wheel 66
Dressing the Wheel 67
Straightening the Crank 68
Grinding and Polishing the Journals...68
Grinding the Flywheel 71

Chapter 6: Connecting Rod Inspection and Reconditioning 72
Inspecting Connecting Rods 72
Measuring Rod Bore Diameter 73
Measuring Center-to-Center Length..73
Checking for Bend and Twist 74
Reconditioning Connecting Rods ...74

Chapter 7: Pushrods and Lifters 82
Measuring for Pushrod Length 84

Chapter 8: Pistons 89
Measuring Piston Skirts 89
Checking Ring-to-Piston Fit 90
Modifying Domes 90
Checking Valve-to-Piston
  Clearance 94
File Fitting Rings 96

Chapter 9: Cylinder Head Inspection, Service and Machining 99
Resurfacing the Deck 101
Measuring Chamber Volume 102
Installing New Guide Liners 104
Refacing Valves and Seats 104
Measuring Valvespring Height 109
Measuring Valvestem Height 109
Checking Spring Pressure 110
Porting Cylinder Heads 110
Final Assembly 111

Chapter 10: Engine Block CNC Machining 112
Milling the Block 113
CNC Terminology 117

Chapter 11: Port Machining 120
Ports and Runners 120
Verifying and Monitoring
  with a Flow Bench 122
Port Matching 123
Intake Manifold Plenums 127
Intake Port Surface 127
Extrusion Honing 127

Chapter 12: Engine Balancing 128
Out-of-Balance Forces
  on the Crank 129
Connecting Rods 131
Pistons 135
Engine Styles 137
Bobweights 138
4-Cylinder Inline Engines 141
Crankshaft 141
Under- versus Over-Balancing 146
External versus Internal Balancing....146
Dampeners and Flywheels 146

Chapter 13: Clearance Checking ...149
Main Bearings 149
Rod Bearings 150
Cam Bearings 150
Cam Thrust 151
Piston-to-Wall Clearance 151
Rod Sideplay 152
Lifter Bore 152
Crank-to-Block Clearance 153
Rod-to-Block Clearance 154
Piston Ring Gap 155
Crank Thrust 156
Valve-to-Piston Clearance 157

Chapter 14: Final Assembly 159
Cleaning 159
Cam 160
Upper Main Bearings 161
Crankshaft and Rear Seal 161
Main Caps and Lower Bearings ...162
Pistons and Rods 164
Timing 168
Oil Pump and Pickup 169
Lifters 170
Heads 170
Pushrods and Rocker Arms 172
Intake Manifold 173
Distributor 174
Timing Cover, Rear Cover,
  Oil Pan and Valvecovers 175
Water Pump 176
Crankshaft Balancer 176

ACKNOWLEDGMENTS

Thanks to the following for their participation and help in the completion of this book: Bill McKnight, MAHLE; Dave Monyhan, Goodson Tools; Scott Gressman, Gressman Powersports, Jody Holtrey, Medina Mountain Motors; Tony Lombardi, Ross Racing Engines; Ron Rotunno, Fel-Pro; Anthony Usher, Rottler Equipment; Sean Crawford and Sebastian Franzen, JE Pistons; Chris Raschke and Zac Kimball, ARP; Bob Davis, Sunnen; Joe and Tammy Baker, Baker Equipment; Roger Carvalho, Winona Van Norman; Dave Metchkoff, LA Sleeve; Bob Fall, Fall Automotive Machine; Dave Johnson, R&R Engine and Machine; Jim Rickoff and Steve Fox, AERA; Charlie Fisher, Fisher Racing Engines; Brian Carruth, Trick Flow; Bob Fall, Fall Automotive Machine; Scott Koffel, Koffel's Place; Mike Anderson, DCM Tech; Martin Freund, Peterson Machine Tool/Viking Corp.; Keith McCulloch, Centroid CNC; Rick Martin, Kennemetal Extrude Hone; and Fox Lake Racing Cylinder Heads.

INTRODUCTION

As an engine builder, you need machine shop services for a stock rebuild, modified, or high-performance engine. Whether you're an avid enthusiast or considering machining as a profession, this volume covers all critical operations of engine machining, so you have a clear understanding of the process and how to perform certain procedures yourself.

Although professionals are often required to perform automotive machining processes, it does not preclude the avid enthusiast from performing some machining and being closely involved in the machining process during an engine rebuild or high-perfomance build.

A typical automotive machine shop contains hundreds of thousands of dollars of machining equipment. Even a hard-core consumer cannot afford, nor is it practical, to buy this equipment. As a consequence, an at-home engine builder needs to contract a qualified machine shop for engine machining services. If you're investing thousands of dollars in an engine build, you need to thoroughly understand these engine machining procedures, so you can guide the process and confirm that the correct results have been achieved. When your head, block, intake manifolds, and many other parts have been machined, you need to inspect, measure, and verify that the components are to specification.

Once all machining is complete, the assembly will be performed either by you or the machine shop. These critical components need to precisely fit together. The tolerances between components is exacting and

INTRODUCTION

can be as little as .0001 inch. It is incumbent upon you to invest in a set of tools to measure and verify the work that has been performed. This includes a C-clamp micrometer, caliper micrometer, dial indicator, dial bore gauge, bore gauge fixture, depth gauge, feeler gauge, pushrod measurement tool, machinist's straightedge, torque wrench, torque plus angle gauge, ultrasonic tester, and other specialty tools and materials for engine building. With these tools, you are able to analyze and evaluate the machine shop work. Equally as important, these tools provide the means to take critical measurements during engine assembly. As a result, you are able to assemble the engine with precision, and this helps ensure that you have a strong-running and reliable engine.

The information provided in this book is intended both for the aspiring engine machinist and the performance consumer. It provides valuable insight into the processes involved in engine machining and assembly. You are given a complete tour of machining necessary for a typical engine build, and beyond that, you are shown the steps to machine engine parts for a build. All the parts of the engine must be compatible and complementary; a certain set of parts requires precise machining so the engine can operate as designed.

In many cases, an engine builder starts with a thoroughly used and tired engine that's in need of a rebuild. In this book, you are instructed how to properly clean all engine components using bead blaster, soda blasting, chemical, and ultrasonic cleaning methods. You're shown how to inspect and evaluate the engine block to ensure that it's a worthy rebuilding candidate. In addition, you learn about the inspection of all components in the engine, so you can identify past problems, current solutions, and determine which parts are worth saving and which ones are not.

When it comes to block machining, main bore aligning, cylinder and cam tunnel honing, and boring are covered. Cylinder sleeving is often required in the engine building process, and that is also revealed. Truing the surfaces of the block deck ensures a seal between the block and the heads. A crankshaft is subjected to all kinds of opposing loads and as it accumulates hours of operation, it can bend, the journals can wear, and suffer other problems.

Measuring, machining, and other parts of crankshaft preparation are covered in detail. Connecting rods are the highest stressed components in an engine, and therefore, if yours are to be reused, they must be thoroughly inspected and properly reconditioned. In particular, the selection and installation of the connecting rod bolts must be done correctly to ensure that there is no failure because a connecting rod failure will likely destroy the entire engine.

You are shown how to install guides, machine and install valveseats, true the deck surface, measure the combustion chambers, and all the other critical steps to returning heads to their full health. Pistons and rings must be properly fitted to the bore of a particular engine block, so the process for fitting the ring to the cylinder and ring filing is covered.

Chapters provide information on rotating assembly balancing, blueprinting, clearance checking, CNC machining, port matching, pushrods, connecting rods, and more. Also included is an overview of final engine assembly tips.

With this comprehensive volume, you will be able to disassemble, inspect, and evaluate the engine components. And with this information, you will be able to make the best high-performance building and engine rebuild decisions, so you ultimately have the best engine to suit your needs. Once the machining has been performed, you will be able to take all the parts, properly fit them, and conduct a professional-caliber final assembly.

CHAPTER 1

ENGINE COMPONENT CLEANING

Prior to test fitting and/or final engine assembly, cleanliness is absolutely critical. This includes every component involved (block, crankshaft, connecting rods, pistons, camshaft, timing system, oil pump and pickup, oil pan, valvecovers, intake manifold, cylinder heads, rockers, pushrods, lifters, timing cover, etc.). There is no such thing as "too clean."

A variety of cleaning methods are available, depending on the application. These include hot tanks, spray cabinets, ovens, airless shot blasting, cabinet media blasting, tumbling, and manual cleaning involving hand or power tools.

Airless Shot Blasters

An airless shot blaster cabinet uses a high-speed impeller that blasts steel shot at the parts as the parts slowly rotate in a cage. This machine does not use compressed air. The steel (or stainless steel) shot is about .030 inch in diameter. After the part has been blasted, the part must then be tumbled in a large tumbling drum to remove any remaining shot. Airless blasting with steel shot is intended for cast-iron parts only and should not be used on softer aluminum parts. Components may only be airless shot blasted after they have been degreased and are thoroughly dry.

Hot Tank Cleaning

Solvents heated at approximately 170 degrees F break down contaminants faster than room-temperature solvents. However, solvents must be chosen carefully to be compatible with ferrous (steel or iron) or nonferrous (alloys) components. After a part has been cleaned in a hot tank, it must be rinsed in hot water and then blow-dried. At this point, steel or cast-iron surfaces tend to surface rust very quickly, so application

An airless shot blaster slings steel (or stainless steel) shot onto the block or cylinder heads as the part is rotated while secured in an adjustable cage. Compressed air is not used. Following shot blasting, the part must be tumbled in a rubber-lined drum to shake any remaining steel shot from the part.

ENGINE COMPONENT CLEANING

of a rust inhibitor is required as soon as possible. Hot tanks are available in various types, including hot-soak and hot-soak with agitation and spray jets.

Jet Spray Cabinets

A "jet" spray machine uses heated solvent and a series of high-pressure spray nozzles. The parts being cleaned are secured in a cage or appropriate mount, on a turntable. The part is rotated during the wash and rinse cycle. Liquids, depending on the application, can include hot water and/or solvents appropriate for the material being cleaned. High-caustic solvents may be appropriate for steel or cast-iron; a detergent-based cleaner is best for aluminum parts.

Cold Solvent Wash

Commonly available parts washers that use a cold (unheated) solvent are useful for degreasing smaller parts such as connecting rods, pistons, camshafts, etc., but this requires allowing the parts to soak and then be hand-brushed or scraped to remove grease and other solvent-soluble contaminants. However, since no pressure is involved, this may or may not remove contaminants from blind holes or passages. Also, this process is

---

Threaded Holes

Regardless of the cleaning method, all threaded holes in the engine block should be inspected and cleaned. Be sure to clean all threaded bolt holes and give special attention to the cylinder head deck and main cap threaded holes. Using a rifle-style bristle brush, scrub all female threaded holes. To make sure that threads are in good condition, and to remove any contaminants/debris, it's a good idea to run a chasing tap through all threaded holes.

Do not confuse this with a cutting tap. Common cutting taps tend to remove metal, which is to be avoided. Chasing taps are specially designed to both clean and re-form existing threads without removing excess material. Especially for main cap bolt holes and the block's cylinder head deck bolt holes, using a chasing tap helps to ensure that the threads are clean while retaining the necessary strength and integrity.

Scrub the block exterior with a clean, soft brush soaked in hot water and Dawn and rinse. I'm not trying to promote the brand of detergent, but for some reason, Dawn seems to do the best job of removing oils and grease. When all internal and exterior surfaces have been thoroughly rinsed, blow clean compressed air through all bolt holes, passages, and exterior surfaces. At this point, when the block is dry, immediately apply a thin coating of clean engine oil to main saddles, lifter bores, and cylinder bores to prevent surface rusting. Cast-iron blocks tend to oxidize (surface rust) very quickly when clean and dry, so this is a good time to mask and paint the block exterior. If the part is not to be painted, apply a thin coat of a rust inhibitor to all surfaces, especially if the part is stored for a while prior to assembly.

All threaded holes in a block should be chased to ensure cleanliness and thread condition. Here, a block's cylinder head deck hole is being chased. Drive the tap with a hand driver only. A variety of sizes is needed to cover all holes. The most critical threaded holes include the block's head deck holes and the main cap holes.

A hot jet spray wash is commonly used to clean blocks, cylinder heads, crankshafts, and more. The table rotates as high-pressure heated solvent or detergent is sprayed.

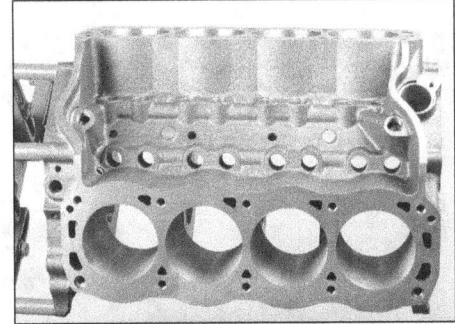

This block has been oven cleaned, tumbled, and washed in a jet spray cabinet to a like-new finish.

AUTOMOTIVE MACHINING: A GUIDE TO BORING, DECKING, HONING AND MORE

time-consuming and is not generally used in an engine builder's shop.

Ovens

Often referred to as thermal cleaning, a dedicated oven can be used to degrease an engine block or cylinder heads. A dedicated cleaning oven "cooks" the component, turning grease, oils, paint, and other contaminants to ash. The component is initially heated to about 375 degrees F to cook off surface vapors, which are then oxidized in a separate chamber at about 1,300 degrees F. The oven's primary chamber then rises to a higher preselected temperature of about 600 to 700 degrees F, for steel or cast-iron components. When the cleaning cycle is complete, which usually takes about three hours or so, all sludge contaminants have been reduced to easily disposable ash. After the component has cooled, it is then washed/rinsed in a hot tank to remove remaining particles.

Aluminum components require more care because extreme temperatures can result in distortion. Typically, aluminum castings cook at about 500 degrees F. This lower temperature also reduces the chance of valveseats and guides loosening in cylinder heads. Regardless of material (steel, iron, or aluminum), the oven temperature must drop very slowly after the cooking stage until reaching room temperature, to prevent metal distortion.

Although a hot tank accumulates sludge and requires periodic cleaning and proper disposal, the use of a cleaning oven eliminates the need to dispose of hazardous waste (sludge), making ovens a bit more environmentally acceptable.

Soap and Water

There are instances where washing/scrubbing and rinsing by hand are applicable, such as performing a final wash and rinse of an already-machined engine block prior to assembly. Using very hot water (as hot as your hands can tolerate) and Dawn dishwashing liquid can produce excellent results. With the block on a stand that allows you to rotate the block, shoot hot water

Although most cleaning ovens are designed to rotate the part during the heat cycles to evenly heat the part, some engine builders like to preheat some parts to cook off any residual oils, prior to glass bead blasting.

This Chevy big-block has been stripped down and placed into a cleaning oven. The block is secured within a tubular cage. With the cage mounted in the oven, the machine rotates the block during the thermal cleaning process to distribute heat evenly, cooking off all grease, paint, rust, and sludge.

This block has been degreased, but surface rust and some contaminants remain.

The same block has now been shot blasted and tumbled. The block is now ready for machining.

ENGINE COMPONENT CLEANING

into all oil and coolant passages, and then pour Dawn into the same passages. Using dedicated (and clean) bristle brushes that are designed for block cleaning, scrub passages as access permits; follow with multiple hot water rinses until all traces of soap are eliminated.

Media Blasting

An enclosed blast cabinet can be ideal for cleaning certain parts, such as pistons, connecting rods, mounting brackets, valvecovers, etc., but the media must be selected carefully. A variety of blasting media is available, including but not limited to "glass bead," crushed walnut shells, crushed corncobs, crushed pecan shells, plastic bead, and soda. Depending on the media, you can accomplish not only cleaning to bare metal, but also lightly deburring razor-sharp edges where desired. Never use

Here, the airless shot blasting process has been completed, resulting in a clean, down-to-bare-metal block that's ready for tumbling. After the block has cooled down in the oven, the block, still mounted in its cage, is moved to an airless steel shot blasting cabinet, which cleans off the ash created by the oven.

The cage is then disassembled and removed from the block. Using the shop's overhead crane, the caged block is removed from the shot blaster.

Finally, the block is placed into a rubber-lined tumbler drum. The drum rotates, allowing the block to tumble randomly. As the block tumbles, any remaining steel shot is knocked loose and removed from the block.

Block Cleaning Brushes

Regardless of the method of degreasing used, always clean oil and water passages with appropriate-sized bristle brushes. A long-bristle rifle brush can be used to clean oil galley passages from the front to rear of a block. Small-diameter rifle brushes can be used to clean oil passages in crankshaft main and rod journals. A dedicated-diameter, long-handled rifle brush can be used to clean camshaft bores. Very small-diameter specialty rifle brushes are also available specifically for cleaning the inside of oil-through pushrods. After brushes have been run through any passage, the passage must then be rinsed with pressurized hot water followed by blowing dry with compressed air. After you're finished with brush work, and before you store the brushes, wash all brushes with hot water and detergent and rinse with hot water to remove any contaminants from the bristles.

Cabinet Tips

Blasting cabinets are wonderful pieces of equipment to have in any shop for cleaning, deburring, and/or achieving a soft "footprint" for planned coatings. However, long-term use creates some wear issues. The viewing window (usually glass) can eventually become etched, even if you're not blasting directly into the window. Although this doesn't affect function, it makes viewing more difficult. Consider installing peel-off clear window film on the inside surface of the glass. Just like peel-off clear film that's used on many race helmet visors, as the exposed layer of film becomes etched/foggy, you simply peel off to expose the next layer, or peel off the existing layer and install a fresh layer. As an example, Goodson Tools & Shop Supplies offers these films (you can cut to fit your window) under P/N GB-FILM. The use of this protective film saves the expense and time of replacing the viewing glass.

Keep an eye on the cabinet door gasket. Especially if the cabinet is designed to open from the top (with the weight of the door continually compressing the gasket), the seal can eventually become compressed, leading to a loss of cabinet vacuum (assuming your cabinet features a vacuum pump) and external media leakage. With the cabinet door closed and matched, when you turn on the cabinet's vacuum pump, your glove arms should quickly be drawn into an extended position (as though they were being inflated). If not, you have a vacuum leak.

Blasting cabinet gloves are always an issue, especially when you're blasting smaller handheld items, where you end up blasting into the glove fingertips. Buy the highest quality gloves available to extend fingertip life (avoid the bargain imported stuff). A variety of glove styles is available, some made as one-piece (glove and arm) and some with replaceable gloves (attaching to the arm sleeve with a clamp). If you're replacing the arm sleeves (whether the arms feature integrated gloves or separate gloves), you need to order them with the appropriate port hole size so that the entry of the sleeves fits your cabinet's ports. Also, make sure that the sleeves are long enough to enable you to reach all the way to the rear of the cabinet. Short arms are annoying, forcing you to stop work and open the cabinet to retrieve an item that's out of reach.

Pay close attention to the cabinet's interior lights. Use only the type of bulb recommended by the cabinet manufacturer. The bulbs must be heavy duty, with outdoor-grade glass that's thick and withstands accidental blasting.

If you expect to rely on your blasting cabinet, keep spare consumables at the ready to avoid downtime. This includes spare light bulbs, gloves, a viewing glass, blast gun nozzle (ceramic or carbide), feed hose, hose clamps, and door seals. Preplanning avoids the need to place an emergency order from an out-of-town supplier while the cabinet sits idle.

Depending on the location of your blasting cabinet, you might consider a freestanding welding curtain that surrounds the cabinet area. Unless the cabinet is located in a separate "dirty" room, this minimizes airborne media dust that can easily scatter throughout the shop.

Prior to glass beading any part, the part should already be thoroughly degreased, removing all grease, oil, and soft sludge. Otherwise, bead sticks to these contaminants, potentially trapping bead in crevices and holes. If a cleaning oven is available, the part may be cooked for a few minutes to remove any oils prior to glass beading. ■

Glass bead blasting cabinets feature rubber gloves that allow the operator to handle and manipulate parts in the cabinet. These gloves are prone to wear and should be inspected on a routine basis. Gloves are available in various sleeve diameters and lengths to accommodate all blasting cabinet models. A blasting cabinet features a glass viewing window. The inside surface of the glass eventually becomes abraded, making it difficult to see through. Depending on how much use the cabinet sees, plan to replace the glass about once each year.

ENGINE COMPONENT CLEANING

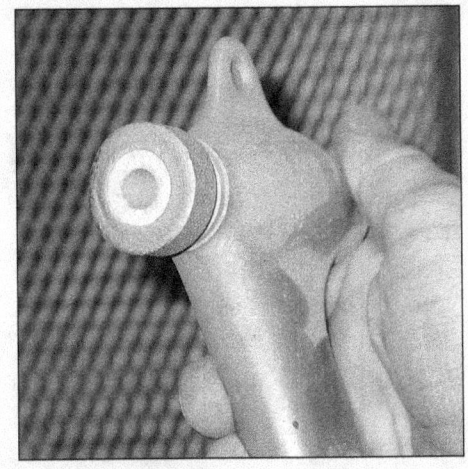

Blasting cabinet guns feature a ceramic nozzle that provides the appropriate media spray pattern. The ceramic nozzles, although very hard, eventually wear, lowering media blasting efficiency. Nozzles are easily replaced. It's wise to keep a few new spares handy.

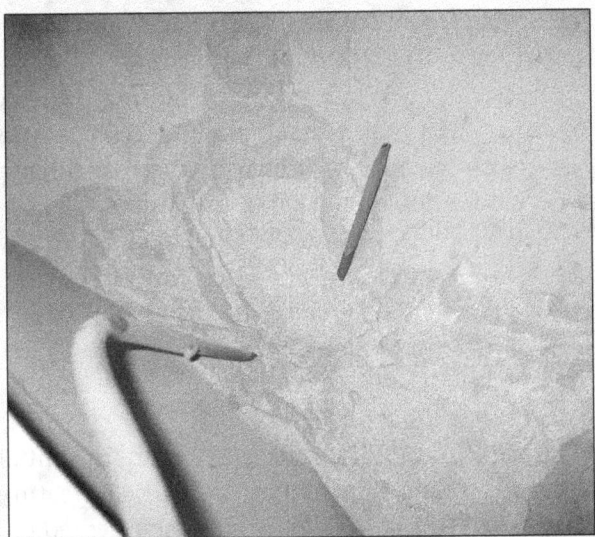

A view of a hopper in a glass bead cabinet. Depending on the cabinet's hopper design, media may start to build up on the tapered walls. In conjunction with airborne moisture absorption, the media is less able to accumulate over the media feed tube. Keeping the hopper full with the required level of fresh media helps to avoid this.

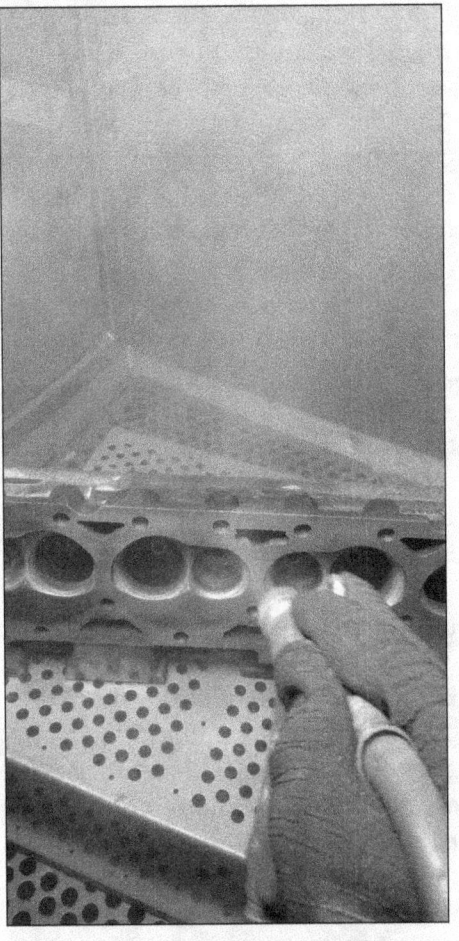

Maintaining a blast cabinet's clear viewing glass and adequate dust vacuum improves worker visibility.

a high-abrasive media such as sand, which is simply far too aggressive. If an abrasive media is used, such as glass bead, the component must be thoroughly and carefully washed and rinsed afterward to remove all bead particles. For that reason, it is not wise to glass bead blast an item such as an intake manifold, because the possibility of particles being trapped inside runners is too great.

If the part to be cleaned features hidden passages that cannot be positively cleaned, avoid blasting with an abrasive media. Also, avoid bead blasting into female threaded holes, since beads can be trapped, and the abrasive action can degrade the thread integrity. After bead blasting, use compressed air to flush all traces of the bead particles. Do not try to initially remove bead particles with a wet rinse, as this can easily cause beads to be stuck to surfaces, possibly in small clumps inside any passages. Also, never use an abrasive media on a part that is wet or features oil or grease. The part must be degreased, rinsed, and dried prior to blasting.

Concerns about potentially contaminating threaded holes with media can be avoided by plugging these holes with temporary bolts. After bead blasting, remove the bolts and manually clean female threaded holes with a chaser tap and solvent. I discuss the use of chaser taps later in this chapter.

Soda (sodium bicarbonate, essentially a form of baking soda) is a nice choice, since it's water soluble and allows easier removal via rinsing. Soda's benefits include being able to clean even surfaces that are still contaminated with oil or grease. Soda does a great job of cleaning, but it does not allow you to soften sharp edges because it's not as aggressive as other media such as glass bead. Although soda might be usable in a conventional blast cabinet, it's best to use a blast system that is designed for soda for highest efficiency and dust reclamation.

Soda Cabinet Blasting

There are distinct advantages to the use of soda, instead of traditional methods using glass bead or plastic. Unlike these other medias, soda easily removes surface grease and oil residue, as well as paint, eliminating the need for a precleaning step. One distinct benefit relates to cleaning an intake manifold (especially a dual-plane-style manifold). The danger when using glass bead (or other abrasive media) lies in the concern for particulates becoming trapped inside hidden/hard-to-reach runner areas, which could lead to disastrous results in a running engine. Because soda is water soluble, entrapment is avoided with a simple water rinse. Any particles that might remain don't pose an abrasion danger (because they're not hard abrasive particles) and effectively break down during engine operation.

Benefits of Soda Blasting
- Soda is granular, suitable for use in pressure pots or in cabinet systems.
- Soda crystals are sharp and provide outstanding cleaning/stripping performance when delivered under relatively low pressure but with high velocity.
- Soda is "friable," meaning that it fractures into smaller particles. This increases cleaning performance while softening blasting impact. Unlike other blast media, soda is relatively soft and doesn't damage metal surfaces.
- Soda is nontoxic and nonhazardous, with a nearly benign pH of 8.2.
- Soda is water soluble and easy to rinse clean.
- Soda leaves no abrasive "grit" that can damage moving parts.

Blasting Media

A wide range of blasting media is available, each with its own characteristics. Depending on the material to be blasted, including cast-iron, cast-aluminum, steel, etc., and type of component including blocks, heads, manifolds, pistons, connecting rods, etc., and the desired surface finish, attention must be paid to selecting the appropriate type of media for the specific application.

Sand
Commonly available silica sand is far too aggressive and should never be used on any engine-related surfaces. This is often used on car components, body panels, frame rails, and suspension parts. But sand is so abrasive that it literally eats away at soft aluminum, pits cast-iron, and does irreparable harm to other steel parts.

Glass Bead
Depending on the specific grade (grit), glass bead media is produced as preformed tiny balls, which, depending on the grade of glass, produce a smoother and "brighter" finish than angular abrasives (results in a matte satin finish). Glass bead, like most blasting media (other than soda), does not act as a desiccant, so the component must be dry and grease-free prior to blasting. Grease, oil, etc., are eventually removed during blasting, but over the long haul, you end up contaminating the glass bead in the hopper. The same applies to layers of paint that flake off easily. Large flakes (larger than, say, your little fingernail) collect in the hopper and eventually clog the feed tube. When/if this occurs, a quick fix is to place the tip of a bolt into the gun nozzle and hit the foot pedal. This causes the bead to "back-flush," temporarily clearing the system for continued use. Regardless, glass bead or any blast media should be routinely changed to remove foreign contaminants and to renew the capabilities of the media.

What most people don't realize is that a huge range of glass bead is available, from very, very aggressive down to ultra-fine grades. All glass bead is not created equal, so pay attention to what you're buying. A fine-grade glass bead produces a matte satin finish.

Crushed Glass Grit
Similar to glass bead in initial appearance, but the particles feature random shapes and sharper edges. This cuts faster and is more aggressive than glass bead, and produces a medium texture.

Soda
Unlike hard and aggressive media such as sand, baking soda (sodium bicarbonate) is able to strip to bare metal without abrading the parent surface. Soda media is "softer" than other types of media and is "friable," which means that the soda crystals break down upon impact (akin to throwing a snowball against a brick wall as opposed to throwing a rock against the same wall). Essentially, soda does the job without damaging

the metal. Because soda is "softer," and because it is water soluble, it leaves no abrasive grit that can damage moving parts (such as hood or door hinges).

Soda is nontoxic and nonhazardous, making its use far safer than other abrasive or chemical stripping methods. However, dry blasting generates a great deal of dust. For this reason, it is recommended that a dust mask be used, as well as eye and hearing protection.

In addition to blasting sheet metal material for body refinishing/restoration, soda is also an outstanding choice for blast-cleaning components such as frames, suspension parts, brake parts, engine components, etc. Because no hard abrasive grit is present, components such as engine blocks, cylinder heads, intake manifolds, etc., can be cleaned and then rinsed without concern for trapping damaging grit particles.

Aluminum Oxide

Depending on blast pressure, this can be very aggressive and leaves a coarse, textured finish. It's economical, but be aware that it cuts very quickly and removes more metal. Used properly (level of blast pressure), you can avoid a too-rough finish.

Speed-Beed

This is a hybrid mix of 50- to 80-grit glass bead and 80-grit aluminum oxide. This provides faster cutting than glass bead but is not as aggressive as aluminum oxide.

Plastic Bead

Generally available in 30- to 40-grit size, plastic bead is good for removal of paint and surface rust. Plastic bead produces less blasting heat. This may be a good choice for cleaning gears, tooling, etc., because it doesn't alter dimensions, and it doesn't etch the surface.

Walnut Shell

Crushed walnut shell (aside from being biodegradable) is relatively gentle and is ideal for preserving surface micro finish while cleaning. Under controlled conditions, it's also useful for those instances where you want to remove paint topcoats but retain the primer layer. Like most media, walnut shell is available in a variety of grit, from extra coarse to extra fine.

Corncob

Corncob is even softer, good for finalizing a nice satin finish. Either walnut shell or corncob can be very effective in removing paint and rust, without eating away at the base metal. And these organic types of media are relatively cheap.

A fine grade of walnut shell or corncob doesn't remove any of the metal, it doesn't etch or scratch softer metals, and the material doesn't imbed into the metal surface. Walnut or corncob are great choices where a finer finish and retention of detail is important.

Steel Grit

A fine grade of steel grit leaves a relatively smooth finish. Steel cuts very fast and lasts longer (because it doesn't fracture, as opposed to aluminum oxide). However, steel grit will likely create more wear and tear on your blasting equipment (nozzle, pickup tube, power head, hose, etc.). It is not for delicate parts or surfaces.

Silicon Carbide

This media stays sharper and lasts longer than other types, but is aggressive and creates even faster wear of blasting equipment.

Tumbling and Vibratory Cleaning

This method involves "tumbling" immersed parts in a soup of dry or wet media, where tumbling

---

> ### A Special Note Regarding Intake Manifolds
>
> Obviously, intake manifolds (single plane or dual plane) feature intake runners. Even after careful degreasing, blasting with an abrasive media can be dangerous, especially when dealing with a dual-plane intake manifold where you don't have easy reach and access to all port surfaces. Fine media particles can embed into the material (or can be stuck in a remote piece of sludge or carbon), increasing the chance of that media eventually being sucked into the engine. If you do decide to blast an intake manifold with, for example, glass bead, you need to make absolutely certain that you eliminate any possibility of trapped particles inside the runners.
>
> If you feel the need to blast and you're worried about leaving harmful particulates behind, soda is the best choice because it's water soluble when rinsed. Even though the soda doesn't pose a threat to the engine, any rust scale, dirt, etc., that's held captive poses a serious risk. Regardless of the type of media you use, you still need to flush the runners surgically. If you do media-blast an intake manifold where you are uncertain about hidden debris, a follow-up cleaning in an ultrasonic unit along with a hot, soapy rinse/flush should remove any remaining contaminants.

CHAPTER 1

Vibratory tumblers may use either a dry or wet slurry of stones. A wet slurry is commonly used for polishing as opposed to cleaning.

or vibration treats the parts. The media can be steel, ceramic, or other material that is available in a wide variety of shapes and sizes. The type of media depends on the desired results, which can include cleaning, deburring, or polishing. Tumblers come in a range of sizes, from small to industrial-large. The parts are randomly rotated in the media mix, with contact among the media particles stripping the parts down to bare metal. Small tumblers are excellent choices for cleaning small items such as valves, valvesprings, retainers, rockers, etc. Unlike blast cleaning, there's no particle or dust cleanup required and no nasty solvents to deal with. To protect valvestems, a piece of runner tubing can be slipped over the valvestem.

Ultrasonic Cleaning

An ultrasonic cleaning system is another option for cleaning delicate parts where you want to avoid abrasives or strong chemicals. The parts are placed into a water tank, and frequencies are induced into the water to essentially vibrate particles loose. For example, this type of cleaning system is popular among shops that restore high-pressure fuel injectors for diesel engines.

Cleaning with Hand and Power Tools

In certain instances, surfaces may be cleaned of heavy buildup of paint, sludge, or carbon deposits if you don't have access to the proper shop equipment. A handheld pneumatic scaler or scraper may be used to remove heavy sludge from a block exterior. A handheld scraper or pneumatic scraper may be used to remove stubborn gasket material. A flared/flat-face wire brush may be used on a drill or pneumatic die grinder on a block exterior, on cylinder head combustion chambers. Again, this is only to remove heavy deposits.

A Roloc bristle pad powered by a drill or die grinder may also be used for these same purposes. However, never attempt to clean or prepare any critical surfaces by hand, such as cylinder head or block decks, intake manifold decks, etc. You can easily damage the surfaces by creating waviness on the decks, which then requires resurfacing to regain proper flatness. You simply cannot obtain a flat surface, because you cannot control your hand and tool pressure adequately enough. Also, do not attempt to hone cylinder bores or lifter bores with the use of a handheld tool. You aren't able to achieve a precise diameter or cylindrical uniformity.

By the way, Scotch-Brite pads, although wonderful for scuffing or cleaning some metal surfaces, have no place in an engine preparation room. The tiny fibers left over from use can easily contaminate not only the engine that you're working on, but any other engines or equipment in the same room. Whether or not you use Scotch-Brite pads during initial cleaning, never have them anywhere near the engine during assembly.

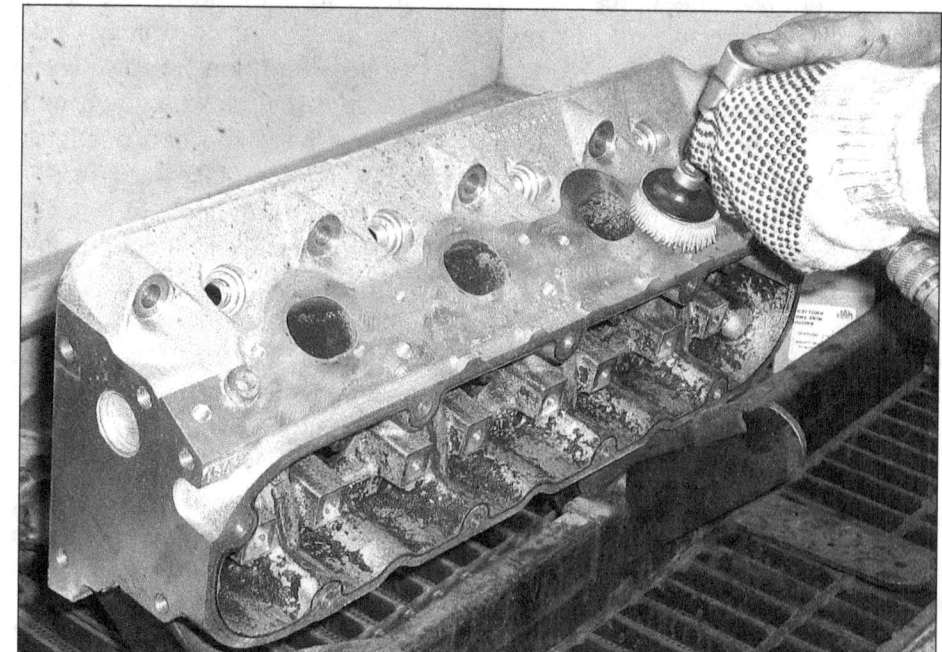

A Roloc bristle head operated with a pneumatic die grinder can be used to remove deposits from various external surfaces.

CHAPTER 2

PRECISION MEASUREMENT TOOLS

Precision measurement tools are a necessity for both machining and assembly procedures. In this chapter I discuss common precision measurement tools and systems that are used on a routine basis in any engine machining shop.

Micrometer

A micrometer is a measurement tool available in various formats, including an outside micrometer, used to measure thickness, length, or diameter; an inside micrometer, used to measure inside diameter of a hole; and depth micrometers, used to measure hole depth.

An outside micrometer features a C-clamp style frame. At the far end is a flat-faced anvil. Facing the anvil at the opposite end of the frame is a flat-faced spindle. The anvil is in a fixed position on the frame. The spindle moves as the micrometer is adjusted. The sleeve features incremented index marks and is stationary. The thimble at the far end of the grip rotates and features additional marks. A lock lever is provided to secure the adjustment in a locked position when required.

An inch-format micrometer features an internal screw drive that features 40 threads per inch. One complete revolution of the screw moves the thread 1/40, which is equal to .025 inch. Each mark on the sleeve represents .025 inch. The beveled face of the thimble has 25 equally spaced lines that each represents .001 inch.

When reading a micrometer, first note the larger lines and numbers on the sleeve, and then look at the smaller lines between the numbered lines. As an example, if the number 3 is visible on the sleeve, that means that you are measuring at least .300 inch. Let's say that three smaller lines after the number 3 are also visible. You now know that the measurement is at least .375 inch (remember that each line indicates .025 inch, so seeing three of these lines indicates .075 inch).

Next, note the lines on the moving thimble to see which thimble line matches up to the last visible line on the sleeve. As an example, let's say that the thimble line is identified as number 8. Because each thimble line indicates a space of .001 inch, that means that you have an additional .008 inch. Because the previously noted measurement was .375 inch, when you add the spindle sleeve mark of 8, the final measurement is .383 inch.

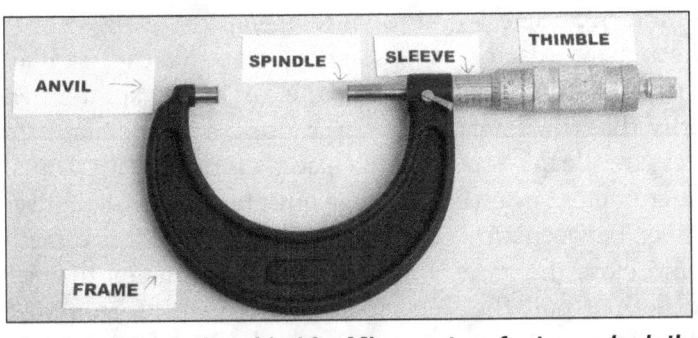

The primary components of an outside micrometer are labeled here, including the frame, stationary anvil, sliding spindle, stationary index marked sleeve, and rotating thimble. Micrometers feature a lock that allows you to lock a measurement for reference. This micrometer features a toggle lever lock. A micrometer set typically includes ranges of 0 to 1 inch, 1 to 2 inches, 2 to 3 inches, and 3 to 4 inches. Also included are three calibration standards and a spanner wrench for adjusting micrometer calibration.

AUTOMOTIVE MACHINING: A GUIDE TO BORING, DECKING, HONING AND MORE

CHAPTER 2

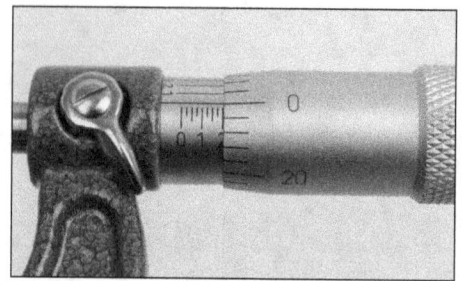

This sample reading shows the number-2 line flush with the chamfered edge of the thimble, with the zero line of the thimble aligned with the horizontal sleeve line, indicating exactly .200 inch.

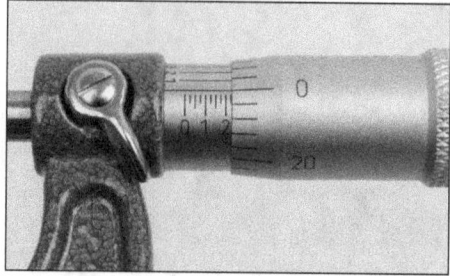

This reading shows one mark on the sleeve greater than the number 2, which translates into .225 inch. The number 2 indicates .200 inch, with one additional line visible at the edge of the thimble. Because each line on the sleeve indicates .025 inch, the measurement shown here is .225 inch.

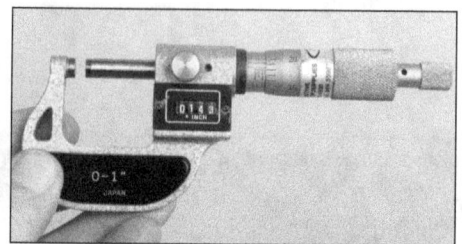

This digital readout micrometer must be properly calibrated. The reading is displayed in the viewing window. The mic can also be read referencing the marks on the sleeve and thimble. Close-up of a digital mic window. The lock on this model is a knurled rotating knob instead of a toggle lever.

A first-time user of a micrometer will likely be intimidated, but with a bit of practice, reading a micrometer becomes much easier.

When measuring a part with a micrometer, adhere to one rule: go slowly. Avoid spinning or twirling the thimble. Work slowly and carefully. Adjust the micrometer to almost the desired opening by rolling the thimble along your hand; avoid twirling it. Place the micrometer onto the part, holding it firmly with one hand. Use your sense of feel to make sure that the axis of the micrometer is perpendicular to the measured surface. Don't rock the micrometer; use your sense of feel. Close the micrometer using the ratchet knob to close the micrometer until the spindle is almost touching the part. Then gently close the micrometer spindle until the ratchet stop disengages by one click.

Always store a micrometer in a protective case when not in use. These are delicate, precision instruments and require care when handling or storing.

"Digital" micrometers are also available; they feature an easy-to-read measurement number in a display window, eliminating the need to read the traditional mark lines. However, it is absolutely critical that either style must be routinely kept in calibration.

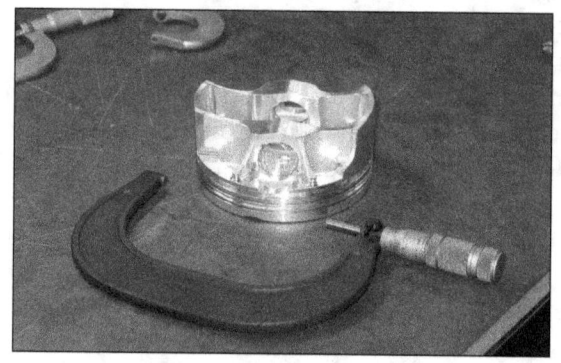

Measuring piston skirt diameters requires having outside micrometers in the range of the pistons that you deal with. When measuring a piston skirt diameter, always measure at the skirt location specified by the piston maker, since a slight taper may exist from the ring area to the skirt bottom.

Calibrating a Micrometer

A micrometer should be checked regularly for calibration because calibration can be affected by wear or damage (dropping it, etc.). To check calibration, first verify that the anvil and spindle surfaces are clean. For a zero-to-1-inch micrometer, insert a clean sheet of paper between the anvil and spindle and close the gap to capture the paper, then pull the paper out. Carefully clean the surfaces but avoid leaving lint on the surfaces. Next, you need a "standard" (also called a checking block), which is a length of steel that has been precision ground to an exact length. Standards are readily available, and many micrometer kits include a set of standards in various lengths. Both the micrometer and standard must be absolutely clean and both must be at room temperature. Using a checking standard, capture the standard between the anvil and spindle. For example, if using a 1-inch standard, and the reading is not exactly 1-inch, the gauge must be recalibrated. Insert the standard onto the micrometer and tighten the micrometer to "feel" (don't overtighten with force). Make sure that the micrometer's anvil and spindle are mated squarely onto the standard (not cocked). Engage the micrometer's lock to prevent it from moving. Hold the knurled thimble

PRECISION MEASUREMENT TOOLS

with one hand. Insert the spanner wrench (included with the micrometer) into the small hole in the micrometer sleeve. Hold the spanner wrench between the thumb and forefinger of your other hand, with your thumb resting on the sleeve. Rotate the spanner wrench to make the correction. If using a 1-inch standard, adjust until the micrometer reads exactly 1-inch. Unlock the micrometer and verify that your reading is exactly 1 inch when measuring the 1-inch standard.

Precision measuring instruments must be kept clean. Even the slightest dust particle can alter your reading. Clean the anvil and spindle surfaces prior to every use. After cleaning with a soft pare or towel, blow dust away with your mouth. Don't use high-pressured shop-compressed air, since the high velocity of compressed air can force dust particles into the tool's mechanism.

Occasionally, apply a drop of precision instrument oil to the spindle where it protrudes from the frame.

Caliper Micrometer

A caliper can be used to measure the outside or the inside dimensions; for instance, the outside diameter (O.D.) of a valvestem or the inside diameter (I.D.) of a hole. Calipers are available in both dial and digital styles. A dial caliper's gauge usually features dial marks in increments of .001 inch. The major dimension is marked on the caliper's slide (for

Standards (measuring block references) are an absolute must, to allow you to routinely check a micrometer for calibration. The three standards, 1-, 2-, and 3-inch lengths, are shown here. These are precision-ground reference blocks and must be handled with care.

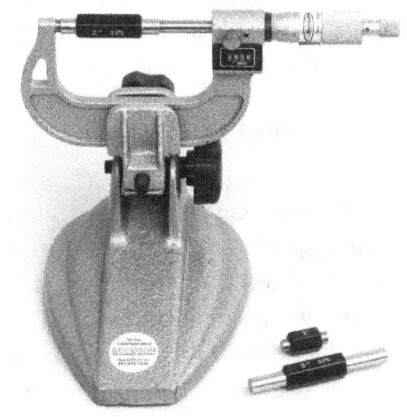

A micrometer stand is highly recommended. This allows you to secure a micrometer in padded jaws, making calibration checks and various measurements without the need to hold the micrometer in one hand while trying to measure a standard or when trying to set up a bore gauge with a micrometer.

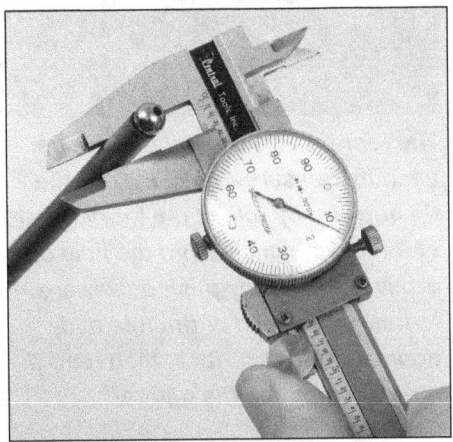

Shown is how to measure the diameter of a pushrod. This example shows a measurement of .3013 inch. Example of a commonly available dial caliper. A dial caliper is essentially a ruler that adds increased measuring precision with the addition of a dial indicator. A dial caliper is very easy to read. This example shows a setting at .5013 inch. The initial distance is represented on the slide, where the inside of the movable jaw aligns with the marks on the slide. Each individual line on the dial represents .001 inch.

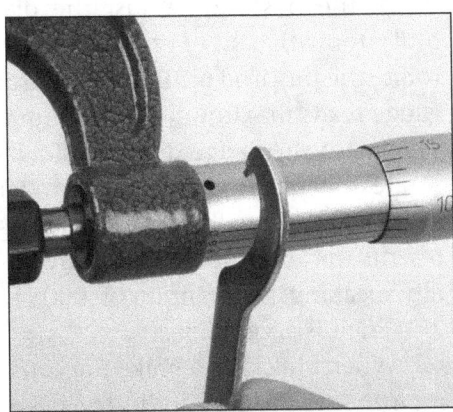

Outside micrometers feature a small hole in the sleeve for the use of a spanner wrench, which allows you to adjust the mic for calibration.

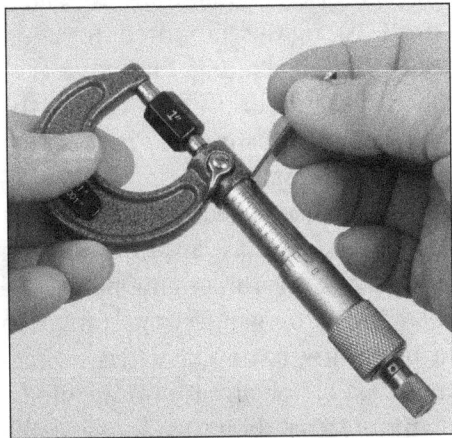

With a measuring standard in place, the spanner wrench is used to adjust the mic so that it precisely reads the standard length. Here a mic is being adjusted so that it reads exactly 1 inch while using a 1-inch standard.

CHAPTER 2

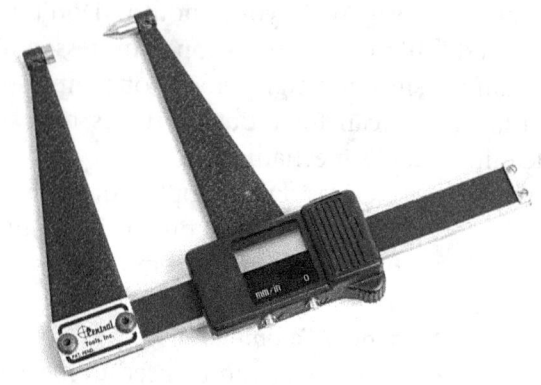

Although a traditional outside micrometer may be used to measure brake rotor thickness, a dedicated rotor thickness caliper is a better choice. The stationary anvil features a precision-ground flat surface, while the sliding arm's contact features a pointed surface.

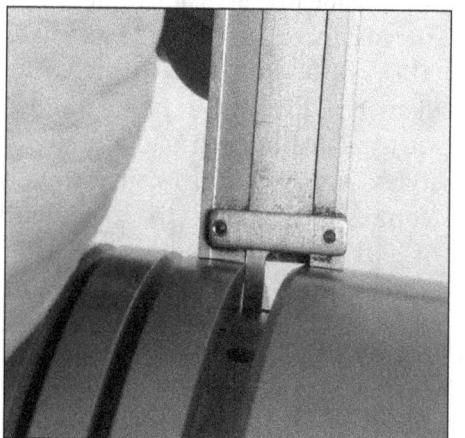

The rear tip of a dial caliper can be used to measure depth. Extend the tip outward by rolling the thumbwheel of the caliper, insert into the hole or groove, and gently push downward to bottom the end of the rule body against the top surface, then read the measurement on the gauge.

instance, 1 inch, 2 inches, etc.) The numbers on the slide that are visible between the caliper's fixed and movable jaws indicate one hundredth of an inch increments (for example, the number 5 indicates .500 inch). The gauge needle further refines the measurement by showing additional increments of .001 inch. When the gauge needle begins to first move away from zero, this represents additional .001 inch of the reading. For instance, if the number on the slide indicates 5, and the gauge needle indicates 13, the reading is .513 inch.

Dial Indicator

A dial indicator features an incremented gauge and a spring-loaded plunger. When the plunger is pushed in, the gauge reading is reduced, depicting how far the plunger moves.

Dial indicators are used in a variety of applications, which determine what type of mounting fixture is required.

Applications include (but are not limited to) measured brake rotor lateral runout, piston position relative to top-dead-center (TDC) in an engine block, measuring crankshaft thrust, measuring runout on a crankshaft, camshaft, valvestem, pushrod, etc. In each case, the dial indicator gauge must be rigidly mounted to allow only the gauge plunger to move.

Regardless of the application, the method of adjusting and reading the gauge is the same.

Let's use checking crankshaft thrust/endplay as an example. In the case of an iron engine block, the dial indicator gauge is mounted to a mounting fixture that has a magnetic base (for an aluminum block, a fixture that bolts to an available threaded hole works). Position the dial indicator so that the plunger contacts the face of the crankshaft snout or other available flat surface. The plunger must be parallel to the crankshaft centerline and not at an angle relative to the crank. Adjust the dial indicator so that the plunger contacts the surface and creates a slight preload (about .050 inch or so). The preload is vital to make sure that the plunger remains in loaded contact with the crank at all times. Using a lever such as a screwdriver, between a main cap and crankshaft counterweight, move the crankshaft rearward as far as it will move and remove the screwdriver. Rotate the gauge dial to allow the gauge needle to read exactly zero. Then use your lever to move the crankshaft fully forward, noting the distance of movement on the gauge. Repeat this reading several times. Move the crank fully forward and re-zero the gauge, then move the crank rearward (the same reading should be seen). Typically, depending on the application, you may see .004 to .008 inch or so of crank fore/aft movement.

The use of a dial indicator is the same for all applications, whether you're measuring for movement or runout. For example, if you're checking pushrods for runout (warp), a special pushrod runout stand is ideal. Lay the pushrod onto the stand and position the dial indicator at the center of the pushrod. Adjust the dial indicator with a bit of preload. Slowly rotate the pushrod until the indicator gauge reads maximum or minimum. Then zero the gauge dial and slowly rotate the pushrod, noting how far from zero the needle moves. This represents the amount of runout. Generally speaking, a maximum of .0005 to .001 inch is acceptable.

When checking a brake rotor disc for runout, the dial indicator needs to be mounted rigidly to prevent the gauge housing from moving. Several methods are available including a mount with a magnetic base and

PRECISION MEASUREMENT TOOLS

A pushrod runout checker features a stand and a dial indicator. Position the pushrod on the stand cradles. Adjust the dial indicator so that the indicator plunger contacts the center of the pushrod radius, and adjust the indicator to create approximately .050 inch of preload, then zero the indicator gauge. Slowly rotate the pushrod and monitor the indicator to measure any pushrod runout. This type of checking tool makes it easy to measure each pushrod for runout/bend. Generally speaking, runout in excess of .001 inch is unacceptable.

A magnetic-base dial indicator can be used to measure a variety of dimensions. In this example, the magnetic base is secured to an iron block deck with the indicator plunger contacting a piston dome, which is one method of checking piston location at TDC (top dead center).

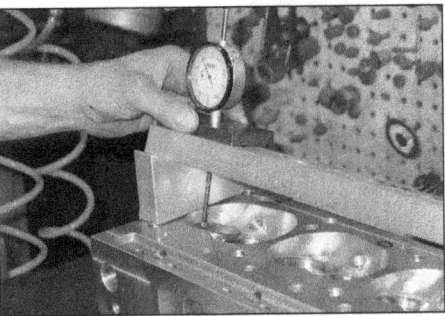

Shown here is a dial indicator being used to measure installed valve depth relative to the deck on a racing cylinder head. A bridge fixture rests on the head deck, with the dial indicator mounted to the bridge. This allows checking to measure each valve's depth, so that the seats can be machined to obtain an identical depth to optimize performance.

Here, a magnetic base dial indicator is used to measure crankshaft thrust. The magnet must mate to a clean, flat surface for proper stability. The indicator is adjusted on the tool's extension rod to locate the indicator plunger onto the crankshaft snout. The magnetic base is secured to the iron engine block.

Here, a dial indicator plunger is set up to contact the front face of the crank snout. Regardless of the point of contact, the indicator plunger must be set up parallel to the crankshaft centerline, not at an off-angle. If the plunger is at an improper angle, the reading will not be correct. Set the indicator up so that the plunger contacts a flat area of the crank, and push the indicator a bit toward the crank to obtain a gauge preload of about .050 inch. Push the crank fully rearward and zero the gauge. Then push the crank forward and observe the amount of travel. The close-up of this dial indicator shows that the crankshaft thrust measures a tad greater than .006 inch. The gauge needle has traveled just past the .006-inch mark. The small dial seen near the gauge center indicates additional travel in .0001-inch increments. This crank thrust reading is approximately .0067 inch.

If you're dealing with an aluminum engine block, you may be able to secure the magnetic base to the face of a steel or iron number-1 main cap. Otherwise, a fixture that bolts to the engine block is needed to mount the dial indicator. In this example, an extension has been added to the indicator plunger, as the plunger contacts the crank's snout base.

adjustable-length rods to position the gauge, or a flexible/locking arm that secures to a solid area such as a strut bracket (the gauge must be mounted to a component that does not move independently, relative to the rotor). Place the dial indicator plunger 90 degrees to the rotor (straight onto the disc surface, not at an angle). The plunger should contact the rotor surface about 1 inch inboard from the disc edge. Adjust the indicator with a bit of preload (about .050 inch), and slowly rotate the rotor until the gauge reads at a minimum point. Zero the gauge needle and slowly rotate the rotor a full 360 degrees, watching the gauge needle. The maximum gauge reading relative to zero represents the amount of rotor runout. Always refer to the manufacturer's runout specifications, but generally speaking, a maximum of about .002 inch should be acceptable.

When using a dial indicator to measure brake rotor runout, the best style of indicator for this task is one that features a ball bearing tip on the plunger. This reduces the variable of contact chatter and provides a smoother, more consistent reading. Dial indicators are available with either a solid or roller tip.

Dial Bore Gauge

A dial bore gauge allows you to measure bore diameter in areas such as main bearing bores, cylinder bores, lifter bores, cam bores, etc. A bore gauge kit includes an array of various length anvil extensions that mount to the tool depending on the bore diameter range that you plan to measure.

Keep in mind that a bore gauge does not allow you to measure a bore diameter directly. The gauge is first

Shown here is a typical bore gauge set. The tool includes a gauge and a selection of extensions and spacer washers to allow obtaining a variety of specific bore diameter applications.

set up to the target diameter and then zeroed. The gauge allows you to read how close the bore is to the target (at target, undersize or oversize, relative to the target diameter).

To set the gauge up, you need a micrometer. First, set the micrometer to the target bore size. For example, if the bore at hand is supposed to be 2.000 inches, set the micrometer at 2.000 inches.

Then, set up the dial bore gauge with the proper anvil extension that is able to accommodate a 2.000-inch bore. Bore gauge kits include a selection of extensions and spacer washers to allow you to adjust the gauge to the specified bore diameter.

Place the bore gauge between the micrometer's spindle and anvil.

Gently rock the dial bore gauge back and forth as well as side to side in the micrometer. Zero the bore gauge dial to zero at the minimum reading found while in the micrometer.

When the bore gauge is then inserted into the bore to be measured, you are able to see if the bore diameter based on the reference in the gauge dial. When measuring a bore, rock the bore gauge back and forth as well as side to side to obtain a precise reading. When the gauge needle reaches a stopping point and

Prior to and during align honing a block's main bore, a bore gauge is used to monitor bore diameter. Here a measurement check is made at twelve and six o'clock. Main bore measurement is also checked at three and nine o'clock and diagonally to check not only diameter but also to check for runout.

then starts to move the opposite direction, rock the gauge to reach the point where the needle stops, immediately before it starts to move in the opposite direction. For example, if the bore reading is .002 inch less than the zero mark, the bore is .002 inch too small. If the dial gauge reads .0017 inch greater than the dial's zero mark, you know that the bore is currently .0017 inch too large. When you know what the bore diameter is, you can then correct by enlarging the bore by boring or honing. If the bore is too large, you can correct (depending on the specific application) by sleeving a cylinder and then honing to size, installing a bushing in a lifter bore and honing to size, or by moving to larger-diameter pistons or lifters, etc.).

PRECISION MEASUREMENT TOOLS

In essence, you're setting up the dial bore gauge for a target bore diameter, then using the gauge to see how much the existing bore deviates from the target diameter.

Setup Tip

Although setting up a bore gauge sounds simple enough, the tricky part is in obtaining a precise point in the micrometer. Basically, you need three hands, because it's difficult to keep the gauge properly centered on the micrometer while holding each tool by hand. You can mount the micrometer on a bench vise, leaving both hands free to manipulate the gauge, but that gets tricky, because overtightening the bench vise even slightly can cause the micrometer to distort.

A better solution is to use a specialty tool that safely secures the micrometer. An example is Goodson's Micrometer Stand (MIC-FIX). This serves as a third hand, freeing both hands to hold the bore gauge. This stand features rubber jaws that secure the micrometer without damaging it.

Another option is to secure the bore gauge itself with a dial bore gauge setting fixture. Goodson's bore gauge setting fixture accepts most popular gauges including Mitutoyo, Phase II, Fowler, Peacock, and others. This fixture does not work with a Sunnen bore gauge, but Sunnen offers an appropriate fixture for its gauges.

Mounting a Bore Gauge with a Setting Fixture

Instead of using a C-frame style micrometer, a bore gauge can be set up using a dial bore gauge setting fixture, such as Goodson's DBG-FIX. This heavy-solid milled steel base accepts a standard (three are included,

Although a bore gauge can be set up by using a micrometer (with the micrometer adjusted to the desired bore diameter), a bore gauge setting fixture eases the task, eliminating the need to hold an outside micrometer. A selection of standards are provided for the 2- to 3-inch range, 3- to 4-inch range, and 4- to 5-inch range, with final adjustment via the built-in micrometer. The bore gauge rests at the pocket end of the setting fixture. The threaded set screws on either side are adjusted an equal distance from the center anvil seen here. This centers the gauge. Do not adjust the set screws tightly against the gauge. Allow .005- to .010-inch clearance at each side of the gauge.

one for the 2- to 3-inch range, 3- to 4-inch range, and 4- to 5-inch range). First adjust the end opposite the adjustable spindle to provide a secure pocket for the end of the bore gauge. An anvil is featured against which one side of the bore gauge rests. Two opposing adjustable set screws, one on each side, are then adjusted to capture the sides of the bore gauge. Adjust the two opposing set screws equidistant from the center anvil. Don't tighten these set screws against the bore gauge. Rather, adjust the set screws to provide .005- to .10-inch clearance. This provides proper alignment of the bore gauge when laced in the fixture, which in turn provides proper alignment to the fixture's spindle and standard.

Insert a standard to the fixture, based on the target bore diameter. Adjust the mic thimble to achieve your precise target diameter. When the fixture is set up, you're ready to adjust your bore gauge

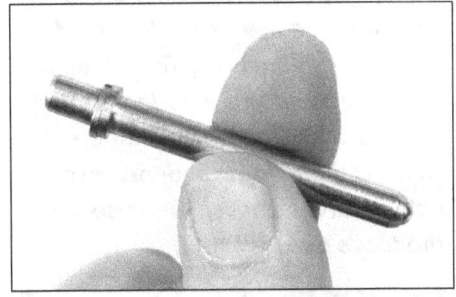

Choose the bore gauge extension that's appropriate for your target bore diameter. The short end seen here inserts into the gauge. To alter the length of the extension as needed, install a supplied spacer washer to the short end of the extension. Here I installed a .100-inch-thick washer. Gauge kits commonly include spacers at .100-, .050-, and .020-inch thick.

Install the appropriate standard (for example, if your target for the bore gauge needs to be set up to check a 3.500-inch bore, install the 2-inch standard that allows setting to a 3- to 4-inch range. Then adjust the fixture's micrometer spindle to obtain a fixed setting at 3.500-inch.

Set up your bore gauge with the appropriate extension and washers for your desired bore diameter. Place the bore gauge in the setting stand. If it is too long to fit, change to a shorter extension or fewer washers. If

CHAPTER 2

Insert the extension to the gauge. Install the threaded collar onto the gauge to secure the extension. The side of the gauge opposite the extension features two rollers that guide the gauge in the bore. The center of the gauge features a spring-loaded plunger that presses against the bore wall. As the plunger is depressed or extended, this movement is seen on the tool's dial indicator.

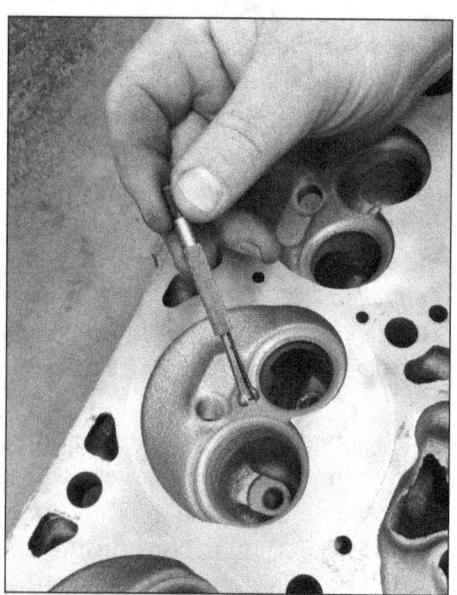

A valveguide bore gauge is required to measure the inside diameter of a guide. Measurements should be taken at the bottom, middle, and top areas of each guide. Here a split-ball gauge is inserted into the guide. The gauge is allowed to relax and expand inside the guide, then tightened to maintain the diameter.

too short, go with a longer extension or add washers as needed. Adjust the bore gauge so that you have a bit of preload on the gauge when placed in the fixture. Rock the bore gauge toward and away from the fixture's micrometer. With the gauge held at its minimum reading, adjust the gauge bezel to obtain zero on the

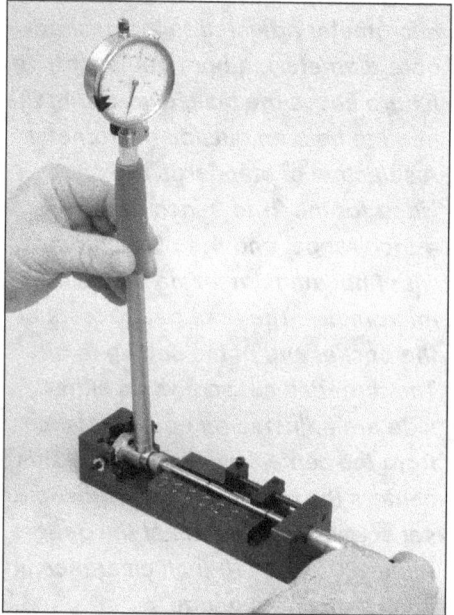

With the bore gauge installed onto the setting fixture, gently rock the gauge forward and rearward, noting the minimum indicator reading. Holding the gauge steady at this minimum reading, zero the dial indicator's bezel so that the needle rests at the zero mark. You now have a zero reference for your target bore diameter. Insert the gauge into the bore (the bore must be clean and free of oil and contamination) and gently rock the gauge in opposite directions, noting the minimum needle reading (where the needle runs to a point and begins to reverse direction). Note the reading on the dial indicator to see how far the bore measures, under or over your target diameter, indicating how far the bore is undersized or oversized relative to the target diameter.

gauge. The bore gauge is now ready to check the target bore.

Depth Gauge

A depth gauge is a micrometer-style tool that features a flat base and allows the tool's spindle to protrude through the flat base. This gauge allows you to determine the depth of a hole, recess, slot, keyway, etc. Securely rest the flat surface against the flat surface with the spindle hole facing the deeper surface to be measured. Rotate the spindle until it gently contacts the surface at the bottom of the hole or recess. Read the micrometer, revealing the

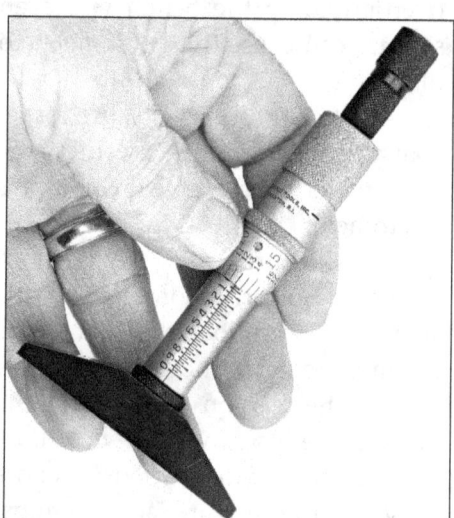

A depth gauge allows you to measure the depth of a hole, groove, recess, etc.

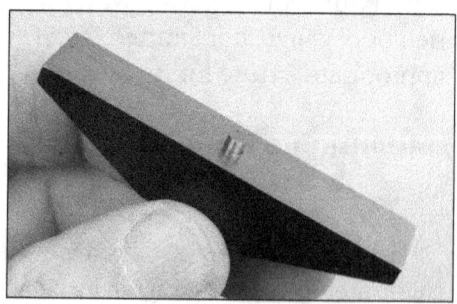

A depth gauge features a spindle that protrudes out of the flat base. Make sure that the base and spindle face are clean of any oil, dust, etc.

PRECISION MEASUREMENT TOOLS

difference in height from the fixed surface to the other surface.

Internal Caliper Gauge

An internal caliper gauge features two arms with small contact tips on the outside of each arm tip. This tool allows you to measure the inside diameter of a hole that is otherwise difficult to access. Compress the arms together, insert them into the hole or recess, and release the arms. The tool features a lock that may be engaged before removing the tool from the hole. The gauge reveals the diameter. This type of gauge is available with either a needle dial gauge or a digital readout.

Measuring Pushrod Length

Pushrod length does not necessarily reflect overall length, depending on the pushrod style. You must consider the oil orifice at the end (if an oil hole is featured). If you measured an existing pushrod using

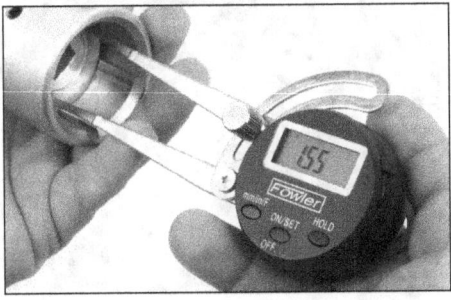

A digital inside caliper allows you to easily measure the inside diameter of a hole. The arms are spring-loaded and the measurement readout is displayed in the viewing window.

Compress the arms together to enter the hole, then release tension. The arms expand away from each other as the arm tips contact the walls. This type of gauge is very easy to use and is extremely accurate.

a large caliper, you'd be fooled by about .017 inch or so (on the short side) because you'd contact the caliper against the small flat at the end that results from the hole opening. If you're using a pushrod checker, this isn't an issue, unless you're also using an existing pushrod that you measured as a reference.

Also, if the pushrod style you intend to use features a top cup (female pocket instead of male radius), you need to remember that your measurement must take place at the female radius seat, not at the outer edge of the cup. The easiest way to accurately measure a cup-equipped pushrod is to drop a steel ball into the cup, take your measurement, then subtract the ball diameter. For instance, if you're dealing with a 5/16-inch cupped pushrod, place a 5/16-inch-diameter steel ball into the cup. Then you can measure overall length (contacting your caliper on the ball). Then subtract the actual ball diameter from this measurement, which provides an accurate length to the radiused seat in the pushrod cup.

If you use a ball to help measure a cupped pushrod, take the time to actually measure the ball diameter using a caliper. Don't just assume that the ball meets an advertised diameter. A 5/16-inch ball should measure .3125-inch in diameter.

Just remember that pushrod lengths refer to the distance between the radiused contact points at each end of the pushrod.

Before you can measure pushrod length, the cylinder head must be fully installed; that means that the head gasket must be in place, and the head fasteners must be fully tightened to their final value.

Verify that clearance between the edge of the valvespring retainer and

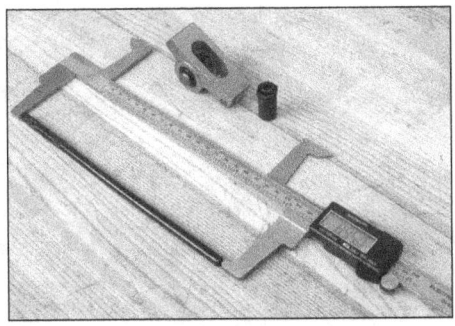

A long-slide caliper can be used to measure pushrod length, or when measuring an adjustable checking pushrod when determining a custom pushrod length. If a cup-style pushrod is being measured, install a ball bearing into the cup during measurement, then subtract the diameter of the ball to determine the required length of the pushrod, from lower radiused tip to the seat of the upper cup. The ball should be sized appropriately for the radius of the cup (for example, 5/16 inch in diameter, or .3125 inch).

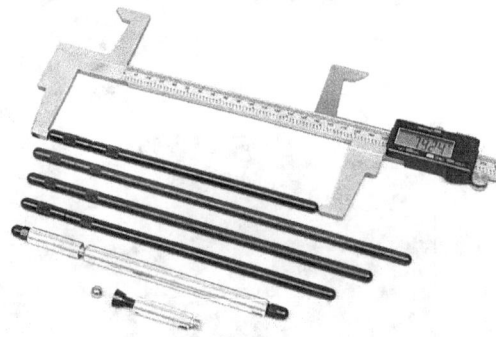

Checking pushrods are available in a wide variety of length ranges and styles.

the underside of the rocker is at least .040 inch.

When measuring for pushrod length, you *must* use the valvetrain parts that will be used in the final assembly, including block, heads, camshaft, lifters, valves, rocker studs, and rockers. When you're ready to measure for pushrod length, the only remaining variable should be the length of the pushrods.

CHAPTER 2

When measuring for pushrod length, swap out a valvespring for a light checking spring. This makes it easier and more precise to rotate the crank and eliminates the tension that a valvespring creates. A heavy valvespring can easily damage an adjustable checking pushrod.

Valvespring Height Gauge

A barrel-style micrometer is available designed specifically to measure valvespring installed height. Obtaining adequate valveseat pressure while avoiding coil bind is critical, especially for extreme valvespring pressures and radical camshafts. Although valvesprings should be tested on a valvespring gauge for seat and full-open pressure, the engine builder needs to be sure that the installed height dimension that's required can be duplicated during assembly. If the measured spring height differs from the target installed spring height, the height can be corrected by adding a shim to the spring seat or by milling the spring seat base.

Valveseat Runout Gauge

Checking the valveguide centerline relative to a valveseat is easily accomplished with a valveseat runout gauge. This gauge features an anvil rod that is inserted into the valveguide. The gauge features an adjustable contact that runs along the valveseat and a dial gauge. Slowly rotating the gauge along the valveseat reveals any runout of the seat relative to the guide. If runout is found, the seat can be resurfaced (or replaced and machined) to obtain zero runout.

Precision Straightedge

When checking a block, cylinder head, or manifold deck surface for flatness/warpage, a precision machinist's straightedge is an absolute must. These tools are precision-ground steel straightedges that allow you to check for deck warpage using a feeler gauge. Do not rely on just any "straight" ruler or piece of scrap steel

A valvespring checker allows you to monitor both spring height and pressure. As you compress the spring to its specified installed height (monitored on a separate indicator), spring pressure is monitored on the tool's pressure gauge.

A valvespring height micrometer is used to measure installed spring height on the cylinder head. The spring height checker is installed in place of a valvespring, with retainer and keepers installed. Adjusting the gauge to remove all slack with the valve in its fully closed position allows you to measure installed spring height. If this measured installed height is too tall for the specified installed height, shims may be added to the spring seat to compensate, or if too short, the spring seat may be machined to remove material.

A precision machinist's straightedge is an essential tool for checking deck surfaces for warpage. The straightedge is positioned front-to-rear on a deck, while a feeler gauge is used to insert between the deck and straightedge. Acceptable warpage limits vary depending on the length and type of cylinder head, intake manifold, or block deck, so referring to published specifications is needed.

PRECISION MEASUREMENT TOOLS

for this procedure. Invest in a dedicated precision straightedge. These are available in various lengths and should be treated with care to avoid nicking the edges or allowing the bare steel precision-ground edge surface to rust. Store in a safe location when not in use.

Rod Bolt Stretch Gauge

Published torque specifications aside, race engine builders have long realized that the correct approach to tightening connecting rod bolts is to stress the bolts into their "working" range of stress, but not beyond. Because OEM connecting rod bolts may vary in terms of their ideal torque by as much as 10 ft-lbs from batch to batch due to variations in heat treating and materials, if the concern is to arrive at both peak bolt strength as well as maintaining concentricity of the rod's big end, the rod bolts should be measured for stretch instead of simply tightening until the torque wrench hits its mark.

In simple terms, to measure bolt stretch, first measure the total rod bolt length (from the head surface to the tip of the shank) in the bolt's relaxed state. Then measure the bolt again after the nut has been tightened to value.

The difference in length indicates the amount of stretch the bolt experiences in its installed state. For the majority of production rod bolts, stretch is likely in the .0045- to .006-inch range. If the stretch is less, the bolt is probably experiencing too much friction that is preventing the proper stretch (requiring lubricant on the threads). If stretch is excessive, the bolt may have been pulled beyond its yield point and is no longer serviceable.

Connecting rod bolt stretch gauges are preferred tools for many performance engine builders. This type of gauge allows you to precisely measure how far a rod bolt has stretched while under installed torque. Shown here are three manufacturers' examples.

A rod bolt stretch gauge features a stationary anvil (seen here at the bottom of the tool frame) and a spring-loaded dial caliper spindle.

Although an outside micrometer may be used to measure the rod bolt length, the most accurate method is to use a specialty fixture that is outfitted with a dial indicator. Excellent examples of this gauge include units from GearHead Tools, ARP, and Goodson Shop Supplies. GearHead's bolt stretch gauge features a heat-treated aluminum frame (with a very handy thumbhole) with a specially modified dial indicator with sufficient spring tension to hold the gauge firmly to the ends of the rod bolt. The indicator can be rotated for right- or left-hand operation, and the lower anvil is adjustable to accommodate various bolt lengths. Goodson Shop Supplies also offers a rod bolt stretch gauge, P/N RBG-4, featuring spherical points for consistent and repeatable readings, and can also be rotated

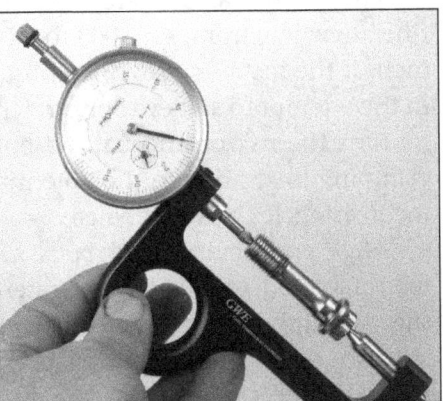

Prior to installing a rod bolt, the bolt is installed to the tool, with a bit of preload on the dial gauge, followed by zeroing the dial gauge. This provides a reference length for the bolt in its relaxed state. The anvil and spindle engage into dimples in the rod bolt head and shank tip.

for right- or left-hand operation. Also, ARP offers its own bolt stretch gauge, P/N 100-9941, designed with .0005-inch increments, with a heavy spring and ball tips.

There is a debate among some engine builders regarding the validity of measuring rod bolt stretch, due to potential compression of the rod material as the rod cap is clamped to the rod. Although this can occur, the use of a stretch gauge remains the best practical method of accurately determining bolt load.

Connecting rod bolts can be viewed as high-tensile springs. The bolt must be stretched short of its yield point in order for accurate, and most important, repeatable, clamping of the rod cap to the rod. Improper or unequal bolt clamping force can easily result in a nonround rod bore.

Stock, or production, rod bolts typically offer a tensile strength of approximately 150,000 to 160,000 psi. However, due to variances in bolt production, tolerances can be quite extreme, with peak bolt stretch occurring anywhere from, say, .003 to .006 inch. If the installer uses only torque in the attempt to achieve bolt stretch, he runs the risk of unequal rod bolt clamping loads, due to the potential inconsistencies between bolts.

High-performance rod bolts are manufactured to much tighter tensile strength tolerances. ARP, for instance, calculates each and every rod bolt for stretch, and the bolt packages include reference data to that effect. The instructions actually recommend that a specific amount of bolt stretch should be achieved on each bolt (ARP cites 190,000 psi as its nominal or base tensile rating, with actual ratings much higher in some applications).

How can unequal/inadequate rod bolt tightness affect the connecting rod big end bore shape? Let me cite an example: If one technician reconditions the connecting rods using torque value alone to tighten the rod bolts, and another technician who is responsible for final assembly uses the bolt stretch method, the final result can be out-of-round bores. This is because of frictional variances. As a result, the assembler using the stretch method may achieve a higher clamping load on one or more bolts as compared to the loads imposed when the rod reconditioner torqued the nuts without regard to actual bolt stretch. When a bolt is tightened with dry threads, as much as 80 percent of the torque can be exerted because of friction, as opposed to bolt stretch.

In a high-volume production rebuilding facility, technicians may not have the time to measure for bolt stretch. However, a slower-paced operation that is attempting to obtain maximum accuracy (for a race engine, as an example) is far better off using the stretch method instead of relying only on the torque method.

A set of connecting rod bolts' instructions may list both a torque value and a stretch range, effectively giving you a choice of methods. Yes, tightening only to a specified torque value is quicker, and measuring bolt stretch requires more time, but the best results are achieved by measuring bolt stretch. So, unless you're in a rush, take the time to measure stretch, tightening each rod bolt to the recommended stretch range. It's all about the quest for precision.

Connecting rod bolt tightening is an absolutely critical aspect of rod installation, to achieve the proper amount of rod bearing crush (contact force between the upper and lower bearing shells that serves to properly secure the bearings to the rod big end bore) and to obtain the correct level of rod bolt stretch and clamping force. Undertightened rod bolts don't provide enough clamping force, and overtightened rod bolts can result in stretching the bolts beyond their elastic range. Either scenario can easily result in rod bolt failure, which in turn results in rod bearing failure and the very real potential for severe damage, including broken and/or twisted rods, damaged or broken crankshaft, broken camshaft, and rods busting through the block.

I cannot overstate the importance of connecting rod bolt tightening. Improper bolt installation results in a ticking time bomb, just waiting to destroy your engine and your wallet.

With regard to tightening rod bolts, there are three potential methods to consider: torque-plus-angle, torque alone, or tightening by monitoring bolt stretch. The only application for tightening rod bolts with torque followed by angle tightening applies to OEM rod bolts that are specified for this type of installation. Any serious builder of a performance engine most likely opts for high-performance aftermarket rod bolts. Generally speaking, if the engine is intended to produce about 450 hp or more, I strongly advise using high-performance rod bolts instead of the OEM bolts. In this book, I focus on the use of these superior quality bolts (as offered by such firms as ARP and others).

When using aftermarket performance rod bolts (or whenever you purchase a set of performance aftermarket connecting rods that include these bolts), bolt tightening instructions will be included, and it's imperative that you follow the instructions.

Based on the rod bolt diameter, bolt grade, length, and application, the maker provides both a torque value *and* a target bolt stretch value. You can then decide which method to use. Some builders prefer to follow the torque spec; others prefer to measure bolt stretch. I always tighten by measuring stretch, because I feel that this provides a more accurate means of achieving the desired clamping load, as well as obtaining equal clamping loads on all of the rod bolts.

PRECISION MEASUREMENT TOOLS

Torque-Plus-Angle

Many late-model OEM engines specify a torque/angle method for a variety of fasteners, including crank pulley bolts, rod bolts, main cap bolts, and cylinder head bolts. An initial torque value is achieved (obviously using a properly calibrated torque wrench). This establishes a specific and initial level of clamping force. Final tightening takes place by continuing to rotate the bolt head by a specified number of degrees. This method, developed by OEM engineers, theoretically eliminates the variable encountered with regard to thread friction. Engineering research has determined that by continuing to tighten the bolt by a certain number of degrees stretches the bolt into its desired range of elasticity for optimum clamping force.

Degree tightening can be accomplished by several different approaches, including placing a dot on the bolt head and observing how far the bolt head is rotated (for example, by 45 degrees, 90 degrees, etc.). This is a crude method, because it relies on your estimation of degree travel. An inexpensive tool that aids in angle tightening is a small degree wheel that is attached to a wrench. The wheel features degree increments and an adjustable needle to establish your zero mark and is observed as the bolt is rotated. The downside is that this requires using your torque wrench for initial tightening, setting the torque wrench aside, grabbing a wrench that's equipped with the degree wheel, and continuing to tighten, while carefully observing the travel.

Another approach involves the use of a digital combination torque/angle wrench. This eliminates the need to switch tools in midstream. By pressing a button, you choose your torque format (ft-lbs or Nm) and your torque value (let's say 35 ft-lbs for example). When the selected torque value is approached, the tool begins to beep and/or LED lights illuminate to let you know that you're getting close. After the selected value is reached, the tool provides an audible alert, as well as the illumination of a final red light and a vibration in the tool handle (the types of alerts may vary among tool brands and models).

After the bolt is torqued, you simply press another button to switch to the angle mode, select the degree, and continue to tighten. The same alerts take place during the angle tightening phase. Depending on the tool model, you can even ratchet the tool during angle tightening without losing the angle reference (Snap-on's TechAngle wrench is an example of this). A number of leading precision tool makers now offer these digital wrenches, including Snap-on, Mac, and others. Granted, they're a bit pricey, but they work well and eliminate the need to use multiple tools. If you're using performance aftermarket connecting rods and high-performance rod bolts, a torque-plus-angle approach is not required.

Ultrasonic Thickness Gauge

A sonic thickness gauge uses frequency bounce-back signals (similar to sonar) to measure material thickness. A thickness gauge is most commonly used to measure an engine block's cylinder wall thickness, prior to overboring, to determine existing wall thickness and to make sure that no areas of a cylinder wall are too thin after the cylinder is bored. Potential thin areas include those adjacent to cooling passages. The sonic gauge is first set up using a checking standard, which is a sample piece of metal that is similar to that of the engine block (since iron castings can vary depending on the makeup of the iron). Some gauge kits will include sample standards of a marked thickness. The gauge is calibrated using the appropriate sample. The gauge probe is then lightly coated with a special grease that promotes a good signal. The probe is then put into contact with the cylinder wall, while monitoring the thickness readout. Cylinder walls should be checked from top to bottom at various clock positions, making note of the thinnest reading.

After calibrating the sonic checker for the type of block material (some sonic checkers include sample standards of various iron compositions; if not, a section of accessible and easy-to-measure area of the block should be measured with a mic or caliper to calibrate the tool), the tool's probe is placed against the cylinder wall, with a light coating of supplied grease that permits accurate measurement.

Cylinder walls should be measured for thickness at top, halfway down the bore, and bottom, at a variety of clock positions. Although engine block designs vary in terms of cylinder wall thickness, generally speaking, a minimum of about .200 inch should be acceptable.

Minimum acceptable cylinder wall thickness may vary depending on the specific type of engine block, but generally speaking, a final minimum of about .200 inch should be acceptable. If a specific block is specified for a minimum of, say, .220 inch, and the cylinder wall's thinnest area currently measures .223 inch, for example, this tells you that a maximum of .003 inch should be removed during boring and honing. A cylinder wall that is considered too thin may be a candidate for sleeving.

Torque Wrenches

The use of a torque wrench allows us to apply a specific amount of rotational force (torque) to a bolt or nut. Torque wrenches are available that provide adjustments in formats including ounce-inch, foot-pounds (ft-lbs), inch-pounds (in-bs), or Newton-meters (Nm). Torque wrenches are available in various designs, including flex-bar style (sometimes called a scale type), dial indicator style, and the common micrometer style (often referred to as a "click" style), as well as digital styles.

With regard to the "click" type micrometer style, "release" models are also available that release upon reaching the preset torque (preventing overtightening), but may not provide an audible click. The release/click type wrench is adjusted by means of a micrometer scale on the handle.

If the torque wrench releases momentarily and/or clicks, this is referred to as a "signal" type. The "indicator" type refers to the visual display units, such as the flex bar or dial indicator style. Newer digital torque wrenches may provide an audible "beep" signal when the setting has been reached, and some may

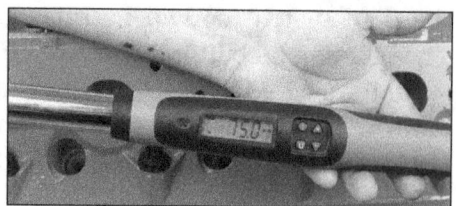

Example of a digital torque/angle wrench. The tool shown here is a Snap-on brand, but other torque wrench manufacturers are also now offering similar technology. Torque is monitored visually via a display window, and an audible beep sounds when the desired torque is achieved. Other models feature a series of green LED lights to alert you when you are approaching the target torque value, with a red light illuminating when the target is finally achieved. A torque/angle wrench allows you to both tighten by torque value and to rotate a fastener by monitoring the tightening angle. Using the Snap-on Tech Angle wrench as an example, press a mode button to enter the torque mode and press the value button until the desired torque is displayed.

feature both a beep and a vibration when the adjusted level has been reached. The grip vibration feature is helpful in a noisy shop environment. Admittedly, this can be somewhat confusing, since there are so many different types available.

Metric scale torque wrenches are available in Newton meters (Nm), meter kilograms (mKg), and centimeter kilograms (cmKg), with Nm being the more common scale. Many torque wrenches provide dual scales for reading in either English or metric formats (for example, a dual scale may offer both ft-lbs and Nm).

Torque wrenches are precision instruments and should be handled as such. Care and storage of a torque wrench is critical in terms of main-

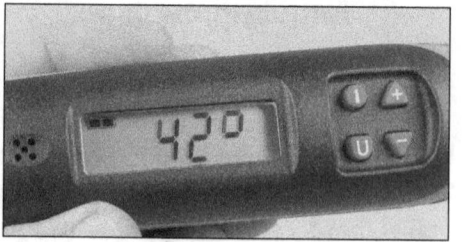

By entering the angle mode, you set the desired angle. When the set angle is achieved, the wrench alerts you via a beep and a vibration in the grip. This is a handy feature for applications where you need to meet OEM torque-plus-angle tightening.

taining calibration. Any adjustable torque wrench (the commonly used micrometer-handled click type, for example) should be set at its lowest torque reading when not in use. This is something that many technicians commonly forget. If left stored at a high-torque setting, the calibration may be affected over a long term. When you're done with the wrench, readjust it to the minimum setting before storing it in the toolbox.

When using an adjustable torque wrench, be careful not to overtighten by applying torque past the release or signal point. With a ratcheting "click" type, the "click" may not be heard at low torque settings, especially in a noisy shop. It's best to become familiar with the "feel" of the release, rather than relying only on the sound of a click.

When using an indicating type torque wrench (such as a flex bar or dial indicator type), try to read the indicator while viewing it at 90 degrees to its surface. Reading the indicator at an off-angle provides errors due to improper line of sight.

Most torque wrenches operate accurately only when held by the center of their handle grips. Don't use cheater bars to extend your grip farther away from the wrench head, and don't grab the handle closer to the wrench head. Only grip the wrench by its designated grip area.

Torque Values and Fastener Clamping

The torque applied to a bolt or stud creates clamping force by stretch-loading, which can be loosely compared to the stretch of a rubber band. When the underside of the bolt head (or nut) makes contact with the parent surface, the additional rotation of the bolt head or nut causes the bolt shank or stud to begin to stretch. The objective is to reach the ideal point where this stretch provides the needed clamping force to properly secure the component being installed. When tightened properly (to specification), the fastener has stretched within its designed elastic range.

When the fastener is loosened, the elasticity allows the shank to return to its normal, uninstalled length. If stretched to its yield point, it can permanently weaken. If the bolt or stud retains no elastic ability, it can't do its job in terms of providing clamping force. If severely overtightened, a bolt can shear.

Bolt or stud diameters are based on the load required for component clamping performance. That's why 1/4-inch bolts may be used in one location and 3/8-inch bolts in another. A smaller-diameter bolt requires less torque value to achieve ideal clamping load, and a larger-diameter bolt requires more torque value to achieve ideal clamping load. Although not a perfect analogy, you can sort of view threaded fasteners as "fuses." The diameter is based on the requirement for the specific job, just as the amp rating of a fuse is based on the requirement for a particular circuit.

Taking advantage of a threaded fastener's clamping load potential isn't a matter of guesswork. Especially for critical fasteners, such as any involved in the brake system, steering system, suspension, engine, transmission, differential, and wheels, all threaded fasteners must be tightened to their specific-application torque value. If you don't pay attention to torque values, it's like buying a set of pistons and sticking them into cylinder bores without measuring oil clearance.

In addition to adjusting the setting and/or monitoring the preset level via a click, listening for a beep, or watching a dial, consider the variables. First of all, is the torque wrench accurate? If it's a cheap one, or if it's been lying around the shop for years, it may be out of calibration. Second, is the fastener being tightened lubricated properly? Third, is the clamping force being created suitable for the diameter and type of metal?

About 90 percent of the torque applied during tightening is used to overcome friction. Friction occurs between mating threads, as well as between the underside of the bolt head (or nut) and the parent material of the object being installed.

Excess friction can occur if galling or "thread seizing" takes place. This is especially common with threaded fasteners made of alloys such as aluminum, stainless steel, and titanium. If galling occurs (at any level of severity), this makes your torque readings inaccurate, since the galling effect will add significant friction at the thread mating area, which results in a severely undertightened fastener.

Several factors can affect fastener tension, including type of material, material hardness, lubrication (or lack thereof), fastener hardness, surface finish/plating, thread fit, and tightening speed.

- Make sure the threads (both male and female) are clean.
- Make sure the threads are in good condition, and free of deformation or burrs.
- When necessary, apply the required lubricant to the threads before assembly (this may involve engine oil, molybdenum disulphide, an anti-seize compound, or an anaerobic thread-locking compound, depending on the situation).
- Keep your torque wrenches clean and calibrated. Depending on their amount of use, consider sending your torque wrenches out for recalibration once per year. Also, store your torque wrenches in a safe place. Don't toss them around the shop. They're delicate instruments.
- When tightening, whether using a common hand wrench or a torque wrench, slow down! The action of tightening quickly can increase friction and heat at the thread area, which can lead to thread galling. Speedy tightening can also lead to inaccurate tightening, as the torque wrench must overcome the increased friction.
- When you reach the torque limit (your desired torque value), approach this slowly and watch the needle or feel for the click or vibration (depending on the style of torque wrench). If you tighten too fast, you may pull the wrench past the preset limit (unknowingly adding a few more foot-pounds of torque).

The use of a torque wrench or other torque value or fastener stretch monitoring device is absolutely necessary for anything engine related (not only cylinder heads and connecting rods, but intake manifolds, carburetors, water pumps, oil pumps, rear seal housings, oil pans, timing covers, valvecovers, exhaust manifolds or headers, power steering pump brackets, etc.). If you own a torque wrench, take the time to look up the torque value for the carburetor fasteners, and adhere to the specs. Tightening anything on the engine by "feel" is more often than not the root cause for annoying fluid or vacuum leaks. The skilled engine builder/assembler never guesses about anything. Undertightening or overtightening can and does lead to problems, ranging from the mildly annoying to the most severe. Don't guess!

Adapters and Extensions

As long as the adapter (socket extension, etc.) is in-line with the torque wrench drive, no compensation is required. However, if an adapter that effectively lengthens the wrench is used (such as a crow's-foot wrench), a calculation must be made to achieve the desired torque value.

For those occasions when a straight socket can't be used, a special attachment might be needed (such as a crow's foot). The use of an offset adapter changes the calibration of the torque wrench, which makes it necessary to calculate the correct torque settings. Following are two formulas for calculating this change:

TW (where the adapter makes the wrench longer) = L ÷ L + E x Desired TE
TW (where the adapter makes the wrench shorter = L ÷ L - E x Desired TE

Where:
E = Effective length of extension, measured along the centerline of the torque wrench
L = Lever length of the wrench (from center of the wrench drive to the center of the adapter's grip area)
TW = Torque setting on the torque wrench
TE = Torque applied by the extension to the fastener

If you want to know where to set the torque wrench when using an adapter that alters the effective length of the wrench, you must calculate to compensate for the adapter. If the distance from the wrench drive to the center of the bolt makes the wrench longer, the final wrench setting must be adjusted to a lower value to compensate. If the distance from the wrench drive to the bolt center makes the wrench shorter, the wrench must be set to a higher value to compensate.

Let's say that you want to torque a bolt to 40 ft-lbs, but you're using a 2-inch-long wrench extension. For the sake of example, the length of the torque wrench is 14 inches (from center of the handle to center of the drive). Adding the 2-inch wrench extension makes the total length (center of grip to bolt-engaging wrench) 16 inches. In this case, you divide the length of the torque wrench (L, from the center of the handle to the center of the drive) by L+E, then multiply that ratio by the desired value.

In this example, the formula works out to: 14 ÷ 16 x 40 = .875 x 40 = 35.

In this example, where you want to tighten at 40 ft-lbs, using a 2-inch extension, you set the torque wrench at 35 ft-lbs.

It's important to orient the wrench extension in-line with the torque wrench itself, to achieve a straight shot from the torque wrench body to the extension. If you angle the extension off-parallel to the torque wrench, this inaccurately affects the applied torque.

If, due to required access of the bolt, the wrench extension needs to be placed 180 degrees (still in line with the torque wrench but effectively making the total wrench reach shorter), and you still want to achieve 40 ft-lbs of torque, you need to compensate for this shorter distance my modifying the formula as TW = L ÷ L - E, x DESIRED TE.

If the torque wrench length (center of grip to center of head) is 14 inches, and the wrench extension is 2 inches long, with the extension effectively reducing grip-to-bolt engagement distance, and you still want to achieve 40 ft-lbs of torque, the new formula is as follows:

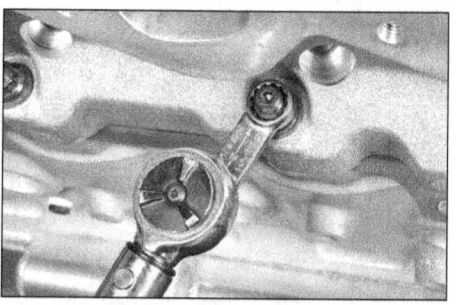

For areas that are difficult to reach that prevent you from using only a socket on the torque wrench, an offset wrench extension may be used. When using an extension that effectively increases the length of the torque wrench, you must adjust the applied torque to compensate. Otherwise you overtighten beyond the desired torque value. The length of the extension must be factored to properly adjust your torque. A wrench extension is marked for its length.

When using a wrench extension on your torque wrench, always keep the extension parallel to the torque wrench body. If it is not parallel/straight, it results in an inaccurately applied torque.

PRECISION MEASUREMENT TOOLS

$$14 \div 14 - 2 \times 40 = 46.6$$

Because the leverage of the setup has decreased, to achieve 40 ft-lbs, you adjust the torque wrench at 46.6 ft-lbs.

- If the adapter makes the wrench longer, you must back off on the torque wrench setting.
- If the adapter makes the wrench shorter, you must increase the adjustment on the torque wrench.

Special Torque/Angle Torque Wrenches

Thanks to advancements in technology, torque wrenches are now available that allow you to achieve both torque value and applied rotation angle without the need for a separate angle gauge.

One example is Snap-on's Techangle series of wrenches. Featuring sensor electronics and digital control and readout, you can preset (program) the torque value you want; or both torque value and final applied angle, depending on your needs. The electronic control allows you to also choose between in-lb, ft-lb, or Nm, plus angle.

An internal gyroscope provides the desired angle sensing.

Here's how it works: you program the desired torque value, and tighten the fastener. When you reach the programmed torque value, the wrench beeps and vibrates.

Then, if you need additional angle rotation, you program the desired angle.

When you continue to apply pressure and reach the programmed angle, the wrench again beeps and vibrates.

The preset angle range is 5 to 360 degrees, with a resolution of 1 degree and accuracy of +/- 1 degree. Unlike the use of a separate angle gauge, where you can't ratchet (with an angle gauge you must start and continue the angle rotation in a steady, one-direction sweep), this tool allows you to ratchet without "losing" the angle memory. Pretty cool.

Two models are currently available, including ATECH2FR100, with a torque range of 5 to 100 ft-lbs; and ATECH3FR250, with a torque range of 12.5 to 250 ft-lbs.

Cam Lobe Checker

Prior to the installation of lifters and pushrods, a camshaft lobe gauge can be used to accurately determine the position of an individual camshaft lobe (for instance, when positioning a cam with a specific intake or exhaust lobe at its base circle, or determining a lobe at its peak, or measuring a lobe from base circle to peak to verify the lobes against published lift specs). This tool features an aluminum tubular body with an adjustable plastic section that expands to lock the body into the lifter bore (adjustable for various lifter bore diameters). At the lower tip is a spring loaded, rounded plastic plunger that contacts the cam lobe. At the top is a gauge. Rotate the camshaft until the lowest reading is obtained (with the cam lobe on its base circle). Zero the gauge needle. As you rotate the camshaft, the gauge shows the lobe ramp and maxes out at peak lift. For instance, if the camshaft lift (not valve lift) is specified at .500 inch, when the lobe has reached maximum lift, the gauge shows the existing amount of lift. You then compare this to published lobe lift. This is a very easy tool to use and offers several applications when you need to monitor the position or base-to-peak travel.

The indicator is zeroed after the camshaft is rotated so that the gauge plunger contacts the camshaft base circle. This gauge allows you to not only locate the base circle, but to measure the cam lobe ramp and peak as the camshaft is rotated. A camshaft lobe checker gauge features an aluminum body, a dial indicator, and a spring-loaded plunger. The plunger is a plastic composite material, placed directly onto a camshaft lobe. The gauge body features an expandable collar that allows you to rotate the body to lock the tool into the lifter bore.

Conversions

Metric
1 Newton Meter = .741 ft-lb
1 Newton Meter = 8.892 in-lb
1 mKg = 7.25 ft-lb
1 cmKg = .870 in-lb
1 nKg = 9.8 Newton Meter
1 Meter = 100 centimeters
1 Meter = 39.37 inches
1 Meter = 3.2808 feet
1 Kilogram = 1,000 grams
1 Kilogram = 2.2046 pounds
1 Newton = .2258 pounds

English
1 in-lb = 1.15 cm.Kg
1 ft-lb = 1.35 Newton Meter
1 in-oz = 28.35 in. gram
1 in-lb = 16 in-oz
1 ft-lb = 12 in-lb
1 foot = 12 inches
1 pound = 16 ounces
1 pound = 453.59 grams

CHAPTER 3

Cylinder Block Disassembly and Inspection

Before you attempt a short-block disassembly, plan ahead. Instead of blindly removing items and scattering them in a pile, reserve a table or workbench to keep all parts organized, even if you plan to replace most or all parts. Also, it's a good idea to take photos during disassembly. These will serve you well during reassembly, unless you are already very familiar with the specific engine design.

Step by Step

Drain all liquids including, engine oil and coolant, and dispose according to state and local guidelines. With the oil pan, water pump and all driven accessories, intake manifold, and flywheel removed, remove all rocker arms and pushrods. Organize all rocker arms and pushrods for original position so that you can determine the location for any unusual wear.

Remove all valve lifters. If flat-tappet lifters are used, remove them one at a time. If roller lifters are used, remove them one pair at a time if they are connected with a tie bar; remove them individually if their orientation is guided by "dogbone" guides. If you're dealing with an LS engine, a plastic lifter "tray" guides a bank of four lifters; the tray is secured with a single bolt. If the engine is a GM LS type, rotate the crankshaft twice. This allows the cam to push all lifters upward to be held in the lifter trays, which eases removal.

Before tearing down a used engine, do yourself a favor and take plenty of photos as a record of parts and their locations. This can come in handy during organizing parts and during assembly.

AUTOMOTIVE MACHINING: A GUIDE TO BORING, DECKING, HONING AND MORE

CYLINDER BLOCK DISASSEMBLY AND INSPECTION

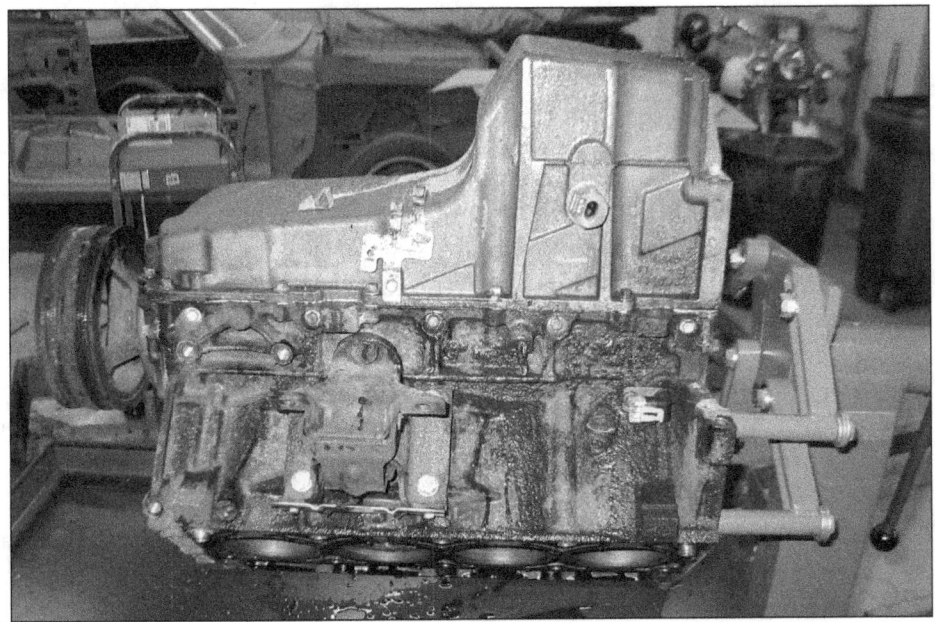

Completely drain the engine of all oil and coolant. After heads are removed, rotate the engine upside down on your stand.

Certain OEM crank dampeners/pulleys require a special tool for removal. This LS crank pulley features tangs at each of the three spokes that accept a specialty puller. Never use a common pulley puller that engages onto the outer rim of the pulley, as this can distort the pulley or dampener.

Rods and pistons may be removed once the heads and oil pickup assemblies have been removed, but the crank dampener, front cover, and rear cover (if so equipped) must be removed prior to crankshaft removal.

If you plan to apply a show-quality paint job to the block, perform any surface smoothing and removal of casting burrs before the block is machined. This type of operation creates an enormous amount of metal particles and dust.

A power tool such as a pneumatic or electric impact wrench may be used for disassembly, but never during assembly. A power wrench makes faster work of disassembly.

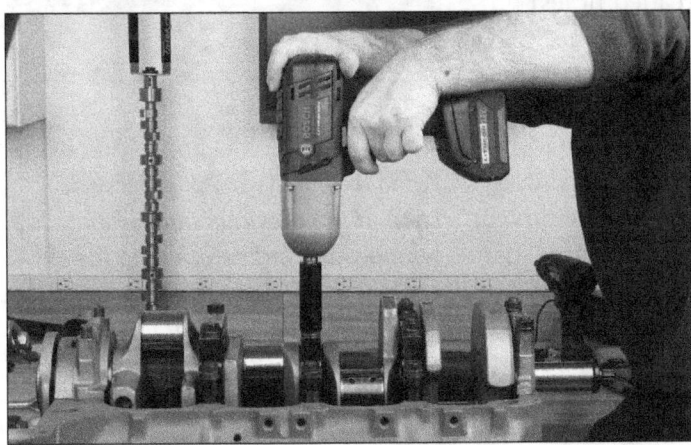

CHAPTER 3

Because you will likely replace all head bolts or studs, removal may be done by hand with a wrench or with a power tool such as a pneumatic or electric impact wrench. Although the heads on a V-engine are interchangeable bank to bank, it's a good idea to label each head before removing, simply from a reference standpoint. Depending on the engine design, the heads may feature additional inboard, smaller-diameter fasteners near the top of the block decks, as found on LS engines. Before attempting to remove the heads, make sure that all fasteners that secure the heads to the block have been removed. Lift the heads from the block. The gaskets may be stuck, or the heads may be slightly stuck onto the deck dowels. If a head seems stubborn to remove, strike the head on its sides with a large rubber mallet to help dislodge it. Avoid hammering a screwdriver between the head and block deck because this can easily damage either deck surface.

Remove the crankshaft's balancer. In most cases this is interference fit to the crank snout, requiring the use of a dedicated balancer removal tool that allows you to smoothly draw the balancer from the crank. Never strike the balancer with any object such as a hammer. The balancer must be pulled off, not pounded off.

Remove the front timing cover. Remove the oil pump and its pickup. If a windage tray is mounted to the block, remove it. Remove the timing system by removing the camshaft gear and the timing chain.

With the block rotated 90 degrees or so for ease of access, remove all connecting rods and pistons. Rotate the crankshaft at/near bottom dead center to gain the best access to an individual rod cap. Remove one piston/rod assembly at a time. Remove both rod bolts and remove the rod cap. Using your fingers or a plastic, brass, or aluminum drift, push the big end of the rod off the crank journal. Continue to push the rod and piston toward the deck until the piston rings have cleared the deck. Use your other hand to capture the piston, to prevent the piston and rod from falling to the floor. As you remove rod and piston assemblies, keep them organized if you plan to reuse the rod and/or piston.

When all rods and pistons have been removed, remove all crankshaft main caps. If the caps are not already labeled for position, do this now using an electric etching pen. Avoid using a hammer and number punch, as this may potentially damage the caps. Caps should also be labeled for orientation (which side of each cap faces forward) if not already marked. Before attempting to remove the main caps, make sure that all bolts are removed. Some blocks, such as vintage Ford FE big-blocks and late model LS engines, feature additional side bolts that engage caps from the outside of the block above the oil pan rails.

By hand, wiggle each main cap to dislodge it. Inserting a pair of used main cap bolts into the cap (but not into the block's threaded holes) provides added leverage. Some main caps may feature a small notch at each side that allows you to dislodge the cap by using a flat-tip screwdriver leveraged against the oil pan rail.

With all main caps removed, carefully remove the crankshaft straight up, avoiding nicking the journals against the exposed edges of the upper main saddles.

Place the crankshaft in a secure location to ensure that it isn't rolled or knocked off of a table or workbench.

After the crankshaft is removed, carefully remove the camshaft. With the crank out of the way, you have better access to the cam, allowing you to guide it out using both hands. Place the camshaft in a secure location to prevent it from being knocked onto the floor. If the cam is to be replaced or is worn, this may not matter, but if the cam is in good condition, you may choose to reuse it or you may be able to sell it.

Using a cam bearing tool and a heavy hammer, remove all old cam bearings. Remove the front number-1 cam bearing first, followed by the second, third, fourth, and fifth.

Work your way from front to rear. Remove all plugs from the block, including coolant jacket

When an engine block enters the shop, if the previous builder installed temperature indicators onto the coolant expansion plugs, check to see if the soft lead center of the indicator appears melted. This indicates that the engine experienced a severe overheating.

34   AUTOMOTIVE MACHINING: A GUIDE TO BORING, DECKING, HONING AND MORE

CYLINDER BLOCK DISASSEMBLY AND INSPECTION

Removing coolant expansion plugs from a block is relatively easy. Simply use a striker (drift or chisel) and a hammer. Place the striker to one side of the plug and hit the striker with the hammer to cock the plug out of position.

When the plug is cocked, use a pry tool to extract the plug, leveraging the pry bar against the block. If the plug happens to fall inside the water jacket, grab it with Vise-Grip pliers and remove.

With main caps fully installed to specified torque, measure each main bore with a calibrated bore gauge. The bore gauge is first adjusted to the main bore specification. Any deviation in terms of diameter and out-of-round is then revealed on the gauge.

If a step ridge is found near the top of the cylinder bore, this is the result of excessive ring wear. If you can feel a ridge with your fingernail, the bore must be refinished to eliminate this ridge. Depending on the amount of wear, this may necessitate overboring to accept a larger piston or it may be corrected by final honing.

expansion plugs and all oil galley plugs. Depending on the engine, the smaller oil galley plugs may be small expansion plugs or threaded NPT (national pipe thread) plugs. Again, depending on the engine, NPT plugs may feature a female hex or a female square drive, so the appropriate wrenches are required. If a threaded NPT plug is difficult to remove, one trick is to heat the surrounding area in the immediate plug area with a torch until it glows. Then immediately apply a beeswax bar to the plug, allowing the wax to penetrate into the threads. This often frees the plug, enabling removal with a wrench.

Block Inspection

When the block has been completely disassembled to a bare block, clean the block using a jet washer or a cleaning oven, followed by jet washing. Although the block will go through additional cleaning after machining, you should clean the block now to properly inspect it. Visually inspect for cracks, cylinder bore pitting, etc. Using a flaw detection method, further inspect for cracks. This can be done with a dye penetrant system or a handheld magnetic particle inspection. Inspect for cracks on the decks between cylinders, cracks in the cylinder bores, cracks at main webs, etc.

Install the main caps, tightening the bolts to specification, and measure the main bore diameters using a bore gauge, comparing your findings to that block's specifications. Record your findings. Using a bore gauge,

CHAPTER 3

Here, after applying a dusting of checking powder, a portable magnetic particle checker is placed across a main saddle to reveal a crack in this upper main bearing saddle. This close-up shows a severe crack in the upper bearing saddle, likely caused by extreme crankshaft dynamic loading during abusive racing use. Here, the crack is bordered by two white marks to make the crack more visible in the photo.

A magnetic particle inspection station features a magnetic ring. The part (in this example a crankshaft) is passed through the magnetic field. After an iron particle liquid is applied, a UV light reveals any cracks.

Check the block's decks in the same manner, from front to rear, above bores, below bores, and across the center of the bores.

measure each cylinder's diameter and record the findings. This provides a reference that helps you to determine if diameter corrections are needed. Even if you plan to overbore the cylinders, measuring the bores now provides a reference.

Although the main caps are in place and the block decks cleaned of any residual gasket material, use a machinist's precision straightedge and a feeler gauge to measure block decks for straightness/warpage. Measuring should be performed lengthwise, from front to rear, above the cylinder bores, intersecting the bores and below the bores. Measure diagonally from the front top corner to the lower rear corner, and from the upper rear corner to the front lower corner. Also check for flatness from the intake side to the exhaust side of the deck, between each cylinder.

As a rule of thumb, the limit of allowable deck surface warpage is as follows:

- With cast-iron heads on a V-6 block, .003 inch or less
- With cast-iron heads on a V-8 block, .004 inch or less
- With cast-iron heads on a straight-6 block, .006 inch or less
- With aluminum heads, tolerances must be tighter; a limit of .002 inch or less in any direction should be acceptable

Inspect each cylinder's walls for thickness, using a sonic wall thickness checker. If corrosion has occurred behind the cylinder wall

When checking for deck warpage, the precision straightedge must be firmly held against the deck, preventing the straightedge from tilting.

This block was never measured for cylinder wall thickness. After oversizing the bores and honing, a small pinhole was found, where the area next to a water jacket had become dangerously thin, aggravated by corrosion inside the water passage. This cylinder then had to be bored out to accept a cylinder sleeve to save the block. It's better to find out before boring and honing.

CYLINDER BLOCK DISASSEMBLY AND INSPECTION

Handheld sonic checking systems are ideal for measuring cylinder wall thickness. Checking this early saves time and aggravation as opposed to finding out that a section of a wall is too thin after having bored and honed. Cylinder wall thickness checks are made at a variety of clock positions, from top to bottom, on each cylinder. The goal is to verify wall thickness at adjacent water jackets. The major thrust side walls were checked at the minimum .288 inch, prior to cylinder oversizing.

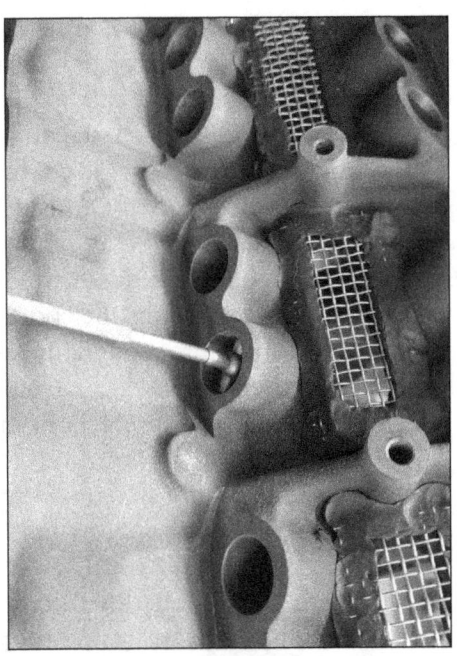

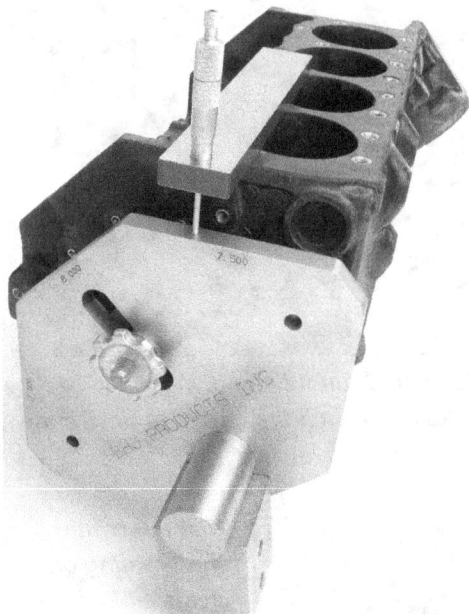

An accurate way to measure block deck height is with the use of a specialty fixture such as the BHJ indexing kit shown here. A bar of the correct diameter is inserted into the main bore. A precision-ground aluminum plate attaches to the bar. The distance from the centerline of the main bore to the top surface of the plate that's adjacent to the deck is 7.500 inches. With a precision flat bar laid onto the deck, a depth micrometer affixed to the bar contacts the upper face of the plate, allowing you to measure the distance from the plate edge to the deck surface by simply adding the fixed 7.500 inches to your micrometer measurement. If you don't have access to this type of fixture, you can use a long caliper to measure from the radius of the main bore to the deck, although you may need to repeat the check a number of times to verify the measurement. (Photo Courtesy BHJ)

If a dedicated valve lifter bore gauge is not available, a telescoping gauge is inserted into the lifter bore. After allowing the spring-loaded gauge anvils to contact the bore walls, carefully tighten the tip of the gauge body to lock the arms in position. Remove the gauge and measure the distance from the tip of each arm with a micrometer.

Also measure the block's deck height and compare your findings to the specification. If the decks have been machined in the past and require additional correction, this can result in the pistons protruding too far out of the decks for your intended application. This measurement refers to the distance from the crankshaft bore centerline to the deck surface. Specialty tools are available for this measurement that allow you to measure from the radius of the main bore to the deck. By measuring from the radius of the main bore to the deck surface, you then add one-half of the main bore diameter to obtain the distance from the centerline of the main bore to the deck.

at coolant jacket locations, or if the cylinders have previously been oversized, sonic testing helps determine if the walls are thick enough to accept overboring. Checking this now will save a ton of grief later on if you skip this and then find out that the walls are too thin after you've gone to the trouble of overboring. Check specifications, but in general, a minimum wall thickness should be in the range of about .200 to .250 inch. If one or more cylinders are found to be too thin, consider installing cylinder sleeves to save the block.

CHAPTER 3

Inspect and clean all bolt threads, especially head bolt holes and main cap holes. Clean each threaded hole using a dedicated thread chaser, not a common cutting tap. A thread chaser cleans and re-forms existing threads; a cutting tap removes metal, potentially weakening the threads.

Measure the existing lifter bores for diameter and out-of-round, using a dedicated lifter bore gauge or a telescoping gauge. Measure each lifter bore from top to bottom, and at various clock positions. Record your measurements for each lifter bore. When you have the lifters that will be installed, measure the lifter diameters and compare to your lifter bore measurements to determine oil clearance. Refer to the OEM or aftermarket specifications to determine if any lifter bore corrections are needed.

Crankshaft Inspection

Inspect each journal for pits, scratches, or gouges. With the crankshaft cleaned, measure all main and rod journals and compare your findings to that crank's specifications.

Inspect the crank for runout. With the crank placed on clean

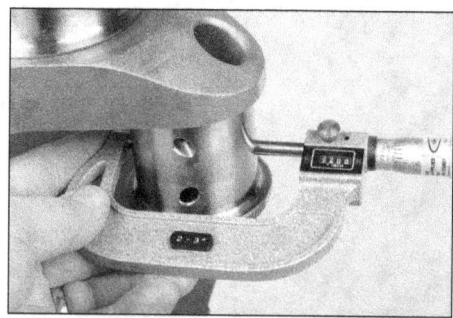

Measure each rod journal carefully and record your findings, and then compare to published specifications.

Crankshaft runout being checked on a dedicated runout stand. You need to rotate the crankshaft slowly on the V-blocks and watch the gauge to determine the measurement.

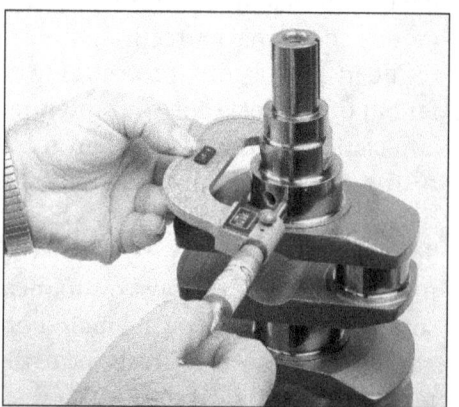

Using a micrometer, measure each of the crankshaft's main journals, and record the diameters. Compare your findings to specifications.

With the crankshaft resting on clean V-blocks, a dial indicator set up at the center main journal allows you to check for crank runout. In some cases, runout may be corrected by using a press to apply pressure to the middle of the crank with the high point of runout positioned at twelve o'clock, pushing the crank about .001 inch or so past zero, in which case the crank should slightly spring back. The goal is to obtain zero runout.

CYLINDER BLOCK DISASSEMBLY AND INSPECTION

Using published rod big end diameter specifications to calibrate the gauge, measure each rod big end diameter to determine size and out-of-round.

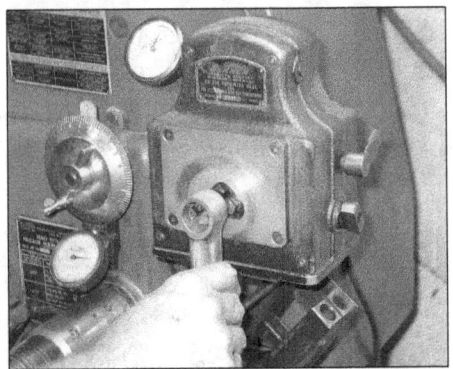

With the gauge adjusted to the rod small end bore specification, measure each rod small end to determine if it meets spec or requires resizing.

Used connecting rods should always be inspected for bend and twist. Using a dedicated rod checker, here a rod is checked for bend. The big end rests on a stationary guide while the upper portion of the checker contacts the wrist pin's upper surfaces. If the upper contacts do not meet the wrist pin evenly, the rod beam is bent. Here a rod is checked for twist with the upper contacts of the checker on the side of the wrist pin. If the upper contacts of the checker do not evenly touch the wrist pin (if a gap is found on one end), the rod has a twist in the beam.

Camshafts may be checked for runout in a similar manner. Here a cam rests on clean nylon-covered V-blocks. If you do not have a dedicated runout stand, you can place the dial indicator's magnet onto a heavy section of flat steel to provide a rigid mount for the indicator stand. Place the indicator plunger onto the center cam journal, adjusting it to apply about .050 inch of preload. After adjusting the gauge to zero, slowly rotate the cam to note any runout on the gauge dial.

V-blocks or on a crankshaft polishing station, locate a stand-mounted dial indicator at the center main journal. Adjust the indicator plunger with about .050-inch preload and zero the gauge dial. Slowly rotate the crank, noting any runout.

Rod Inspection

If the original rods are planned for final assembly, use a magnetic particle inspection system to check each rod for cracks. Also check each rod for bend and twist.

Any issue, including cracks, bend, or twist, deformation of the big end requires rod replacement.

Cam Inspection

If the cam is to be reused, inspect camshaft journals for signs of scratches or pitting. Inspect lobes for signs of excessive wear or pitting. Any faults indicate the need to replace the cam.

Also inspect the camshaft for runout. This can be done on a dedicated camshaft checking station, or by placing the camshaft onto a pair

CHAPTER 3

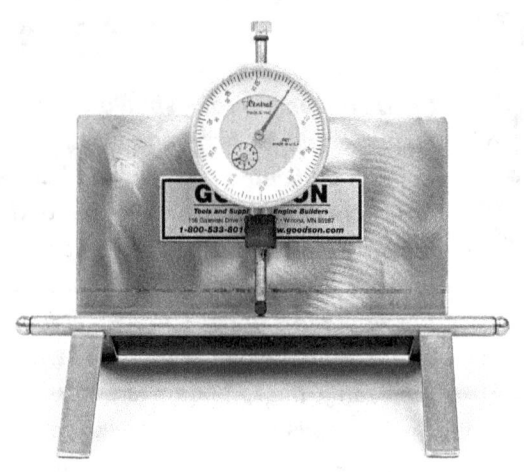

Check all used pushrods for runout. Here a pushrod is placed onto a pushrod checker. The dial indicator plunger contacts the middle of the pushrod, adjusting the plunger with about .050-inch preload, with the gauge then adjusted to zero. Slowly rotate the pushrod and note any runout. Generally speaking, runout in excess of .0015 inch indicates the need for replacement.

Inspect each rocker arm's pushrod cup for excessive wear, as seen in this example of a factory original LS rocker arm.

of clean V-blocks. Position a dial indicator at the center camshaft journal. Adjust the dial indicator plunger onto the journal and apply a preload of about .050 inch, then zero the indicator gauge. Slowly rotate the camshaft, noting any runout. Runout should be less than .0015 inch. If a cam is bent it should be replaced. Do not attempt to straighten it.

Inspect the cam's distributor drive gear, if the engine features a cam-driven distributor. Check for wear and tooth damage. If the camshaft features an eccentric lobe for a mechanical fuel pump, inspect the lobe for excessive wear. Also inspect the fuel pump rod for tip wear.

Pushrod Inspection

If you intend to reuse the pushrods, or if you simply want to check the condition, place each pushrod onto a runout checking stand that features a dial indicator. Contact the center of the pushrod with the indicator plunger, and apply a bit of preload, perhaps .050 inch, and zero the dial. Slowly rotate the pushrod and watch the indicator gauge. Any runout of .001 to .0015 inch or more indicates that the pushrod has experienced excessive load and should be replaced.

An alternative is to slowly roll the pushrod on a perfectly flat surface such as a pane of glass. If the pushrod does not roll easily and smoothly and any wobble is found, this indicates that the pushrod is bent.

Also inspect each pushrod for scratches or nicks, signs of heat-related bluing, and inspect the ends of the pushrod for excessive wear. If any damage is found, replace the pushrod. If the pushrod features an oil passage, check to make sure that the passage is clear and clean.

Rocker Arm Inspection

Examine all rocker arms for excessive wear, including all pivot points and surfaces that contact the pushrod and the valvestem tip. If the rocker arms feature needle bearings at the trunion pivot, inspect for bearing cage looseness and for missing needle bearings. Some OEM rocker arms that feature trunion needle bearings are incapable of handling high engine RPM, resulting in needle bearing damage, where the needle bearings are no longer captured and may exit the rocker, scattering these bearings throughout the engine. If the engine was equipped with full-roller rockers that feature roller bearings at the trunion and at the rocker valve tips, inspect for smooth roller operation.

Cylinder Head Inspection

First make sure that the head deck is clean and free of any debris or gasket material. Measure cylinder head decks for flatness using a precision straightedge and a feeler gauge in the

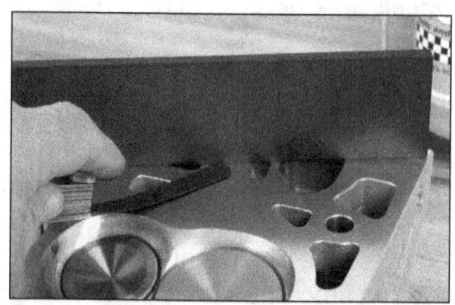

Measure cylinder head for warpage in several planes. When checking in a diagonal path, the straightedge is placed between opposite corners. For example, front lower corner to rear upper corner, and from front upper corner to rear lower corner. Also check for warpage in a straight line from front to rear, at each side of the combustion chambers, and across the center of the chambers.

CYLINDER BLOCK DISASSEMBLY AND INSPECTION

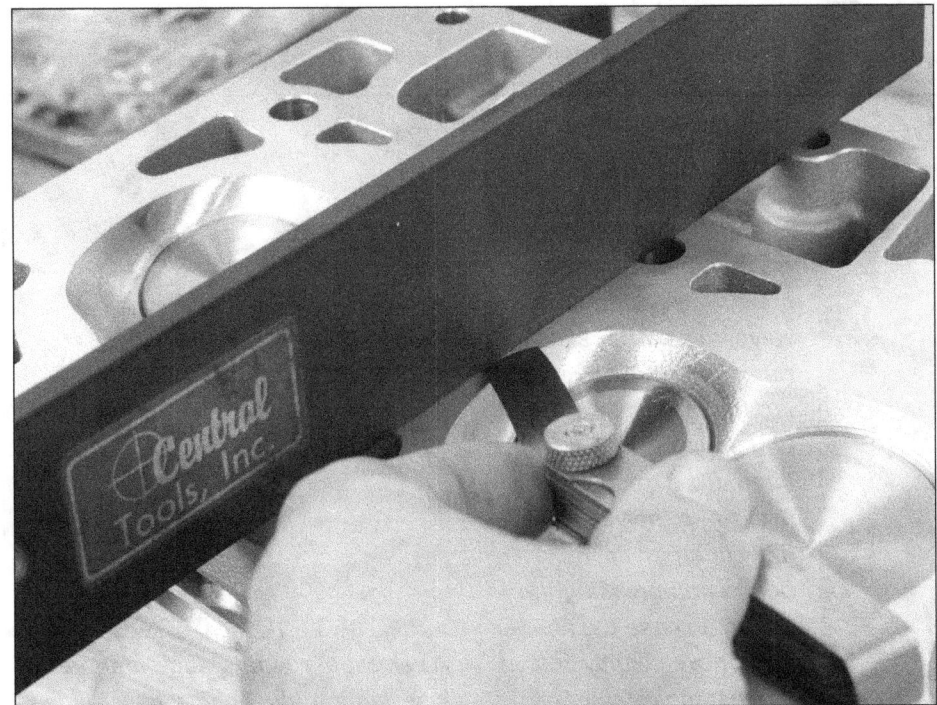

Also check for warpage across the width of the head, from the intake side to the exhaust side, between the combustion chambers.

Precision machinist's straightedges are available in various lengths. Always use a length that contacts the entire surface being measured. Use only a quality steel straightedge that is precision-ground. Never rely on a common ruler or on a section of scrap steel that you might assume is straight.

same manner used when checking the block's decks. As a general rule, a minimum acceptable warpage from front to rear or when measured diagonally is .004 inch or less for iron heads and .002 inch or less for aluminum heads, with .001 inch or less along any 3-inch span.

Disassembly of the cylinder heads involves removal of valves, valvesprings, locks, and retainers. A manual or pneumatic valvespring compressor tool is used to compress the valvespring. This large C-clamp-shaped tool features one side that's a flat disc, and it's placed onto the valve face, holding the valve stationary. The opposite side of the tool features a C-shaped clamp that engages onto the spring retainer. As the tool compresses the spring, the valve locks, or keepers, are exposed. These two-piece locks are removed with your fingers or with a small pencil magnet. After the locks are removed, the tool is relaxed, decompressing the spring. The retainer, spring, and valve may then be easily removed.

For the sake of reference, especially if you plan to reuse the valves and springs, keep all parts organized for location.

Prior to compressing the spring, place a hollow tube or a socket wrench onto the retainer, avoiding contact with the valvestem tip. Retainers may have seized onto the locks, which makes it difficult to separate the retainer from the locks. Strike the tube or socket with a soft-faced hammer to dislodge the retainer. Before attempting to remove a valve, inspect the valvestem tip for burrs. If any burrs are present, this makes valve removal difficult and can result in damaging the valveguide. In this case, use a small abrasive stone or emery cloth to remove any burrs.

CHAPTER 3

A pneumatic valvespring compressor tool makes easy work in compressing valvesprings during disassembly or assembly. The C-clamp side of the tool engages onto the valvespring retainer. Compress the spring and remove the valve locks. After slowly relaxing and then removing the tool, the retainer and spring is removed by hand. It's a good idea to first strike the valvestem tip with a plastic mallet before compressing the spring, in case the keeper locks have slightly seized against the retainer or valvestem groove.

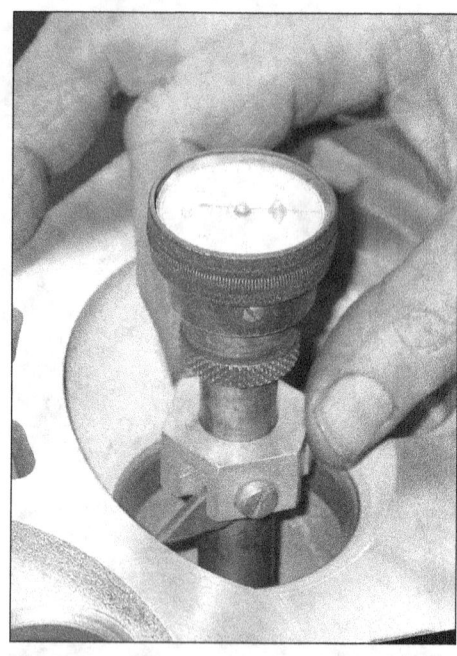

A valveseat runout gauge mandrel is inserted into the head's valveguide to locate the centerline. The gauge probe contacts the valveseat. As the probe is slowly rotated, the gauge dial indicates any runout.

Valves that are in good condition and are intended for installation are secured in a setup fixture, allowing the valveguide bore gauge to be calibrated to valvestem diameter.

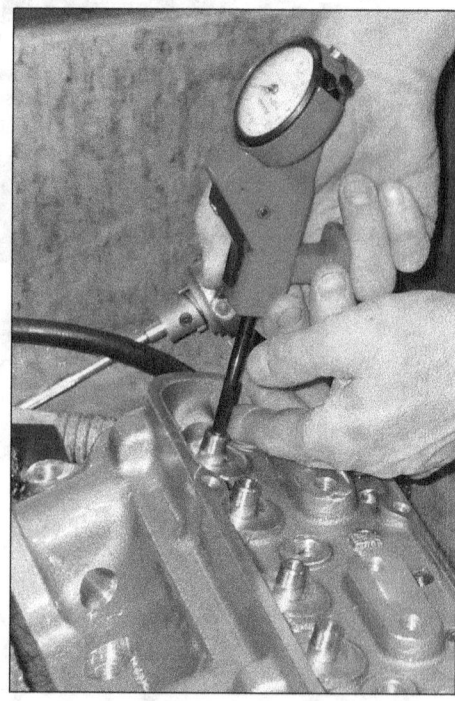

The valvestem bore gauge is then inserted into each valveguide to determine the oil clearance between the valvestem and guide.

CYLINDER BLOCK DISASSEMBLY AND INSPECTION

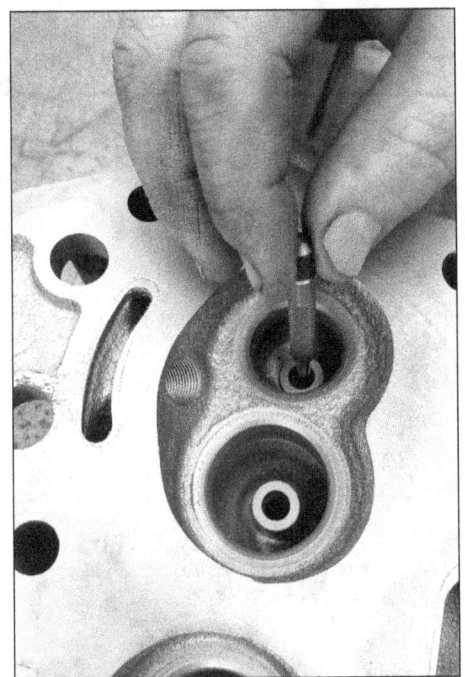

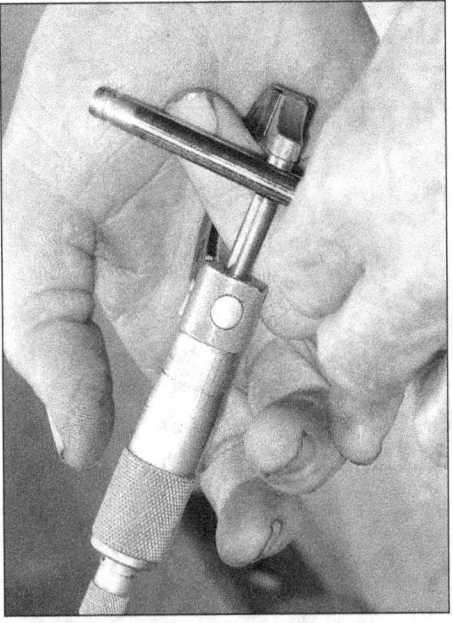

With valves removed, inspect each guide and seat for runout using a valveguide runout gauge. The gauge mandrel is inserted into the guide from the valveseat side. The angled probe of the gauge contacts the valveseat. Slowly rotate the gauge, noting any runout. If any runout is found, this indicates

Valvestems are measured with a micrometer, with thickness checks performed near the tip, at the center, and above the valve throat. Any thickness measurement that is under specification indicates excessive wear and the valve should be replaced.

A small split-ball gauge may be used to measure valveguide bore diameter. The ball gauge is inserted into the guide and adjusted to contact the guide walls.

An option to using a magnetic particle inspection is a dye penetrant kit, which allows you to inspect for cracks. A dye penetrant kit includes a surface cleaner, a dye penetrant, and a developer. Prior to using a portable magnetic flaw detection unit, a small bit of iron powder is applied to the area to be inspected. Spray the cleaner to the surface, which prepares the area for the penetrant.

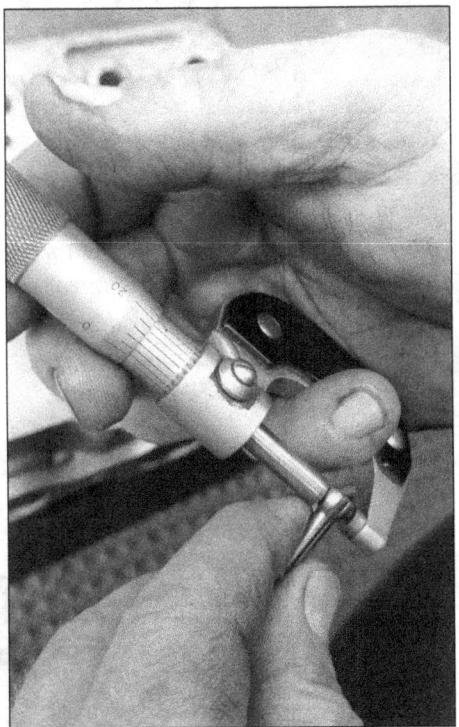

After removing the ball gauge from the guide, a micrometer is used to measure the ball diameter.

When the cleaner is dry, spray the penetrant.

AUTOMOTIVE MACHINING: A GUIDE TO BORING, DECKING, HONING AND MORE

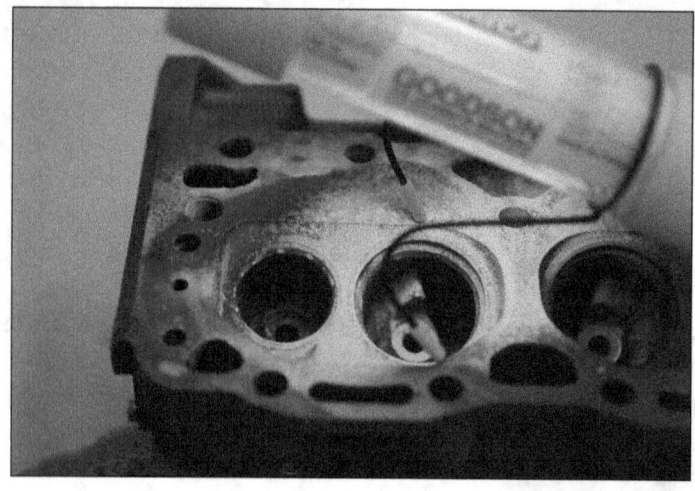

After applying the developer, the area is inspected with a UV light.

This close-up reveals a tiny crack at a spark plug hole.

Iron powder is applied to the inspection area. When the surface is energized, the particles are pulled into any existing cracks.

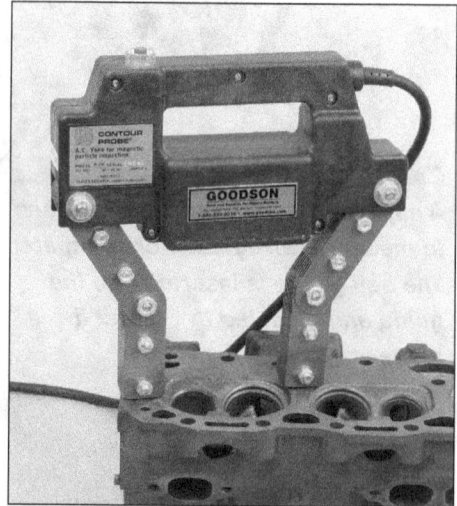

A portable magnetic inspection system consists of an electric-powered two-pole magnet and a bulb dispenser filled with iron powder. With the magnet placed on the surface of ferrous components, such as an iron head, the magnet is energized, creating a magnetic field between the poles.

the need to restore/replace the valveguide.

Using a valveguide bore gauge, inspect the diameter of each valveguide and record the findings. Refer to the specifications for the specific engine and compare this to your findings to determine if guides need to be replaced.

Inspect the cylinder heads for cracks, especially between valve pockets. Cast-iron heads can be checked with a magnetic particle inspection or a dye penetrant, while aluminum heads require the use of a dye penetrant.

Inspect all threaded spark plug holes for thread integrity, especially on aluminum heads. Depending on the thread condition, damaged threads may be restored using a chaser tap or by drilling the hole(s) oversize and installing a threaded insert.

Cracks are visible as the particles concentrate in a crack, slightly standing up. Here, a crack is found between two valveseats.

CHAPTER 4

CYLINDER BLOCK MACHINING

In this chapter I provide an overview of what's involved in preparing the engine block, addressing main bore honing, cylinder bore boring and honing, lifter bore correction, block deck resurfacing, and a brief outline regarding "blueprinting" the bare block.

Rough Edge and Obstruction Deburring

Before corrective machining, take the time to remove any casting burrs in the block that can affect the flow of fluids and/or areas that can present potential stress risers. Using a die grinder and the appropriate bits, remove rough casting flashings from oil drain-back passages in the lifter valley, sharp edges that could contribute to future stress cracks, etc. Performing these tasks at the very beginning eliminates the risk of damaging freshly machined surfaces.

Main Bore Align Honing

Main bore honing (also called align honing) is often necessary due to block core shift and block warpage, when main caps have been replaced, or when main caps have stretched due to excessive loading. Align honing allows you to establish the correct bore diameter, eliminate any out-of-roundness and achieve proper centerline alignment of the main bore, in all main bearing locations, from the front cap to the rear cap.

First and foremost, make sure that all main caps are placed in the proper order and location. This is especially important when dealing with a previously built/used engine block.

Here, a die grinder is used to notch the base of cylinder bores for connecting rod bolt clearance.

To remove any potential stress risers, use a die grinder and appropriate cutting bit to remove any casting flashings in the block.

Here, oil drain-back hole edges are smoothed out in the lifter valley of a vintage Mopar block, removing large flashings that remained after block casting. This provides more efficient oil drain-back.

All OEM and aftermarket main caps feature a stamped location number (1, 2, 3, 4, 5, etc.). In addition to location, orientation of the cap is critical. Some main caps feature an arrow, which always points toward the front of the block. In the case of some block designs, such as the GM LS family of blocks, each main cap features a different design on each side of the cap. One side is flat and the opposite side features a slight extension at each end. On the LS engines, number 1, 2, 3, and 4 main caps must be installed with the flat side facing the front of the block and the end-extension side facing the rear. Number 5 main cap is the opposite: the flat side faces the rear of the block.

When dealing with new performance aftermarket steel billet main caps, the caps must be honed to size. Cap makers generally machine the bores on the tight side, to allow you to final-hone the main bores to desired diameter.

Main bore align honing allows you to create a uniform bore location and diameter from front to rear. Especially when dealing with a used block, it is possible that the main bore centerline has shifted due to block distortion as a result of metal stresses and thermal expansion and contraction. Any shift along the centerline axis of the main bore results in uneven main bearing clearances. Whenever machining any block, it's imperative to check (and correct when necessary) the main bore diameter and alignment. Correction to the main bore may be performed by line boring or align honing. A line boring machine uses a cutting bit that machines the final bore with the cutting bit on a bar that establishes the correct bore centerline, with the cutter machining one bore location at a time. Align honing requires a main bore honing machine that features a horizontal bar that is equipped with honing stones. As the bar rotates in the bores, the bar is slid back and forth, honing all main bore locations at the same time.

If alignment correction is needed, the main caps may be shortened slightly by grinding material from the mating faces and then reinstalled on the block. Depending on the existing bore diameter and/or out-of-roundness, a minimal amount of material is removed from the caps, generally to the tune of about .002 to .003 inch or so. By shortening main caps and align honing to create a new round bore, you have effectively moved the crankshaft closer to the camshaft by one-half the distance of the amount removed from the main caps, which can cause loose timing chain issues. For example, if the caps were shortened to create a .002-inch undersize of the main bores, honing back to original size moves the crankshaft .001-inch closer to the camshaft tunnel. This small movement of the crankshaft centerline shouldn't cause any problems. If the crank centerline moves excessively, and if the timing chain fit is too loose, a special-order timing chain may be available to make up the difference to maintain proper timing chain tension.

Before align honing, install main caps using the same bolts or studs that will be used during final assembly. If using main cap studs, install studs finger-tight. The clamping force is achieved when the nuts are tightened.

Whenever changing main caps, the block and main caps must be align honed. When upgrading to new steel billet main caps, be aware that new caps are slightly undersized to allow you to hone to the desired main bore diameter.

Before main bore align honing, install all main caps and fully torque to specification, and check each bore for size and roundness with a calibrated bore gauge.

CYLINDER BLOCK MACHINING

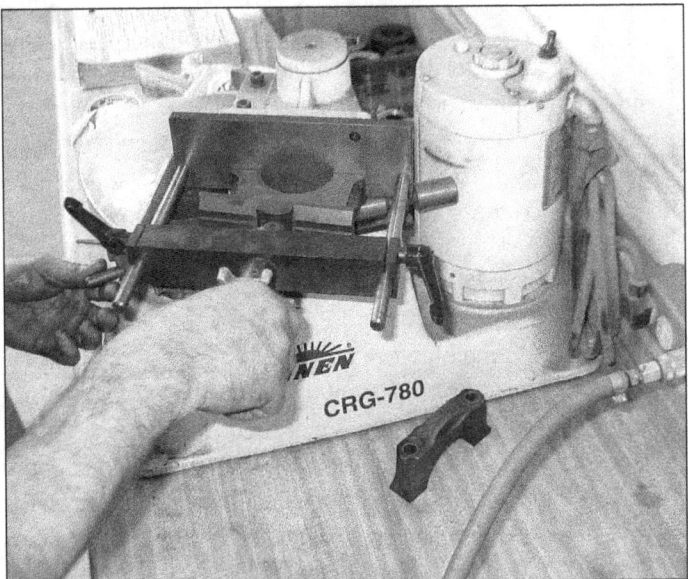

Here a Mopar 383 block is prepped for align bore honing with all five main caps fully installed.

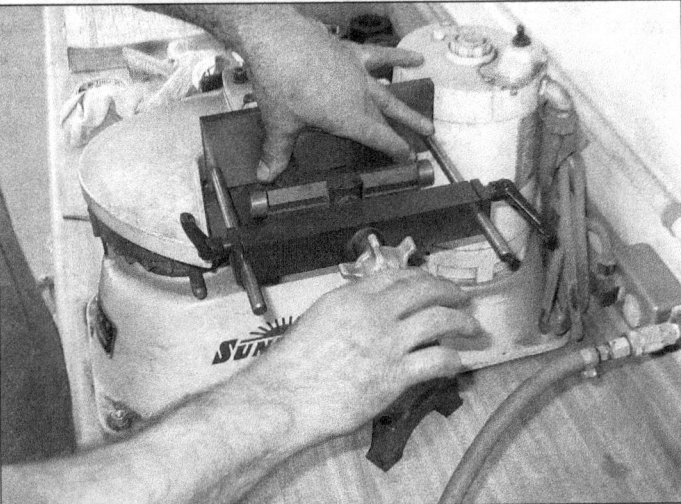

Here, a main cap face is ground as the operator sweeps the cap across the grinding stone.

Main caps are shortened using a dedicated main cap grinding machine. The main cap is clamped onto the machine's fixture. With the cap in a vertical position, the cap's mating surfaces are ground. With the cap in the horizontal position, the cap faces are kissed by the grinding stone to verify that a perfect 90-degree angle is obtained between the mating surface and faces.

Only remove the minimum amount of material from the caps to allow you to establish a new round bore. This is done on a main cap grinding machine. Pay particular attention to the thrust bearing main cap. Before removing material from the mating surfaces, first grind one side of the cap 90 degrees to the mating surface. This ground side is then placed on the flat fixed jaw of the grinding machine when grinding the cap's mating surfaces. Grinding the side of the cap first provides a flat register when grinding the mating surfaces, to prevent the cap from tilting, which affects thrust bearing clearance.

After the caps are ground, lightly deburr sharp edges from the parting lines that might otherwise interfere with bearing clearance and bearing crush. The main bore is then align honed on a main bore align honing machine, in several passes to re-create the necessary bore diameter and to create a straight axis through all bores. The grinding stones on the honing bar are adjustable for diameter. After a few initial passes, the bores are measured with a calibrated bore gauge to monitor the increase in bore diameter. Further honing and gauge checking is performed in stages until the desired bore size is achieved.

On some block designs, especially those that feature side "pinch" bolts, such as the old Ford FE side-bolt blocks and current GM LS blocks, you're severely limited as to how much material may be removed from the cap mating surfaces. Shortening the caps too far can prevent side bolt hole alignment. An alternative is to bore or hone the main bores to a greater-than-original diameter, with the difference taken care of with the use of oversize-outer diameter main bearings. Do your research beforehand to make sure that oversize–O.D. main bearings are available for the specific block at hand.

Operating an Align Honing Machine

Align-honing an engine block is often required for three common reasons. First, when an engine has been operated for many thousands of miles, the heat and stresses imposed on the block can result in block distortion, which can cause main bore misalignment. Second, if operational loads imposed by the rotating assembly have gradually distorted the main caps in a vertical direction, this could result in an out-of-round condition. Third, if an engine ran in a severely overheated condition, main bearings may have stuck to the crankshaft and spun inside the main bearing bore, causing main bore scoring.

Align honing ensures not only that the main bores are round and to size, but also are aligned from front to rear of the block. To align hone a block, a horizontal honing machine is required. Because some align honing machine operations vary, you need to cover a specific machine. For the purposes of this sidebar, I cite the Sunnen CH-100 machine as an example, which provides a roundness and alignment accuracy to within .005 inch.

Before align honing, make sure that all main caps are numbered for position and direction reference. Remove all main caps and grind the mating surfaces on a cap grinder, removing perhaps .002 inch. This creates a smaller, non-round bore when the caps are installed, allowing the honing process to establish a new, round hole. Then, install all main caps, torqueing to the specified value.

Mount the block onto the align honing machine, with the block upside-down.

Retract the honing stones on the hone unit fully by inserting a key into the end of the honing bar and turning it counterclockwise. Follow the machine's operating instructions to center the honing bar in reference to the block's main bore centerline. This can involve a dial indicator checking operation, which I don't have space here to explain in detail.

When the honing bar is centered, expand the honing stones by turning the key clockwise and turning the stone feed-up knob clockwise. Slide the honing bar out of the main bores and measure the main bearing bore diameters with a dial bore gauge. This determines how far undersized they are in relation to the main bore diameter specification for the specific block. Slide the honing bar into the main bore with the honing stones at twelve and six o'clock. Loosen the clamp handle, roughly align the machine's roller support with the six o'clock position of the main bore, and retighten the clamp handle. The front of the hone unit rests on the roller support.

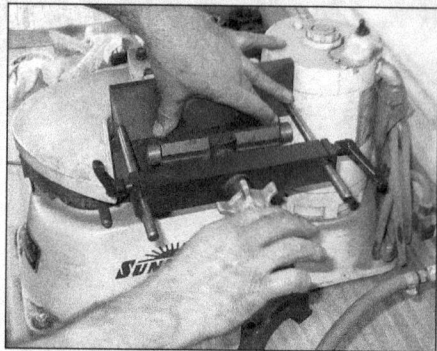

Prior to align honing, the main caps are prepared. Each cap is first ground flat on one side to produce a true 90-degree angle of the mating cap surface. Using that flat surface as a reference, the mating faces are then ground to slightly reduce the main bore diameter in an un-round state. Align honing then creates a round bore at the desired diameter.

Honing stones must be kept clean and cooled with a continuous application of honing fluid.

Lift the end of the hone unit and slide the hone unit into the main bores. Loosen the clamp handle and lower the roller support. The centerline of the main bearing bore should be in approximate alignment with the honing bar's quick coupler. Tighten the cradle clamp. Connect the hone driver to the quick coupler. Set the overstroke at each end of the stroke to ensure that the stones remain inside the bores during the stroking process.

Adjust the cutting pressure so that the honing stones automatically advance in diameter during the honing operation. Rotate the cutting pressure control dial clockwise with a chuck wrench until the zero mark lines up with the witness mark.

CYLINDER BLOCK MACHINING

Turn the stone feed-up knob by hand clockwise as far as it will go, then back off two turns counterclockwise.

With the machine's front door raised and latched, push the start lever to start the honing oil. Lower the oil bar. This automatically turns on the flow of oil onto the honing bar. While standing behind the drive motor, grasp the carriage/motor handle. Depress the button on the handle to turn the drive motor on, and then manually stroke the bar within the main bores with an even back and forth motion to preset the stroke stops. Release the button on the handle to stop the honing bar from rotating.

If the bearing bores are on the minimum size of specification and the caps were not ground, hone for 10 to 20 seconds. If the caps were ground by about .002 inch, hone for about 40 seconds. Disconnect the honing unit at the quick coupler and measure the bores for size and out-of-round using the dial bore gauge to determine if additional honing is required to establish the target bore diameter.

This is a very brief overview of align honing. Always follow the operating manual instructions for the specific machine. ∎

Also be aware that some blocks are very sensitive to distortional stresses, such as many aluminum blocks. Although main cap fasteners must be tightened to specification prior to align honing, other factors may influence the block and create stresses that can affect the main bore alignment, such as cylinder head fastener tightening. In some applications it may be necessary to install deck plates onto the block decks to simulate the installed heads, prior to align honing.

Another aspect to consider involves front and rear crankshaft seals. If the crankshaft centerline moves excessively (for example, more than .001 inch), this may result in the crankshaft not being located at the center of the front and rear seals due to a nonconcentric fit between the crank and its seals, which can easily lead to nasty oil leaks. If this is the case, it may be possible to relocate the front timing cover by drilling the cover mounting holes a bit oversize to allow you to center the front seal to the crank. The rear seal area, depending on engine design, might be addressed in the same manner, or by remachining the rear seal housing. This may not be necessary, but always check if the main caps have been reduced in height.

Although align honing is usually the preferred approach because it removes material from all main bore locations at the same time, instances do occur when align boring is required. For example, if you're swapping the center three OEM main caps to steel billet aftermarket caps, but retaining the front and rear OEM caps, line boring allows you to address the individual steel caps instead of having a main bore hone attempting to "average" the material removal on all caps. If you happen to deal with a block that features stepped-size main bores, line boring will be necessary to achieve the correct individual bore diameters.

If you're dealing with an engine for which no published oil clearance specifications are readily available,

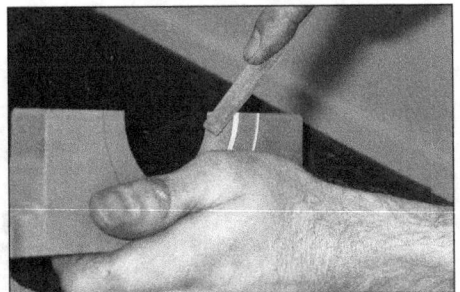

Main cap bearing parting edges are lightly filed to remove sharp edges and burrs.

Front and rear edges at the bearing parting lines are also lightly filed to remove sharp edges.

Maine Bore Measurements

Following is an example of determining main bore size:

Crankshaft journal diameter (inches)	2.3500
Upper bearing thickness (inch)	.0620
Lower bearing thickness (inch)	.0620
Oil clearance desired (inch)	.002
Target main bore diameter (inches)	2.476

With the honing bar in place in the main bore, honing coolant nozzles are positioned to provide lubrication and cooling for the honing stones.

Multiple light passes are made through the main bore, with the honing stones adjusted as needed in increments to achieve the final desired bore diameter.

A dedicated main bore honing machine is required to correct a block's main bores for both diameter and bore-to-bore alignment from front to rear of the block. Note the coolant/lubrication spray bar positioned above the honing bar.

you can approximate the requirement for the final main bore diameter by considering the crankshaft journal diameter, main bearing thickness, and a generally accepted oil clearance of .002 inch.

Perform a test fit of the crankshaft (with at least three main bearings in place) and connecting rods (with bearings) to check for rod-to-block clearance, especially if you're using a longer-stroke crankshaft and aftermarket connecting rods. Check for clearance between the rod big ends and rod bolt heads to the block. Mark any interference areas, remove the crank and rods, and relieve the block as needed for clearance. Generally speaking, you want a minimum of about .080 to .100 inch of clearance.

Cylinder Boring and Honing

Cylinder overboring is required to correct for bore damage, excessive bore taper, or out-of-round in addition to accepting oversize pistons. Actually, whenever boring to an oversize, piston replacement is required. Cylinder boring involves machining the bore walls with a cutter, to be finished up to final diameter and surface finish on a honing machine. The boring operation is not performed to achieve the final diameter. The boring operation must leave a small amount that will be removed during cylinder honing. Generally speaking, you should leave about .004 to .005 inch of material that will then be removed during the honing process.

Before boring, you must determine the diameter of the pistons to be installed. Piston diameter dictates the required finished bore diameter. Carefully measure your pistons using a micrometer, but only at the skirt location specified by the piston maker. Do not assume that you should measure at the very bottom edge of the piston skirt; a slight taper is designed into the pistons. You must measure only at the location recommended by the piston manufacturer. Today's performance piston makers do an outstanding job of manufacturing their pistons to very precise tolerances, but you should never assume anything. You should measure each piston for diameter. If diameters vary by more than .001

Prior to main bore align honing and after each honing step, each main bore is carefully checked with a bore gauge, checking for both diameter and roundness. The bore gauge is gently rocked to be able to read maximum bore diameter, comparing the reading to the desired diameter that was previously calibrated to the bore gauge.

CYLINDER BLOCK MACHINING

During test fitting, especially when using an increased stroke and aftermarket performance connecting rods, always check for clearance between rod bolt heads and the block, and between rod big end bosses and the block.

Always test fit the crankshaft and rods prior to major block machining, especially when planning to increase crankshaft stroke, to check for rod-to-block clearance issues. Here you see an interference issue between a rod bolt and the block.

A slight notch has been ground at the bottom of a cylinder to clear the rod bolt. Don't wait until all block machining has been finished only to discover that a clearance issue exists.

inch, plan to final-hone each cylinder dedicated to each piston.

For example, if the application starts with a 4.000-inch bore and plans to oversize by +.030 inch to achieve a 4.030-inch bore, don't assume that the finished bored and honed cylinder should be taken to 4.030 inch. Always measure piston diameter, adding the recommended piston-to-wall clearance.

As a specific example, during block machining of an LS race engine, I planned to obtain a 4.185-inch bore, using a set of custom JE pistons. The piston diameter, measured .275 inch from the skirt bottom as specified by JE, measured out at 4.1795 inches. The cylinders were then bored on the first pass at 4.155 inches, followed by boring to 4.180 inches. This left the remaining .0055 inch to be removed during honing (JE recommended a piston-to-wall clearance of .0055 inch). Boring was accomplished in two stages to reduce the frictional heat generated by material removal.

Boring is generally accomplished with either a boring bar or on a CNC machine. A boring bar allows you to bore one cylinder at a time, and if set up properly allows you to achieve good results. However, keep in mind that a boring bar fixture indexes the bar relative to the block deck. If the block deck isn't flat and "square," the cylinder will be bored off-angle relative to inboard/outboard or front-to-rear of

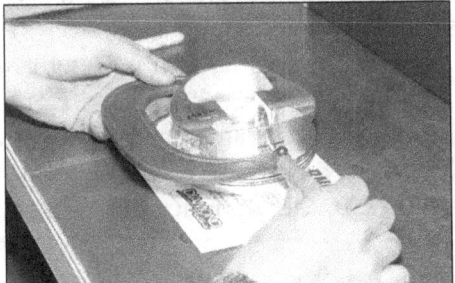

Prior to cylinder boring or honing, always measure the piston diameters of the pistons that will be used. When piston diameter is known, final honing can be accomplished to obtain the required piston-to-cylinder wall clearance. Be sure to measure piston skirt diameter precisely at the skirt height location specified by the piston maker.

Cylinder bores are machined to a rough size, leaving approximately .003 to .005 inch for material removal during honing. It is absolutely critical to measure the piston skirt diameter and to determine the piston-to-wall clearance specified by the piston maker prior to boring.

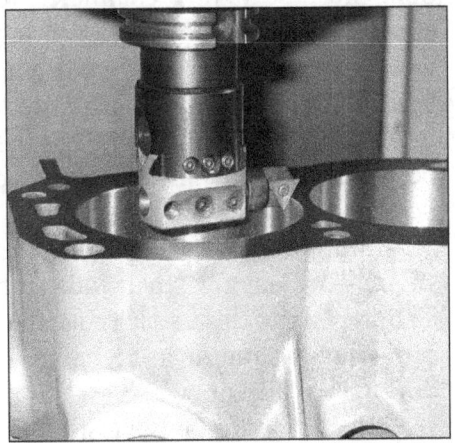

After decks are milled on a CNC, a cutting bit creates a slight chamfer at the top of each cylinder bore. CNC cutting provides a precise and uniform chamfer at all cylinder locations.

CHAPTER 4

the deck. If you're using a traditional boring bar, the block decks should first be checked (and resurfaced if needed) to verify that the deck is parallel to the crankshaft centerline. On a CNC machine, a reference is taken from the crank centerline, avoiding this potential issue.

Cylinder boring should be accomplished by alternating bore locations to reduce the potential distortional effects of heat buildup effecting adjacent cylinders. Instead of boring cylinders in progression from the front to rear (cylinder 1, 3, 5, and 7 for example), bore number 5, followed by number 1, followed by number 7, and then number 3 cylinder. This gives the previously bored cylinder a bit of time to cool before boring the cylinder that's next to it.

The boring cutter should be allowed to travel about .500 inch past the bottom of the cylinder (depending on block design) to provide adequate clearance for the honing stones during the honing operation, to avoid having the honing stones bottom-out against a lip.

The top edges of each cylinder bore must be lightly chamfered to allow entry of piston rings during final assembly. This must be done either after boring or after deck resurfacing, where a sharp edge has been created. Chamfering may be done either using an abrasive cone on a drill or on a CNC machine and should be about 1/32-inch wide. The chamfer eliminates a sharp edge that can cause piston rings to hang up during final assembly.

After the bores are oversized on the boring machine, the block is then moved to a honing machine. Do not try to hone by hand, using a power drill and a honing ball. This is only for lightly deglazing an existing bore where no size corrections are being made. Final honing must be performed on a dedicated cylinder honing machine.

A honing machine allows you to mount the block with the block deck facing upright at a 90-degree angle from the main bore centerline. The machine's honing stone head features a flexible mount that compensates for slight off-angle conditions.

Bore mounting the block to the honing machine, all main caps must be installed and fully torqued to specification. To further compensate for potential block distortion, always install a deck plate to each block deck, using the same fasteners that will be used during head installation. Installing deck plates simulates cylinder head installation. This is recommended because the block may be prone to cylinder bore distortion after the heads are installed.

By installing deck plates, the block is then stressed in its final assembled condition, allowing you to create a more precise cylinder wall profile, reducing or eliminating cylinder out-of-round or taper when the engine is assembled. The use of deck plates is no longer a "trick" procedure aimed at only race engines. This improves the cylinder bore shape on any engine, with resulting benefits in terms of reduced friction, smoother engine operation, improved performance, and potentially improved fuel economy. A cylinder bore that is more precisely honed to final shape reduces engine operating friction and resistance.

The honing fixture features a set of four honing stones, adjusted for bore diameter. The honing machine allows the operator to adjust and monitor honing speed, strokes per minute, and honing dwell. Dwell refers to the amount of time honing is allowed to spend at any given bore height location. If the machine's monitor tells you that it's seeing more resistance at the bottom of the cylinder, for example, you can then allow the honing stones to "dwell" a bit longer at that location, compensating for any cylinder bore distortion. Honing stone types and grades are selected for various applications and operator preferences. Generally, a diamond-particle stone cuts faster and lasts longer than vitrified stones. Some machinists prefer to use a rougher diamond stone to "rough-in" the honing, switching to a finer stone for final sizing, finishing with a "plateau" honing brush. The brushes, mounted onto the fixture in place of honing stones, serve to provide a finished surface that eliminates microscopic peaks, evening out the surface finish's peaks and valleys. This provides faster piston ring seating and superior oil retention on the cylinder walls.

Different honing stone makers identify their stone grades with (often) proprietary numbers, which may or may not represent actual grit grades. You need to refer to your brand of honing stones for grit level identification. Using Rottler stones as an example, initial honing might be done with 275–325 diamond stones to near-final diameter, followed by perhaps four passes with 500-grit stones for final honed size. Again, this is followed by approximately four passes with plateau brushes.

Honing oil is applied constantly to the stones as they travel through the cylinders. The oil provides cooling and self-cleans the stones.

Just as operations were done to alternating cylinder locations during boring, the same procedure is used during honing. Avoid honing from one cylinder to the next, to allow

CYLINDER BLOCK MACHINING

Prior to cylinder bore honing, a deck plate is installed to the block deck to simulate the clamping force of an installed cylinder head. This stresses the block to an "assembled" state, allowing you to more closely achieve ideal cylinder roundness. This is necessary because cylinder bore distortion occurs when the heads are installed. Use of a deck plate helps to reduce or eliminate the effects of the installed cylinder head clamping force. Always use the same type of cylinder head bolts or studs that will be used during final assembly. A used, already-crushed cylinder head gasket is installed between the block and deck plate to more closely simulate final assembly. Here, a deck plate is torqued to specified value, following the same tightening pattern that will be used during head installation.

With a deck plate installed and torqued, honing with the appropriate grade of stones begins. To reduce the effect of heat transfer between cylinders, bores are honed in an alternating manner. For example, cylinder number-1 is rough honed, followed by rough honing number-3, etc. This allows time for the heat generated in the first cylinder to dissipate before honing the adjacent cylinder. Rough honing is then followed by honing with a finer grit stone package.

The honing operator is able to adjust the expansion pressure of the honing stone package as the honing process achieves the final cylinder diameter.

The honing stones stroke up and down while coolant is applied. The deck plate simulates the installed cylinder head to apply stress to the block, which influences cylinder bore shape and minimizes unwanted bore distortion.

Cooling liquid is constantly applied during all stages of honing. This transfers heat from the block and aids in keeping the honing stones clean.

The honing operator is able to adjust honing by tailoring dwell, strokes per minute, and RPM to accommodate the desired cylinder wall finish.

CHAPTER 4

Here, a honed cylinder is finished using plateau honing brushes. This "averages out" the peaks and valleys that result from stone honing, allowing more immediate piston ring seating.

After the cylinders have been honed with stones, a final step preferred by many engine builders involves a final-dress of the cylinder walls with "plateau" brushes. These abrasive brushes obtain a more uniform final surface finish, eliminating any microscopic "peaks" that were created during honing. Plateau finishing tends to improve cylinder wall lubrication and effectively "evens out" the honed surface. This also promotes quicker piston ring seating during initial running of the engine. Plateau brushes are generally run on the honing machine at about three to four passes, simply to provide a final finish.

any heat buildup to subside between adjacent cylinders.

Honing Stone Selection and Ring Type

Ra stands for "roughness average." Ra is an arithmetic representation of surface finish in terms of the height of the surface peaks and valleys, in millionths of an inch. The smaller the Ra number, the smoother the surface finish. It's important to create the correct type of surface finish for the type of piston rings to be used.

Chrome and cast-iron piston rings require a slightly rougher Ra finish, in the range of 25 to 35 Ra. If a too-fine surface finish is obtained, hard chrome rings may not be able to seat properly, resulting in a certain amount of blow-by and reduced cylinder pressure, along with possible oil leakage past the rings into the combustion chamber. Softer moly-faced piston rings require a somewhat smoother finish, in the range of 10 to 20 Ra. If a too-rough surface is achieved and moly rings are used, premature ring wear can result. In addition, low-tension rings may tend to bounce and chatter during piston travel.

When honing for chrome or iron rings, honing stones in the range of 220 grit should be adequate. For moly-faced rings and today's lower-tension piston rings, a grit range of 400 should be appropriate.

Rough honing with 70-grit stones can be done for removing an initial .003 to .005 inch of cylinder wall material, if needed. Finish honing for chrome and iron rings should be done with 220-grit stones with a feed rate of 40 to 45 percent. Finish honing for moly rings requires less feed rate at about 25 percent. The honing machine should be set up initially at a rotating speed of about 155 rpm, with a rate of about 60 to 61 strokes per minute. The honing machine is easily adjusted for RPM, feed rate, and strokes per minute.

Cylinder Sleeving

A damaged or excessively worn cylinder may be restored by installing a cylinder sleeve. A quality sleeve designed for use in a cast-iron block provides the same hardness characteristics of cast-iron. Wall thickness may be 3/32 or 1/8 inch, depending on the application. A sleeve insert is not to be viewed as a "Band-Aid" fix or as a detriment to performance. Properly installed, a sleeve provides all of the performance and durability required.

The cylinder is first bored or honed to the diameter required for the proper interference fit of the sleeve. The sleeve relies on a tight interference fit to prevent it from moving within the block. Generally, the interference fit in a typical cast-iron block is in the range of .002 to .003 inch, but it's important to follow the specific recommendation of the sleeve manufacturer. Installing a sleeve in an aluminum block generally requires a greater interference fit. Again, follow the press-fit recommendation from the sleeve maker. When the cylinder has been oversized to accept the sleeve, there are several methods of installation to consider. A huge misconception exists regarding heating and cooling when dealing with a cast-iron block. Some engine builders recommend that the cylinder must be heated to expand the cylinder diameter, or the sleeve may be cooled to contract the sleeve O.D. to allow installation. If the cylinder is to be heated, do not

CYLINDER BLOCK MACHINING

Shown here is a GM LS7 block, cut in half. The original sleeves are integral, in place during the casting process. Resleeving requires boring out the original sleeves and interference-fitting stepped sleeves that are Siamesed together at the deck surface. (Photo Courtesy L.A. Sleeve)

The parent bore is bored oversize to accommodate the specified bore-to-sleeve interference fit. (Photo Courtesy L.A. Sleeve)

try using a torch. The block must be uniformly heated in an oven to about 400 degrees F. Some builders prefer to cool the sleeve in a refrigerator to allow it to contract. The sleeve is then installed into the cylinder, but this must be done quickly before either the block or the sleeve begins to return to room temperature.

When dealing with a cast-iron block, both methods (heating the block or cooling the sleeve) have drawbacks. As soon as the sleeve starts making contact with the block, temperatures begin to transfer between the two materials very quickly. If the sleeve was cooled, as it enters the block, the only area that stays cool is the area that's still exposed above the deck. A preferred method is to install the sleeve with both the block and sleeve at ambient temperature, using a press-in fit. Apply a very thin oil such as WD40 and press the sleeve into the cylinder.

When dealing with an aluminum block, it's a different story. A highly respected engine builder that I know prefers to bore the cylinder to accommodate a .001-inch interference fit, although some sleeve makers call for a fit of as much as .004 inch when installing a sleeve into an aluminum cylinder (again, follow the sleeve maker's specs). Then he heats the block to 200 degrees F, with the sleeve at 70 degrees F and installs the sleeve by hand. The block is then allowed to cool to room temperature. After the block has cooled, he taps the liners down or installs a torque plate to make sure the liners are seated.

Prior to installing the sleeve, you may apply a thin coating of green

Sleeves installed, prior to final deck resurfacing. (Photo Courtesy L.A. Sleeve)

Sleeves installed and deck resurfaced to make the sleeves flush with the deck. (Photo Courtesy L.A. Sleeve)

Certain block designs require a stepped boring to accept a stepped sleeve. Stepped sleeves provide a positive stop for sleeve location. (Photo Courtesy L.A. Sleeve)

AUTOMOTIVE MACHINING: A GUIDE TO BORING, DECKING, HONING AND MORE

Loctite 290 to the cylinder wall to obtain additional securing of the sleeve. After you have applied the Loctite, you must install the sleeve quickly. If you stop at some point, the sleeve seizes in place before it's fully inserted.

When the sleeve has been installed, the block is then placed onto a resurfacing machine to machine any excess exposed sleeve material flush to the block deck.

The sleeve is then honed to the diameter needed for the required piston-to-wall clearance.

As an example of saving a block with the use of a sleeve, I recently had a Mopar 383 block machined, only to find that one of the cylinders had a small pinhole, the result of corrosion that had attacked the wall from the cooling jacket side. The cylinder was overbored, a cooled sleeve was interference-fit, decked, and honed to size. The engine ran all day on a dyno, pulling 657 hp and 642 ft-lbs of torque. Subsequently, the engine was used by a drag racer, to date running two full seasons without an issue. Sleeving is absolutely an acceptable remedy to save a block, as long as it's installed properly.

If one or more cylinders require sleeving, sleeve installation must be accomplished before final honing of all cylinders and before final deck resurfacing.

Lifter Bore Honing and Bushings

One of the key aspects of accurizing (blueprinting) an engine block is correction of the lifter bores, not only for diameter for proper lifter oil clearance, but for precisely creating a lifter bore that is alignment- and angle-corrected, thereby correcting

If lifter bores need to be restored due to wear or other irregularities, a bronze bushing can be installed. With an index bar inserted in the cam tunnel to register the centerline of the lifter bore, a stepped reamer enlarges the lifter bore to accept the bronze liner.

any tolerance flaws that may have resulted from engine block mass production. Misaligned lifter bores can result in premature camshaft wear and improper cylinder-to-cylinder valve timing. Correct geometry for the lifter bore can be achieved either with the use of specialty fixtures such as offered by BHJ's Lifter Tru indexing fixture, or on a CNC machine.

When the centerline and angle have been determined, a reamer is used to enlarge the lifter bore. The bronze bushing is then press-fit into the enlarged bore. Bushings are available in a variety of diameters and lengths to suit any application. Bronze lifter bushings are generally installed with about a .002-inch interference fit.

After the bushings are installed, the excess bushing material exposed above the parent bore is spot-faced and lightly chamfered. The bushing inside diameter is then honed or machined to achieve the desired lifter oil clearance. Any oil feed passages in the parent bore must be aligned with an oil hole in the bushing, based on the specific engine application.

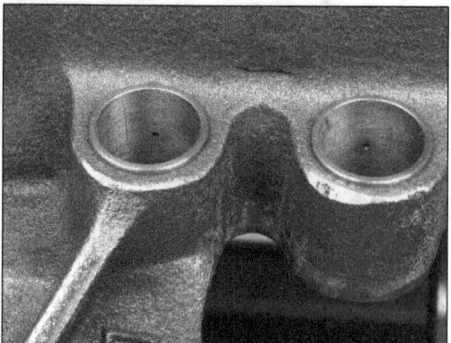

With the bronze liner interference-fit to the lifter bore, the bushing is then honed to size, obtaining the required oil clearance for the lifter. Note the oil holes in the bronze bushings, which must be aligned to the oil feed holes in the lifter bores during liner installation. In certain engine designs, builders prefer to restrict the oil feed by using an oil hole in the liner that is smaller than the OEM oil passage in the lifter bore. The example shown here is a vintage Pontiac big-block.

Block Deck Resurfacing

Engine block decks require resurfacing due to existing deck warpage, to correct deck squareness or deck height, to restore deck surface finish, or all of these factors. When restoring a used engine, the rule of thumb is to remove as little material as possible. With most production engine blocks, deck height and deck squareness may not be precisely true to design. Due to potential casting core shift and/or mass production machining, the decks may not be ideal. One bank may be higher than the opposite bank. The front of a deck may be taller in the front and shorter in the rear. Or the inboard/outboard deck angle may be slightly off relative to the cylinder bore centerline.

When building a performance engine, the block should be "accurized" by machining the decks perfectly

Deck resurfacing on CNC provides a perfectly flat finish while correcting for any original deck angle issues.

The block is set up on the resurfacing machine with the crankshaft centerline parallel to the cutting head. Here an operator checks the deck surface with a dial indicator to make sure that the lowest point of the deck is cut, ensuring that the entire deck is machined parallel to the crankshaft centerline. The cutting head, with the built-in dial indicator, is carefully moved from front to rear of each deck to determine the start of the resurfacing process.

To ensure that each block deck is milled at a 90-degree angle to the crankshaft centerline, a specialty fixture is attached to the block that provides a precise angle reference.

Many older OEM blocks feature large casting flashings that can interrupt coolant and oil flow.

parallel to the main bore centerline and machined to achieve the same deck height on each bank. If you're dealing with a brand new aftermarket block, manufacturers may often provide excess deck height, allowing the builder to achieve exactly the deck height he desires.

Block decks may be resurfaced by either grinding or milling. Grinding involves the use of a machine equipped with an abrasive wheel, while milling uses hardened CBN (cubic boron nitride) or PCD (polycrystalline diamond) cutters on a rotating head, with CBN cutters designed for machining cast-iron and PCD for aluminum). Because today's engines increasingly use MLS (multi-layer steel) cylinder head gaskets, which require a finer surface finish, milling achieves a superior result.

Measurement checks should be performed prior to any surfacing operation. Measure block deck height from the main bore centerline to the top of the decks, at the front and rear of each deck, and record these findings. This allows you to roughly determine how much material needs to be removed to equalize deck height and to obtain the proper deck angles. For example, a block's specified deck height might be 9.240 inches. But when measured, the front of the left deck might be 9.240 inches, while the rear of the same deck might measure 9.245 inches. The opposite deck might measure 9.246 inches at the front and 9.242 inches at the rear. In theory, you should be able to machine to achieve a deck height of 9.240 inches on both decks.

You then need to measure the decks for distortion (warp). Using a

CHAPTER 4

The block is adjusted on the resurfacing machine while using a dial indicator on the edge of the specialty indexing plate. This ensures a true "squaring" of the deck relative to inboard/outboard of the deck surface, again, relative to the crank centerline.

Prior to milling the deck, the cutting head is passed slowly across the deck from front to rear while monitoring the dial indicator. Here the dial indicator has moved to the rear of the deck. Careful measuring prior to milling informs the operator of how much minimum material removal is required to obtain a straight and level deck.

Older-style resurfacing machines such as the one shown here use a larger diameter milling head with the head sweeping across the deck in an arc.

Deck cuts are performed in stages with multiple cut passes instead of trying to remove material in a single pass.

precision machinist's straightedge, lay the straightedge on the center of the deck from front to rear and use a feeler gauge to check for distortion. With the straightedge positioned on the deck, try to slip a feeler gauge between the straightedge and the deck surface. The generally acceptable limit is .004 inch from front to rear.

Place the straightedge front-to-rear inboard of the cylinder bores and check. Next place the straightedge from front-to-rear along the outboard deck surface.

Next place the straightedge diagonally from corner to corner (in both

58 AUTOMOTIVE MACHINING: A GUIDE TO BORING, DECKING, HONING AND MORE

An example of a deck that has been resurfaced. Any "shadows" indicate low spots that might appear if the deck is warped, which then requires further cutting passes.

planes in an X pattern). Again, the acceptable warp limit is .004 inch along the entire length in each location. Also, any warpage of more than .002 inch along any 6-inch length is unacceptable. Also measure from inboard to outboard of the deck between each pair of cylinders. Maximum allowable warp is about .0015 inch. Any warpage that is beyond these limits requires resurfacing.

To machine the decks to achieve deck squareness, you can either use a specialty fixture, such as offered by BHJ or resurface on a CNC machine. The specialty indexing fixture serves as an index. This large steel plate attaches to the front of the block, indexing to the main bore centerline. The plate features upper left and right surfaces that are 90 degrees to the crank centerline. These plate edges are then used as reference points when setting up the resurfacing machine to allow you to mill the decks parallel to the main bore centerline and achieving a 90-degree angle relative to the crankshaft. If machining on a CNC machine, the machine program allows you to easily position the block to achieve squareness and identical deck heights.

Surface finish is critical to provide a proper sealing surface between the head gasket and block. The type of head gasket to be used must be considered when deciding on surface-finish Ra. Composite-type head gaskets can accommodate a surface finish on a cast-iron block in the 60- to 120-Ra range, if a cast-iron cylinder head will be used. If an aluminum head is planned, the gasket must be allowed to move a bit on the deck surface due to expansion and contraction rates, so an Ra finish of 20 to 50 is better suited with a cast-iron block and aluminum heads. If you plan to use multi-layer steel (MLS) head gaskets, the surface finish needs to be finer. If the MLS gasket is uncoated, a surface finish of 20 to even as fine as 7 Ra is needed. If the MLS gasket is coated, this is a bit more forgiving, with its coating compensating a bit for a rougher finish, so decks finished with an Ra of 50 to 60 may be adequate. Just remember that MLS head gaskets require a smoother block deck finish.

The only way to actually measure the Ra finish is with a special instrument called a profilometer. This is an electronic device that features a fine-tipped stylus (similar to that found on a record player needle). The stylus drags across the surface slowly, reading and displaying the Ra finish. Not all shops have a profilometer, as they're fairly expensive. You can achieve the desired Ra by operating the resurfacing machine at specific rotational speed and feed rate. After initial cuts have been achieved with the CBN or PCD bits, and you're after an Ra in the mid- to low-teens, the final cutting pass should be fairly high, in the range of 1,000 to 1,500 rpm, with a fairly slow feed rate of less than 2 inches per minute of feed rate. If a rougher finish is desired, slow the RPM and slightly speed up the feed rate.

If too much deck material is removed from the block, this can result in poor intake manifold alignment when dealing with a V-block. In addition, as you remove block deck material, you bring the cylinder head closer to the pistons, increasing compression ratio and potential piston-to-head or piston-to-valve clearance issues. For engines that feature a distributor that installs through the top of both the intake manifold and the block, excessively reducing deck height can also lead to misalignment of distributor-to-camshaft gears if the top of the block is machined to restore intake port alignment.

Also, if the distributor passes through the intake manifold, there is the potential for binding of the oil pump intermediate shaft (for engines where the oil pump is driven by the camshaft gears), when the distributor installed height is lowered. If the distributor installs through the top of the block, and the upper block front and rear rails have been machined to regain intake manifold alignment, you may need to space the distributor by adding shims at the distributor base, at a thickness equal to the amount that was machined from the block rails.

If decks are reduced in height below the original specification, the top of the block and the intake deck of the heads may be machined to compensate to restore port and intake bolt alignment. Different engines require specific height reduction ratios to determine how much material should be removed from the top of the block and from the intake decks of the cylinder heads.

Citing a generation 1 small-block Chevy engine as an example, you can

CHAPTER 4

Block Ratios

Following are ratios for each type of block, again based on the cylinder head's included angle:

Block Type	Included Angle of Head (degrees)	Top of Block Ratio (:1)	Head Intake Ratio (:1)
90	95	.90	1.3
90	90	1.00	1.4
90	80	1.20	1.7
90	75	1.40	2.0
90	70	1.70	2.3
60	90	.60	1.2
60	80	.70	1.3
60	75	.75	1.4
60	70	.80	1.5

Step 1: Determine the head's included angle.

Step 2: Determine how much material is to be removed from the block decks.

Step 3: Multiply the deck removal X [times] the top of block ratio to determine how much material to remove from the top of the engine block.

Step 4: Multiply the deck removal X [times] the cylinder head intake ratio to determine how much material to remove from the intake deck of the cylinder heads.

generally use a 1.2 ratio for correcting the cylinder head intake decks and a ratio of 1.7 for machining the top of the block. Multiply these ratio numbers by the amount that was removed from the block decks. For example, if .008-inch was removed from the block decks, you multiple .008 by 1.2 to remove intake deck material. Multiply 1.7 by .008 to remove material from the top of the block.

If the block decks were reduced by .008-inch:

.008 x 1.2 = .0096-inch (for head intake deck removal)

.008 x 1.7 = .0136-inch (for top of block removal)

The ratios used for material removal from cylinder head intake decks and the top of the block depend on the included angle of the cylinder head combustion-side deck and the head's intake deck. A protractor can be used to determine this angle. Don't blindly assume that a specific head features a specific angle.

Material removal ratios differ between 90- and 60-degree engine blocks.

Although intake manifold port and bolt alignment issues can often be resolved by resurfacing the intake decks of the cylinder heads and the top of the block, if excessive material is removed from the block decks, instead of removing material from the intake side of the heads and the top of the block, the issue can sometimes be resolved simply with the use of a thicker-than-stock head gasket. Performance gasket manufacturers offer head gaskets in various thicknesses, especially with regard to MLS gaskets, which are made using layers of stainless steel in between the upper and lower sealing surface lay-

A simple protractor enables you to measure the angle between a cylinder head's combustion and intake deck surfaces. This example is an inexpensive digital protractor obtained from a local discount chain's tool department. As an example, here I measure a 90.45-degree angle with a protractor between the cylinder head combustion deck and intake deck on a 5.0L small-block Ford head.

ers. Companies such as Cometic can custom make just about any thickness you need, within reason.

Pay particular attention to the block decks' cylinder head bolt holes. If enough material is removed from the block decks to bring the bolt hole threads flush to the deck, the result can be that the top threads are pulled upward as the head bolts are tightened, possibly interfering with head gasket sealing. All head bolt holes should either be countersunk or chamfered. If the holes were not originally countersunk and the threads are flush with the deck after resurfacing, take the time to slightly chamfer the top of the bolt holes.

Threaded Hole Preparation

Never assume that threaded holes in the engine block are in good condition or have been tapped properly. As part of block preparation, inspect all threaded holes. You don't want to find problems during final assembly. Inspect and correct now. Although thread condition is important at every location, the most critical are cylinder head bolt holes and main cap bolt holes, because these areas experience the most stress.

An older or used block may have damaged threads or threads that are burred or contaminated. Run a chasing tap through each threaded hole. Do not use a common cutting tap, as this may remove too much material, weakening the threads. A chasing tap is designed to "re-form" and clean threads, as opposed to removing material. Chaser taps are available for all common inch and metric sizes.

Even when dealing with a brand-new OEM or aftermarket block, although thread condition may be fine, it is possible that some holes have not been tapped deep enough. When dealing with a new block, take the time to prefit and test-install. I've encountered brand-new high-quality aftermarket performance blocks where holes have been drilled deep enough, but threads have not been cut to the required depths at hole locations for the water pump, timing cover, oil pump, etc. Take the time to check before final assembly.

If dealing with a used block, check all bind holes to make sure that debris hasn't collected at the bottom of the holes.

Block Blueprinting

The term "blueprinting" is widely misunderstood. People often note that their engine has been "balanced and blueprinted," when this simply is not the case. By simply having the crankshaft and rotating assembly balanced, they mistakenly assume that the engine has been blueprinted.

Blueprinting refers to a very extensive "accurizing and optimizing" of the block and all engine components. As far as the block is concerned, this entails correcting all of the out-of-tolerance aspects of block geometry. When a production block is cast, it is common for a certain amount of "core shift" to occur when the block is cast. This means that the cylinder bores and/or lifter bores may not be exactly located per the engineering design. Bores may be a bit off-center and off-angle relative to the main bore centerline. Block decks may be

When accurizing a block on CNC, one of the first measurements taken is a reference of the existing main bore centerline. Here a digital probe contacts the main bore indexing bar.

The CNC probe also reads camshaft bore centerline, providing the operator with information that will be used when correcting lifter bores.

CHAPTER 4

With the block secured in the CNC center, a digital probe measures all deck surfaces, providing the operator with existing deck height and angles. This information is then used to determine the required deck milling to establish decks that are parallel to the main bore centerline.

slightly nonparallel to the main bore centerline, and decks may be different heights on each bank. The main bore and camshaft bore might not be precisely centered, and the distance from the main bore centerline to the camshaft centerline (in an overhead-valve block) might not be exactly where it's supposed to be.

This usually isn't enough to create a problem, but for high-performance and racing applications where optimum performance is critical, the block is not providing optimum durability and performance in terms of potentially increased friction and less-than-ideal valve timing.

By blueprinting, all aspects of block geometry are referenced from the main bore centerline. If cylinder bores are not precisely centered, the bores can be overbored to create a precise centerline and bore angle. The same holds true for lifter bores. Correcting cylinder bores requires the use of larger-diameter pistons. If lifter bores require correction, bores are oversized to establish proper geometry. They are then treated to bronze bushings, which are honed to size to provide required lifter oil clearance. Decks are corrected by indexing off of the main bore centerline, with decks milled perfectly parallel to the main bore centerline and to equal deck heights.

Two methods are available to accurize the engine block. One method involves the use of highly specialized indexing fixtures that are attached to the block, providing precise reference points that allow corrections on traditional machine

Blueprinting a block on a CNC machining center involves taking existing measurements using digital probes. Each cylinder is referenced at inboard, outboard, front, and rear coordinates. This provides the computer with a reference regarding the existing centerline location of each bore. Here, a probe notes a cylinder bore's inboard radius.

shop equipment. Another approach is available through the use of CNC machines, where a digital probe establishes existing dimensions and geometry, then machines the block via a written program that corrects any out-of-specification issues. CNC machining is precise, repeatable, and allows block accurizing in a much quicker time frame. Block optimizing can be accomplished with either approach. CNC machines are very expensive, so even shops that cannot afford this technology can still provide the service with the use of specialty fixtures at an investment of a few thousand dollars, as opposed to a CNC machining center that can easily run in the hundreds of thousands of dollars.

Further blueprinting techniques apply to all engine components, including cylinder heads (verifying that all combustion chambers are of equal volume, valves are all at the same installed seat depth), crankshaft (verifying that main and rod journals are of correct diameter and that all rod throws are exactly to specified length and are identical in length), connecting rods (verifying that all rods feature identical center-to-center lengths), pistons

Here, the CNC machine's digital probe reads the existing rear radius of a cylinder.

CYLINDER BLOCK MACHINING

(verifying equal dome volumes and compression heights and correct piston ring groove dimensions), valves (verifying that all intake stem heights are identical and all exhaust stem heights are identical), camshaft (checking journal diameters and all intake and exhaust lobes for lift and ramp angles, etc.), carefully matching intake manifold to cylinder head intake port alignment, cylinder head deck height, verifying identical rocker arm ratio, etc.

In short, there's more to blueprinting than most folks realize.

Blueprinting is just not required for a street application, but when the engine is required to produce optimal power and optimal durability, the blueprinting process is critical. Blueprinting requires an extensive amount of shop time and skilled labor, so expect to pay a premium for this work.

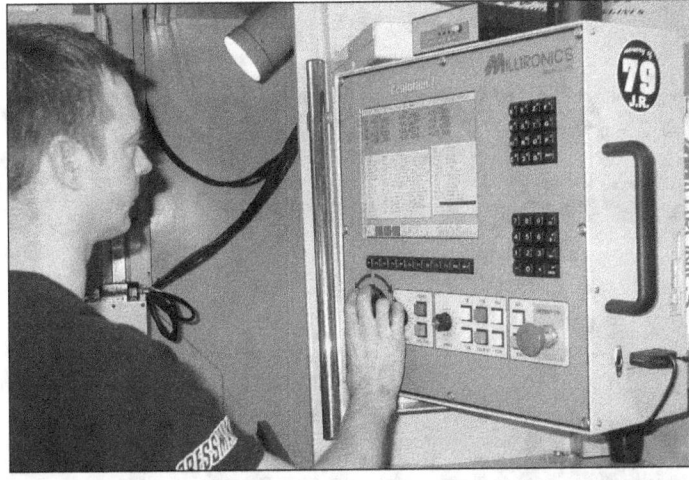
When all block dimensions have been digitally recorded on CNC, the operator uses a program to specify desired cylinder bore diameter, deck cut depth, and lifter bore diameter.

Cylinder bore centerline location correction can be handled on a conventional boring station with the use of a precision indexing fixture. This provides a guide for the boring operation to place the cylinder centerline in the correct location when overboring.

If CNC machining is not available, lifter bore geometry corrections can be handled with the use of specialty fixtures that provide a precise guide during the blueprinting process.

Here, lifter bores are corrected on a CNC machining center. The CNC program automatically adjusts block angle and location to achieve a precisely located centerline for the lifter bore.

CHAPTER 5

CRANKSHAFT MEASUREMENT, GRINDING AND PREPARATION

This chapter focuses on preparation, setup, and crankshaft journal grinding.

Refer to Chapter 3 for information on measuring crankshaft journal diameters and checking for crankshaft runout to determine if the crankshaft is slightly bent. Chapter 3 also discusses checking the crankshaft for cracks using a magnetic particle inspection (commonly referred to as Magnafluxing).

If main and/or rod journals are damaged, the journals may be reground to undersize.

Depending on the severity of journal surface damage, polishing the crank journals may correct minor scoring or blemishes. If polishing does not bring the surface to specification, the crankshaft must be reground.

Measuring the Crankshaft

When measuring the existing journal's diameter, be sure to check for taper. Using a micrometer, measure the journal at each outer edge, near the fillet radius. Any differ-

Crankshaft journal grinding, whether performed on a new crank during manufacturing or during a regrind to save a used crank, requires absolute precision to achieve a true on-center for each journal, in addition to correct diameter and surface finish, while avoiding unwanted taper or out-of-round.

Crankshaft grinding machines are available in a variety of sizes to handle the smallest single-cylinder crank to the largest industrial crankshafts. This Berco unit is an example of a unit that can handle all automotive and light-truck diesel cranks. (Photo Courtesy Berco)

CRANKSHAFT MEASUREMENT, GRINDING AND PREPARATION

ence in these measurements indicates that a taper exists. Taper tolerance specifications can vary among manufacturers, but generally speaking, any taper that exceeds .0005 inch is unacceptable. Excess journal taper allows oil to escape from the sides of the bearings.

Also measure the journal for out-of-round. Using a micrometer, measure journal diameter at several clock positions. An out-of-round condition of more than .0005 inch or a taper of more than .0005 inch requires regrinding.

When measuring journal diameter, keep in mind that the crankshaft might have been reground previously. Typical reground undersizes include .010, .020, or .030 inch. If a crank has been reground in the past, the shop performing the work should have stamped or etched the undersize onto the front face of the forward counterweight as a reference. However, just because you don't see an undersize marked on the crank, don't assume that this has not been done.

Always check for crank runout. If the crank is to be reground, the crank must be straightened first. Grinding a bent crank creates a host of problems, including changes in stroke and imbalance, and because of internal stresses imposed during grinding and during engine operation, the runout can worsen as the crank springs further off-center. For a crankshaft that has one or more journals damaged to the point where the journal cannot be ground to accept a limit of available undersized bearings, the journal(s) may be welded to build material up, then ground. Welding can be done using specialized submerged-arc or gas-shielded welding processes, which I won't delve into here. In most cases, the cost of a replacement crankshaft provides a cheaper (and quicker) alternative. Weld repair and grinding is an avenue to pursue if the crankshaft in question is of a vintage nature and new units of its type may not be readily available.

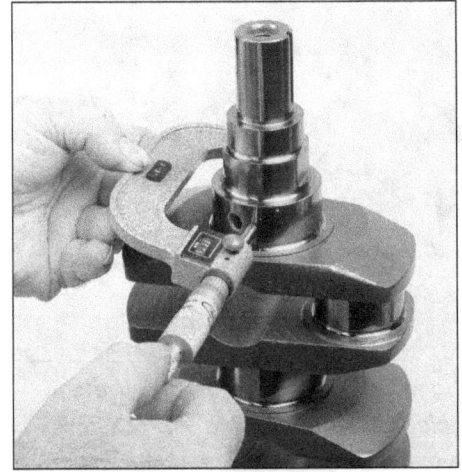
Measure each main journal for diameter at a variety of clock positions to check for diameter and out-of-round.

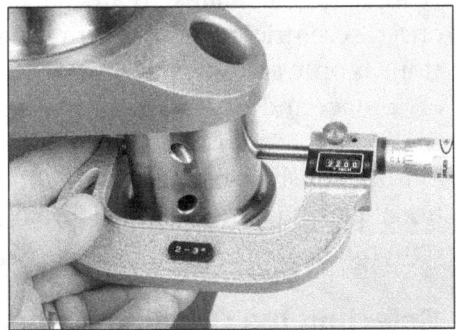
Measure each rod journal for diameter, out-of-round, and for taper, by measuring close to the fillet at end of the journal surface.

Check for taper by measuring journal diameter at each end of the journal.

This crankshaft has been etched from the manufacturer to indicate the stroke length. When regrinding is complete, undersizing should be marked on the face of the front counterweight as well. For instance, if mains were undersize ground by .010 inch and the rods by .010 inch, the mark should read ".010/.010." If mains and rods have been undersized differently, for instance .020 inch at the mains and .010 inch at the rod pins, the mark should read ".020/.010."

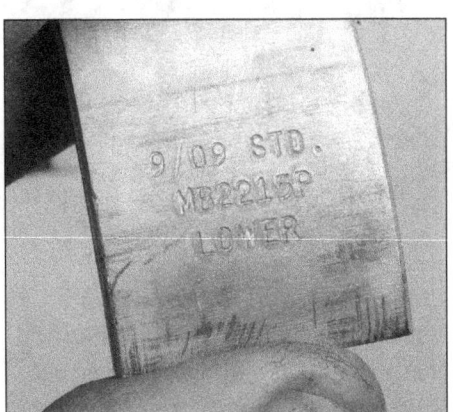
Main and rod bearings are factory stamped to indicate size. STD indicates standard size. If the bearing is marked ".010," this indicates that the inside diameter of the bearing is sized for a journal that has been ground undersize by .010 inch. The outer bearing diameter remains at the standard size, with the bearing shell thicker to accommodate the smaller-diameter journal.

CHAPTER 5

Prior to grinding, check for runout on a runout stand and dial indicator. If runout exceeds about .0015 inch, the crank should be straightened.

For journal measuring in your assembly area, a V-block crankshaft rest with clean plastic-padded V-blocks provides a safe and convenient method of handling.

If the crankshaft is fitted with a toothed reluctor wheel, care must be taken to avoid damaging the wheel during grinding. If the technician opts to remove the wheel, be aware that wheel installation requires a special indexing tool fixture to register the wheel properly.

If welding is to be done, the crank requires straightening after each journal has been welded. The crank should also be stress relieved after welding. Hardened cranks can soften as a result of welding and should be tested with a portable hardness tester. If rehardening is needed, this is commonly done by nitriding. However, due to the high heat involved, journal diameters may slightly grow and may also go out of round. If the crank is to be nitrided, the crank should initially be ground to the high limits of tolerance, then nitrided, then finish-ground to size.

Corrective crankshaft grinding is performed on a dedicated crankshaft grinder that features a large-diameter abrasive stone wheel. To regrind the main journals, the crankshaft is set up on the machine so that the crankshaft is chucked onto a pair of DC motors that are synchronized for rotational speed. A large-diameter grinding stone wheel is positioned vertically. When grinding main journals, the crank is adjusted on the chucks to rotate the crank on its main centerline axis.

If rod journals require grinding, the crankshaft must be indexed on the machine so that each rod journal is centered to the machine's rotational axis. When adjusted for grinding a rod journal, as the crank is rotated, the mains rotate on an offset eccentric path. The grinding stone is only adjustable for the depth of contact and width traverse along the journal. To grind a journal, that journal must be placed in a rotational path that indexes the journal's centerline.

Selecting the Grinding Wheel

Grinding stone wheels are available in a range of abrasive grains, grit sizes, and hardness grades. One stone is not suitable for all crankshaft applications. The wheel must be suited for the type of crankshaft material. For grinding a cast-iron crank with a Rockwell hardness of 35 Rc or less, a semi-friable abrasive is a good choice, where minimal thrust grinding is needed. Friability refers to the abrasives' characteristics for fracturing. A very friable abrasive tends to break down faster, requiring more wheel dressing. A semi-friable wheel still allows fresh cutting crystals to be exposed to the work piece as it wears, but it lasts longer.

For forged or modular iron cranks, a suitable abrasive is capable of removing more material, handling larger radii, and dressing thrust grinding. Moreover, a wheel that is less prone to loading and that holds its shape longer is more suitable. For extremely hard steel such as is found on diesel cranks and high-performance and/or billet steel cranks with a hardness of 35 Rc or more, a wheel featuring friable and semi-friable abrasives is a better choice. These cut cooler and require less wheel dressing to hold their shape. CBN (carbon boron nitride) wheels provide excellent cutting and last longer, and are ideally suited for high-production grinding.

The grinding wheel should be checked for cracks or damage before use. In addition to a visual inspection, tap the wheel with a wood or plastic hammer. A good vitrified wheel (where material bonding is in good condition) provides a clear ringing tone. If the wheel is cracked, you hear a dull sound.

Grinding wheels are marked with a maximum operating RPM speed. The speed rating must match that of the machine's spindle speed. Before a grinding wheel is installed to the crank grinding machine, the wheel should be checked for balance and rebalanced if necessary.

According to Goodson Tools, install the grinding wheel on a wheel center and snug the cap screws, but do not tighten fully yet. Mount the wheel on a balancing arbor and place it on a balancing stand. With the arrow on the wheel pointed as directed, loosen the screws to allow the wheel to settle downward on the wheel center, then gradually torque the screws to the recommended specification. Do not rotate the wheel until all screws are secure. Remove the balancing weights from the wheel center and allow the wheel to rotate to its rest position. Using a piece of chalk, mark the twelve o'clock position, which is the lightest area of the wheel. Install two balancing weights approximately on the horizontal centerline, then move the weights up toward the top of the wheel hub.

If the wheel holds its position with the mark at twelve, three, six, and nine o'clock, the wheel is properly balanced. If the wheel freely rotates back to twelve o'clock, move each weight slightly upward again until balance is achieved. If the chalk mark moves to the bottom six o'clock position when allowed to rotate freely, move the weight in the opposite direction. After mounting the wheel to the machine and dressing the surfaces, remove the wheel and check balance again. Don't allow coolant to run onto the wheel when making this check, as this can saturate the wheel in isolated spots and can mask an imbalance.

Dressing the Wheel

Frequent wheel dressing provides a clean and even cutting surface. Always run the machine's coolant during dressing to reduce frictional heat buildup, which can cause the diamond particles in the dresser bit to loosen and separate. According to Goodson, the best results are obtained if the diamond is brought into contact with the center of the wheel face. Feed the wheel to the dresser a maximum of .002 inch, then traverse left and right off the edge of the wheel. This must be done fast enough to prevent surface glazing, but slow enough to minimize spiral lead marks. A rapid traverse removes large amounts of material quickly. A slower traverse produces a more desirable finish but doesn't remove material as quickly.

When you grind the crank journals, it's important to duplicate the original corner radii (fillet radius) to prevent potential weakening of the crank. A slight radius at the fillet is required, where each end of a journal features a soft "blending" radius, as opposed to a sharp 90-degree corner, which can potentially result in a stress failure under severe load. When dressing the wheel for the crankshaft involved, position the diamond dresser bit facing the front. Slide the holder back, and position and lock the radius adjuster at the desired dimension. Then slide the diamond holder forward until the diamond contacts the radius adjustment stop. Tighten the diamond holder, unlock, and retract the adjustment stop. Feed the wheel into position fully forward. Using a fine feed rate, bring the diamond into contact with the front face of the wheel and dress full width. Then back the wheel away from the diamond .004 inch. Loosen the swivel lock and remove one of the stop pins so that the upper swivel can be rotated through 90 degrees of travel. Although pivoting the diamond through its 90-degree arc, bring the wheel into contact and dress off the required amount from one corner of the wheel. Repeat this process for the opposite side of the wheel edge.

Diamond dresser tools must be kept sharp. Rotate the diamond 30 to 45 degrees after each dressing operation.

CHAPTER 5

Here, a crankshaft is checked on a crank-straightening stand. While the crank rests on clean V-blocks, and with a dial indicator contacting the center main journal, the crank is slowly rotated to determine the amount of runout. This crank revealed an excessive runout of .008 inch.

Straightening the Crank

If the crankshaft has more than enough runout, this must be corrected before attempting journal grinding. Carefully bending the crank by applying controlled pressure to the center main journal can straighten the crank. With the crank resting on V-blocks, it's rotated to obtain the highest point at twelve o'clock, monitored by a dial indicator. Downward pressure is then applied at the twelve o'clock position. This may be accomplished either by striking the journal with a soft brass drift or by hydraulic pressure. Commonly, depressing the center main downward past the zero runout target is necessary because the crank likely springs back due to the memory in the iron or steel material. Pushing the center by the same distance as existing runout likely has no effect.

As an example, I recently witnessed a crank that was found to have .008-inch runout. After the operator pushed the center main by .170 inch, the crank sprang back to result in gaining only .001 inch of runout reduction, improving runout from .008 to .007 inch. The operator was forced to repeat the push several times, eventually exerting a push of .220 inch before runout was corrected to zero. Careful experimentation coupled with operator experience is required to obtain zero runout.

Using a hydraulic pump connected to a clamp that is placed onto the center main, the operator applies pressure, bending the crank in the opposite direction of the highest point of runout. Bending the crank slightly past the zero point is necessary to compensate for crank spring-back. This practice requires experience and usually several attempts to obtain a zero runout.

Grinding and Polishing the Journals

Grinding to an undersize (to accept .010-, .020-, or .030-inch undersize bearings) should be consistent. Undersizing is relative to the original journal diameter specification. For instance, if a journal's spec diameter is 2.200 inches, grinding to a .010-inch undersize involves reducing the journal diameter by .010, to 2.190 inches.

All main journals should be ground to the same undersize, and all rod journals should be ground to the same undersize. For instance, all main and rod journals might be ground .010-inch undersize, or mains by .020 inch and rods by .010 inch. Never undersize only select journals. All mains should be the same size and all rod pins should be the same size. This allows you to use the same size main bearings on all main journals and the same size bearings for all rod journals. By having all rod journals sized identically, you also avoid potential balance issues.

Some shops prefer to grind rod journals before grinding the mains. The crankshaft is offset mounted for stroke length, with the center of the rod journals centered to the true center of rotation. By adjusting the machine's chucks, the main journal is offset from the center of rotation by half of the stroke length. For example, if the crank features a 4.00:1 stroke, the offset is adjusted by 2.00 inches. The abrasive wheel is adjusted to the desired grinding depth, so that it stops plunging when the calibrated depth is achieved. A built-in dial indicator allows verifying journal diameter.

To grind main journals, the chucks are adjusted to place the center of the mains at the true center of rotation. This not only grinds the main journals to the desired undersize, creating a profile with no taper and no out-of-round, but ensures that when the crank is installed to the block, that the crank centers to the front and rear crank seals. Each DC motor's chuck is adjusted to obtain the on-center point.

Attention must also be paid to the crankshaft's thrust bearing surfaces. Dressing these surfaces with the side of the wheel, if needed, involves removing only enough material to obtain a smooth surface that is 90 degrees to the journal, with both thrust sides parallel to each other.

Prior to grinding main journals, each DC motor's chuck is carefully adjusted to establish a true center of rotation. Here, the operator adjusts the rear flange end chuck.

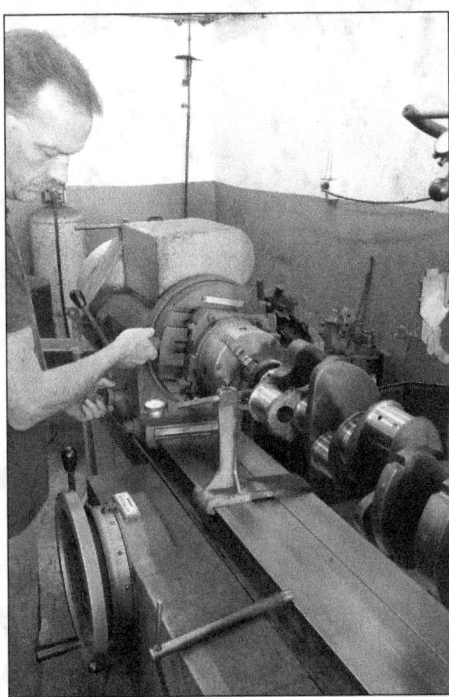

Here, the operator adjusts the front nose chuck to obtain true center.

Before grinding mains, the steady rest fixture provides support to the bottom and front of the center main to prevent the crank from deflecting during grinding.

A built-in gauge allows the operator to monitor the amount removed during grinding.

Notice the smooth blended radius at the fillet area. A sharp angle cut here can promote a stress area.

CHAPTER 5

Here, a rod journal is ground. The rod journal has been placed at the true center of rotation. Careful chuck adjustment is required to avoid creating an out-of-round condition. The operator continually monitors and verifies material removal during the operations.

A manually operated grinder features a control wheel at the left side that allows the operator to traverse the grinding wheel left/right to traverse across the journal. An operating wheel on the right controls the wheel's plunge contact to the journal.

Because the center of the crankshaft may have a tendency to sag a bit due to its own weight, a stand-off support contacts the center main at the front of the machine to provide support. The stand-off features slippery and protective nylon pads that don't damage the surface. The stand-off support also features a front support contact, preventing the crank from deflecting forward as stone wheel pressure is applied from the rear.

A steady rest fixture is also adjusted to contact the rod journal to be ground. This rest features nylon pads that don't damage the ground finish.

Pay close attention to oil holes in each journal. It's necessary to remove any burrs or sharp edges. Oil holes must be chamfered after grinding to remove sharp edges and to promote oil flow. The leading edge, based on direction of crank rotation, features a longer chamfer to provide a more efficient oil path for quicker oil wedging between the journal and bearing.

Here, a main journal is being ground. It is critical that the crank rotates on its true center.

Coolant is continually applied during grinding to reduce frictional heat and to flush the surface.

CRANKSHAFT MEASUREMENT, GRINDING AND PREPARATION

As the crank rotates on its axis, the polishing belt is forced against the journal surface lightly. This removes tiny burrs created by grinding and achieves the desired surface finish. A variety of belt grits are available, depending on the machinist's preferences. Some builders prefer to use a 420-grit belt, followed by using a fine Scotch-Brite belt.

A fine journal polishing creates the desired surface finish and softens any irregularities from oil hole edges that have been chamfered.

When all journals have been ground to size, the oil holes in each journal now feature sharp and abrupt edges. The oil hole edges must be chamfered to protect bearings from sharp edges, to remove potential stress risers, and to promote oil flow. Using a great deal of care to avoid damaging the ground surface, chamfer the holes with a tapered abrasive stone on a die grinder tool.

After grinding has been accomplished, the journals must be final-polished to achieve the proper surface finish. This removes the microscopic burrs that result from the grinding process. Using a dedicated crankshaft polisher and a fine-grit polishing belt, the crank is rotated while a polishing belt runs across the surface. The journals are polished in both directions of rotation to optimize burr removal. Polishing belts are available in abrasive levels from 240 to 600 grit. Some builders prefer to start with a 420-grit belt, followed with a final polish using a fine Scotch-Brite belt.

Following the journals being polished, the crank must be thoroughly washed and cleaned, followed by a thin oil coating to prevent surface rust.

The hardness of the journal surface may be compromised by grinding to an undersize. For a crankshaft that has been hardened by nitriding, for example, grinding to a .010-inch undersize may remove the hardened surface depth, requiring the crank to be renitrided to regain surface hardness.

Grinding the Flywheel

A flywheel (for applications that use a manual transmission) needs to be checked for flatness and for surface finish for proper clutch engagement. A CBN flywheel grinding stone is recommended for resurfacing on cast-iron flywheels. CBN grinding stones are suitable for resurfacing many types of cast-iron flywheels. They also create less dust while grinding, and they last longer.

CBN is an abbreviation for cubic boron nitride. This material is nearly as hard as diamond and almost four times as hard as aluminum oxide. CBN is a better choice than diamond-dressed stones primarily because CBN lasts longer.

Because there is no substantial porosity in the CBN grinding wheel, large amounts of clean flywheel grinding coolant is required at the contact area during grinding. The coolant lubricates, cools, and carries away debris created during the grinding process.

CBN stones don't need to be dressed as frequently as vitrified abrasives, but they do require an occasional dressing. Never use a dresser attachment on the grinder. For best results, dress with a handheld dresser stick (such as Goodson's DS-CBN).

It is highly recommended that a filter sock is installed on the coolant returning to the sump to minimize debris that returns from the sump to the grinding wheel.

CHAPTER 6

CONNECTING ROD INSPECTION AND RECONDITIONING

Connecting rods are critical components that connect the pistons to the crankshaft. Connecting rods experience a great deal of stress as the crankshaft pushes the rods and pistons upward during the compression stroke and are pushed downward under the firing stroke. Potential areas of damage include the rod's big end (the end attached to the crankshaft's rod journal), bend or twist of the rod's beam, and potential cracking. Conditions that can lead to damage include overheating due to inadequate lubrication and excessive stress that may result from detonation or over-revving.

Construction and design of connecting rods varies, depending on the application, but most connecting rods are made of cast-iron, forged steel, powdered metal (PM), billet aluminum, or titanium. Decades ago, cast-iron was most common for production vehicle engines, while forged rods were installed in many high-performance production engines.

Today, powdered metal is the material typically used for the majority of production street engines. Billet aluminum or titanium rods are often selected for some racing applications because these lightweight rods reduce reciprocating mass, which is critical in order to lighten operating loads. Many OEM rods today are made from powdered metal that feature a fractured parting line between the rod saddle and rod cap. These are commonly referred to as PM rods.

Inspecting Connecting Rods

When inspecting used rods, each needs to be inspected for center-to-center length, big end bore diameter, small end bore diameter, big end bore out-of-round, rod bend, rod twist, and for cracks.

Also check for discoloration. If a rod shows a blue coloration, this indicates that it has experienced excessive heat and its strength has been compromised due to changes in material hardness. If a rod shows blue heat damage, it's best to discard it and replace with a new rod. Rods

Aftermarket performance connecting rods are precision machined and weight-matched. Although each rod should be checked for bore sizes, a matched set from any of the leading rod makers should be ready to install with no corrections required. Shown here is a set of H-beam rods. Performance rods are offered in both H-beam and I-beam styles. The vast majority of performance rods are designed for use with free-floating wrist pins.

CONNECTING ROD INSPECTION AND RECONDITIONING

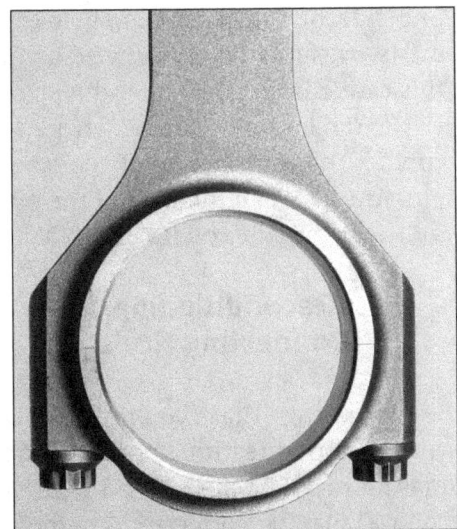

Before measuring any rod's big end bore for diameter and out-of-round, the cap must be fully tightened to the rod maker's specifications.

are placed under tremendous stress, and if one fails, it will destroy the engine. If you are going to reuse connecting rods, then you should Magnaflux the rods so you can see if there are any cracks or other damage.

Measuring Rod Bore Diameter

Both rod bores should be checked for diameter, as well as for out-of-round. Big end and small end bore diameters can be measured with a bore gauge, measuring at both vertical and horizontal planes. Refer to the specified diameters for the rods at hand. If the small end diameter is too tight, honing to the correct size is possible. If small end diameter is too large, the small end may be honed oversize and fitted with a bronze bushing that is then honed to final size (depending on rod design). Big end bores should also be measured

If the small end of a bushed rod does require repair, the bushing can be bored out and replaced with a new bushing that is then honed to size.

both for diameter and out-of-round. Depending on the extent of distortion, the big end may be reconditioned. Rod big end bores, regardless of the style, must be sized to specification and any out-of-round cannot be tolerated. Any deviations must be corrected by reconditioning or replacing the rod.

Measuring Center-to-Center Length

Center-to-center (CTC) distance represents the distance from the center of the rod's big end to the center of the small end. For example, a rod specified as having a center distance of 6.125 inches should measure that value from the center of the big end bore to the center of the piston wrist pin bore.

Before measuring CTC distance, the rod cap must be fully installed, with rod bolts fully tightened to specification. This may involve a torque value, or in the case of many OEM rods, an angle-plus-torque value. If you're using performance aftermarket rods and rod bolts, always follow

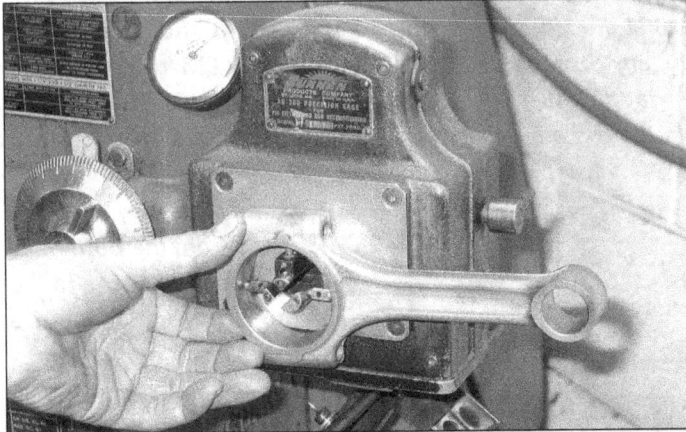

Measuring the diameter of a rod big end is easily done on a shop's rod honing machine that features a bore gauge. The gauge is adjusted to the specified diameter. The rod big end is then placed onto the gauge to check for both diameter and taper.

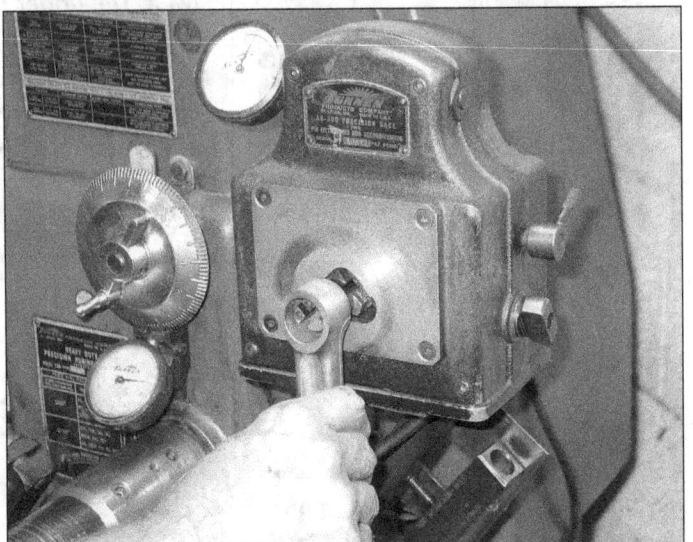

The rod small end, or wrist pin bore, is also measured for diameter on the rod hone's built-in gauge.

the maker's specs for bolt tightening.

One method of measuring CTC distance is to first measure the small end and big end bore diameters, and record these numbers. Then, using a caliper, measure from the top of the big end bore to the bottom of the small end bore and record this number. Then add 1/2 of the big end bore diameter, then add 1/2 of the small end bore diameter. This is easier than trying to measure actual center-to-center distance in one measurement check.

Checking for Bend and Twist

As a result of extreme use, it is possible that bending or twisting distorted the rod's beam. Using a dedicated connecting rod alignment checker, check for bend and twist. With the rod big end secured on the fixture, install a wrist pin to the small end. The upper fixture on the checker contacts the exposed areas of the wrist pin on the sides of the pin. If the upper fixture does not contact the wrist pin fully on both ends, you have a gap between the fixture and

Inspecting a connecting rod for bend. The upper fixture of the checking tool is placed onto the top surfaces of the wrist pin. A feeler gauge is then used to check for any difference in gap between each side of the wrist pin and the checker. Here, a rod is checked for twist. The upper contact of the checking tool is placed against the sides of the wrist pin. Again, any deviation checked with a feeler gauge indicates any amount of twist in the rod beam.

one side of the wrist pin. If a gap exists, the rod beam is twisted. In this case, discard the rod and replace it. Next, relocate the upper fixture to contact the top surfaces of the wrist pin. Any gap on either side of the pin indicates that the rod is bent.

Reconditioning Connecting Rods

Assuming that you're dealing with rods that feature flat rod-to-cap mating surfaces, the big end bore of the rod may be corrected by removing .002 to .003 inch from the parting line mating surfaces of the rod and from the cap, using a dedicated rod grinder. This makes the big end bore smaller and intentionally slightly out-of-round, which is then corrected by honing the big end back to the specified diameter, establishing a round bore at the same time. To achieve equal rod lengths at all cylinders, the same amount of material must be removed from each rod and rod cap for all rods.

This cannot be done with PM rods, because the rod-to-cap mating surfaces are uneven. A brief explanation of PM rods is included later in this chapter. If a PM rod big end is out-of-round or too tight, the only way to save the rod is to hone to an

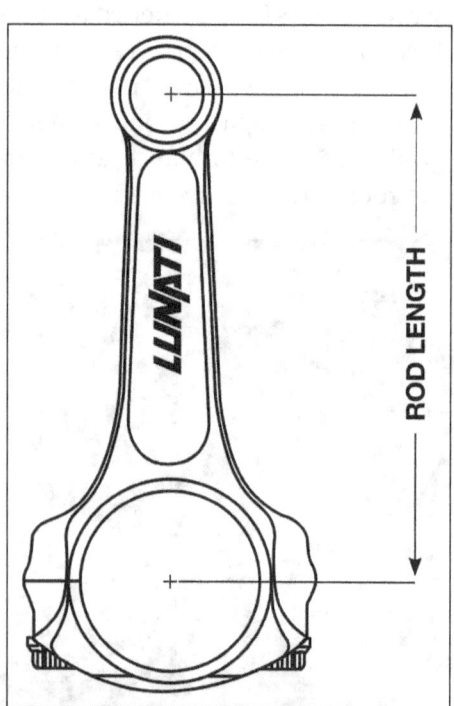

A connecting rod's center-to-center length represents the distance from the centerline of the bog end bore to the centerline of the wrist pin bore.

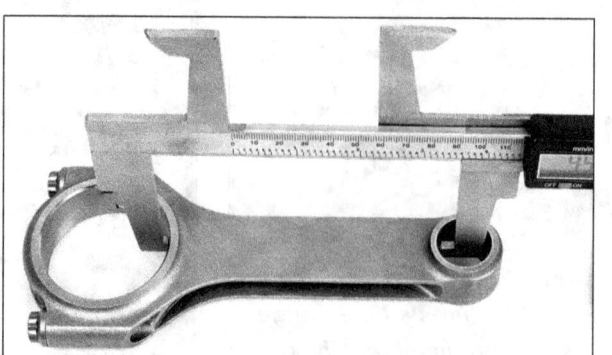

Using a caliper, the distance from the bottom of the small end bore to the top of the big end bore is measured. In this example, you measure 4.555 inches. If the big end bore diameter measures 2.214 inches and the small end bore diameter measures .926 inch, you add one-half of each bore diameter to the first measurement (1.107 + .463 + 4.555) to obtain a center-to-center rod length of 6.125 inches.

CONNECTING ROD INSPECTION AND RECONDITIONING

oversize, assuming that oversize-O.D. rod bearings are available for your particular application. Otherwise, a damaged PM rod must be discarded and replaced.

When reconditioning a rod big end (other than a PM rod), after the cap and rod are ground, use a fine flat file to remove the sharp edges at the mating surfaces. Then install the cap to the rod using new rod bolts. If the rod features captive rod bolts that are interference fit to the rod, use a hydraulic press to smoothly press the rod bolts into place. The rod bolts (or nuts, depending on style) are then tightened to the specified torque value with the rod secured in a bench-mounted rod vise.

A micrometer is adjusted to the specified I.D. that the rod requires. The micrometer is then placed onto the rod honing machine's built-in gauge, adjusting the gauge to zero. This provides the reference point to allow checking big end bore size in between honing procedures.

The honing machine's mandrel is then set up for the diameter of the rod big end. Initial honing is usually done with a slightly rougher-grit honing stone. When the big end has been honed to within about .001 inch of the desired size, the operator switches to a finer-grit stone.

With cooling lubricant applied to the upper and lower areas of the honing stones, the rod is placed onto the mandrel, with the rod beam resting on a stationary guide rod. As the mandrel rotates, the operator manually runs the rod in and out along the length of the honing stones. After each honing phase of about five or six passes, the rod is removed from the mandrel and checked on the machine's gauge to verify how much material has been removed. The

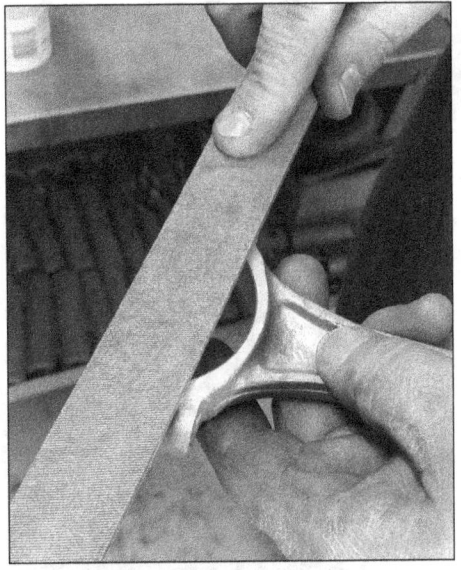
Prior to grinding caps and rods, run a file across the sides to eliminate any potential burrs that prevent the rod or cap from seating squarely in the grinding machine.

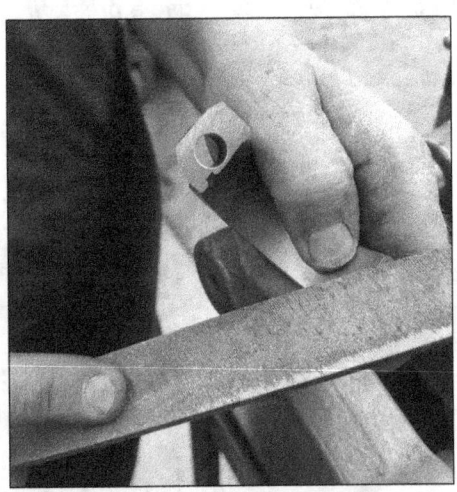
Inspect the freshly ground cap mating surface to verify that surfaces have been dressed, with no low spots. After grinding the mating surfaces, run a fine file across the mating surface edges to remove any sharp edges.

The secured rod is swept back and forth against the grinding wheel, removing .003 inch. A dedicated rod grinding machine is mandatory for resurfacing rod and cap mating surfaces.

Here, a rod cap is secured to the rod grinder. The operator grinds the cap mating surfaces, removing .003 inch.

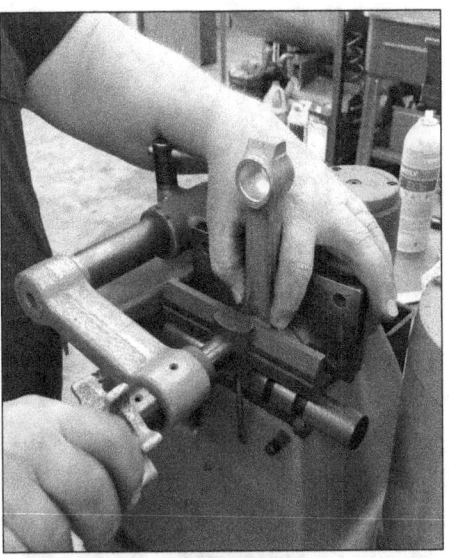
The rod is positioned on the rod grinder in the same manner.

process repeats until there is about .001 inch remaining, at which time a finer honing tone grade is installed, finish-honing to the zero mark on the machine's gauge.

Depending on the design, a press-fit pin may be featured in the small end, where the wrist pin is interference fit to the rod small end, with oil clearance between the pin and piston pin bores to allow the pin to rotate within the piston's pin bores. On the other hand, a full-floating pin design is free to rotate both within the rod's small end and the piston. This allows heat and friction to be distributed to both

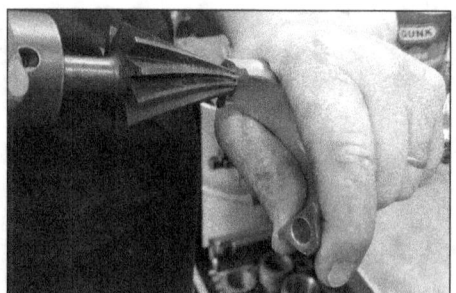
After mating surfaces have been ground, lightly de-burr the rod bolt holes with a tapered reamer.

After a micrometer has been adjusted to the desired inside diameter of the rod big end bore, the rod honing machine's checking gauge is adjusted to zero.

For rods designed to use a press-fit rod bolt, new rod bolts are smoothly pressed into the rod with a hydraulic press. Never hammer the rod bolts in place.

Brass support bars are located on the opposite side of the mandrel's honing stones. Here, the bars are adjusted to center the stones within the rod big end bore.

With the rod secured in a rod vise, both rod bolts are tightened to specified torque value.

Various grades of honing stones are available for rod reconditioning. Initial honing strokes are performed with a slightly aggressive grit stone. As final size is approached, the operator switches to a finer-grit set of stones. The rod big end is positioned on the honing mandrel, with the rod beam resting against a stationary support rod to prevent the rod from rotating during honing.

Powdered Metal Rods

Although connecting rods may be made with cast-iron, forged steel, or machined form billet stock, powdered metal rods (often referred to as PM or "cracked cap" or "fractured" rods) manufacturing involves a specialized powdered mixture of alloys placed into a cookie-type mold. This powdered mix is then both heated (to melt and flow) and pressurized. The process results in a surprisingly strong product that requires only big end and small end honing and bolt thread tapping (no additional exterior finishing is required).

Because the rods are made as one piece, the caps must be separated by a fracturing process. With the rod secured in a fixture, the cap parting line area is scored, and the cap is literally snapped off without losing any mating surface material. The resulting parting faces are uneven instead of being flat. This results in perfect mating between rod and cap because no material is lost during the separation. The cap fits to the rod precisely (mirror-image surfaces). The cap is now dedicated to its original rod, and when mated and the bolts are tightened, the parting line is invisible to the naked eye. If this uneven mating surface is disturbed, rod-to-cap alignment is lost.

The best approach, if resizing is necessary, is to avoid disturbing the irregular cracked mating surfaces altogether. Instead, it may be possible to hone the big end to an oversize that accommodates the fitting of oversized-O.D. rod bearings. Unfortunately, these oversized bearings are not yet available for all cracked cap applications, so check with your bearing suppliers before committing to this. If available, though, bearings may be obtained that feature a standard size I.D. and a .010 inch larger O.D.; or in an undersized I.D. (to accommodate an undersized ground crank) and an oversized O.D. to accommodate an enlarged connecting rod big end.

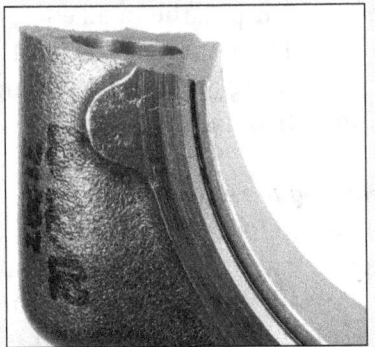

Powdered metal (PM) rods are often referred to as "cracked cap" or "fractured" rods because the rod caps are created by snapping the caps from the rod. No material is lost during this fracturing process, and it provides a perfectly matching mating face between rod and cap. Although this may look like a crude method, it works very well to lock the cap to the rod with perfect alignment. Never modify the mating surfaces. Doing so prevents correct cap mating. Use great care not to damage the fractured mating surfaces.

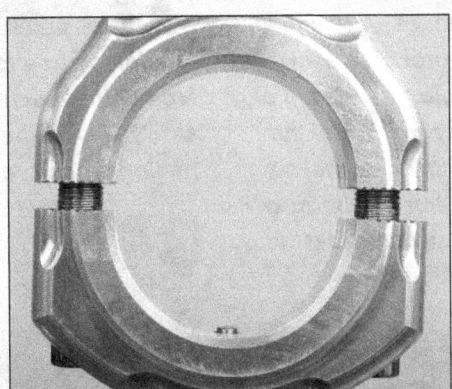

Some exotic racing aluminum rods may feature a serrated tooth profile on the rod and cap that provides precise registration of the cap to the rod. Although this mating design is machined, this is essentially the same principle that is used on cracked-cap PM rods, wherein each cap is precisely matched to its rod.

A cracked-cap powdered-metal rod's cap mating surfaces are uneven on purpose. Each rod and cap's mating surfaces are unique to that rod and cap. Here, a cap is placed in position but not tightened yet. Note the uneven-looking parting line.

Here, the same cap on its PM rod has been tightened to specification. Note how the parting line has essentially disappeared from view. The cap and rod are mated together perfectly.

CHAPTER 6

As the honing mandrel turns, the operator glides the rod in and out along the honing stones. A gauge at the rear of the mandrel area allows the operator to monitor as the big end bore diameter increases. When the big end bore gets closer to final size, at about .001 inch short of the zero mark, the operator switches over to a set of finer honing stones.

In addition to a load control at the face of the machine, a remote foot switch allows the operator to increase honing stone pressure.

After each phase of a series of passes, the big end is checked on the sizing gauge to see how close the big end bore size is approaching the zero mark.

The rod big end bore is continually checked for size and honed progressively until the gauge reads zero.

the rod small end bore and the piston. Because this design features no interference fit to the rod, the pin is easily inserted by hand. In addition, a wire C-clip or a flat-wound spiral clip at each end holds the pin in position and prevents it from sliding out. The clips secure into grooves that are machined into the outer ends of the piston's pin bores.

If the rod features a press-fit wrist pin and the pin bore of the rod is damaged and requires oversizing, the only way to save the rod is to obtain an oversize-diameter wrist pin. Depending on the application, these may be available in a .002-inch oversize. Otherwise, the rod must be replaced. If the rod is designed to use a free-floating pin, the small end may be restored by removing the existing bronze bushing and installing a new bushing, then honing to size.

Numbering the Rods and Caps

Connecting rods *must* be matched with their original rod caps. When rods are manufactured (or reconditioned), the big end (rod bearing end) is honed with the cap attached and fully tightened to

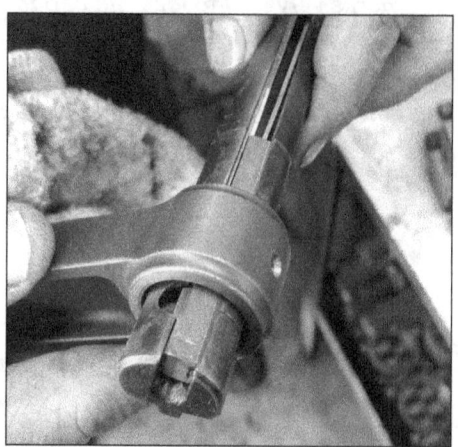

If a rod small end is to be resized, a mandrel and stone set of the appropriate size is installed to the honing machine.

specification. *Never* mix up your caps, because it guarantees a diameter and out-of-round problem that kills your rod bearing clearance.

To aid in keeping rods matched to their respective caps, each rod and its cap should be numbered (with matching numbers). Quality performance aftermarket rods are usually laser-etched with matching numbers, and these may be factory-assigned sequential numbers such as matching three-, four-, or five-digit numbers. If your rods and caps are not numbered (as is usually the case with OEM rods), you need to number them. Bore location numbers are the easiest to use. Simply follow the engine's firing order to identify each rod for its location by placing the numbers on one side of the rod big end (just above the parting line) and the side of the cap (just below the parting line on the same side). For example, for No. 1 rod, place a "1" on the rod and "1" on the cap, etc.

If your rods and caps are not already numbered for matching identification, it's advisable to mark them yourself. However, avoid stamping the numbers by using a steel number punch and a hammer. If you don't have a very skilled feel for this, you can easily distort the rod bearing bore, depending on the amount of force applied, which may be difficult to control. The safe method is to etch the numbers. Because not every shop has access to a laser etcher, a simple and inexpensive electric etching pen (available at most hardware stores) can be used without damaging the rod or cap.

Rod Bolt Tips

The quality and strength of the rod bolts is absolutely critical for high-performance applications.

Rods and their caps must remain together as a matched set at all times. Aftermarket performance rods are laser etched on one side of the rod big end saddle and cap. Both rod and cap feature the same number; numbers are only applied on the same side. This makes it easy to keep rods and caps matched, as long as you pay attention.

Always purchase the best rod bolts available such as those offered by ARP, A-1, and others. Rod bolt tightening is also of critical importance to obtain the desired clamping force. Depending on bolt design, bolts may be tightened by monitoring torque value and stretch, or by the use of a torque-plus-angle approach. A torque-plus-angle method is primarily used only for OEM (original equipment manufacturer) rod bolts, where the specifications specifically call for torque-plus-angle, for a specific engine application.

If you're using aftermarket performance rod bolts, in the majority (if not all) cases, manufacturers provide both a torque specification and a stretch range (giving you a choice of tightening methods).

For rod bolts that are to be tightened by the torque method, pay attention to the bolt maker's instructions regarding thread lubricant, since this can differ with the use of oil versus a specific moly lubricant. Rod bolt (and performance rod) makers provide two different torque values: one with the use of engine oil as a lubricant and one with the use of a specific moly lube. Specified torque value is always a bit lower with moly, because moly decreases thread and underhead friction. Moly-based lubricant decreases friction and as a result, the torque value is slightly lower as opposed to the use of engine oil. Also, before installing rod bolts, apply lube to both the threads and to the underside of each bolt head.

It's important to follow the proper rod bolt tightening procedures, not only for final assembly, but whenever measuring big ends during inspection.

Speaking of rod bolts, consider replacing them during future service. Rod bolts don't last forever, due to the stretching involved when you obtain clamping force as well as the stresses they endure during engine operation.

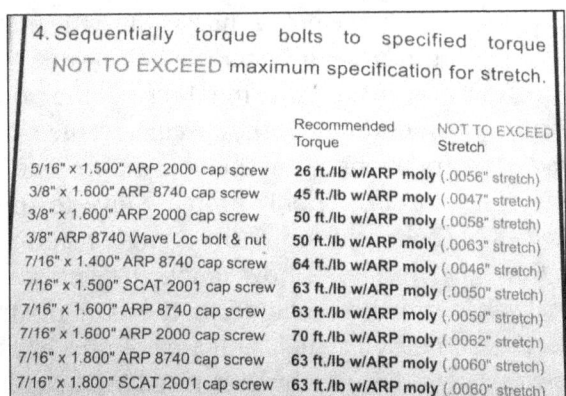

Performance aftermarket rods are supplied with torque and bolt stretch specifications. The chart shown here specifies the use of ARP moly lubricant. With that lube applied, the appropriate torque values and maximum allowable bolt stretch are listed.

CHAPTER 6

Torque-to-yield (TTY) rod bolts, those that require a torque-plus-angle tightening method, should never be reused. Even high-performance rod bolts should be replaced after they've been torqued by a certain number of cycles during initial build and subsequent rebuilds. There is no golden rule for rod bolt replacement, but a high-performance or racing application is a good candidate for bolt replacement during every future teardown and reassembly. The cost of a set of rod bolts is far less expensive than dealing with the severe engine damage that can result from bolts that can potentially fail.

Monitoring Bolt Stretch

Instead of only achieving a torque value by tightening the rod bolts, a preferred method involves monitoring rod bolt stretch as torque is applied. As any bolt is tightened to its specified value, it begins to stretch in length, entering its "elastic" range. If undertightened, you may have insufficient clamping force. In the case of rod bolts, this can result in inadequate rod bearing crush and loosening of the cap during operation, which results in lower oil pressure, bearing damage, rod failure, crankshaft damage, and even block damage. If the rod bolts are overtightened to the point where the elastic range is exceeded, the bolts don't have enough clamping strength, resulting in potential bolt failure, followed by damage to rods, crank, and block. By monitoring bolt stretch during tightening, you are able to more precisely verify that the bolts have been tightened within the specified range. Performance rod bolt and rod makers include both torque and stretch values in their instructions.

High-performance rod bolts feature a dimple at each end of the bolt. This allows the use of a rod bolt stretch gauge, which features a pair of tapered contact tips. To measure bolt stretch, you first zero the stretch gauge to the bolt with the bolt in its relaxed, free state. Place the bolt onto the gauge, with the anvil contacts resting in the bolt's dimples, then zero the gauge (rotate the gauge bezel to align the needle to the zero mark). Remove the bolt from the gauge and apply the proper lubricant to the bolt threads and under the bolt head.

Install the rod bolt to the rod and torque to the specified value recommended by the bolt maker. Then install the bolt stretch gauge to the bolt and note the gauge reading. This shows how much the bolt has stretched relative to the bolt in its relaxed state. Compare your findings to the stretch range listed by the bolt or rod maker. If your reading shows that you have not entered the elastic range, further tightening is required. Some builders prefer to apply a bit less torque initially, then they check stretch and apply additional torque until the bolt has stretched by the amount specified. You want to avoid overstretching the bolt beyond the specified maximum because this can weaken the bolt.

The stretch monitoring process is repeated for each rod bolt, requiring you to first zero the gauge to each bolt prior to installation. It's time-consuming but allows you to determine the bolt's clamping force more accurately.

Removing and Installing Caps

When servicing rod caps off the crankshaft, during inspection and measuring procedures, the rod must be handled carefully to avoid creating bend or twist issues or creating nicks that can result in rod beam stress failures. Avoid using a bench vise to hold rods while removing or installing rod caps.

When removing caps from rods, a slight interference fit is common due to clamping forces, or where guide bushings in the rod fit tightly

GM LS original connecting rod bolts usually feature a straight-shanked bolt with a centering dowel sleeve. High-performance aftermarket rod bolts, such as the ARP bolt seen here on the right, feature an undercut shank with a larger-diameter area under the bolt head that centers the bolt, eliminating the need for the separate sleeve.

Before installing a rod bolt, it must be first cleaned and then treated to a film of the appropriate lubricant on both the threads and the underside of the bolt head. Rod bolt and rod makers specify the torque value for using oil or moly. You must follow the torque specs for the lubricant being used.

CONNECTING ROD INSPECTION AND RECONDITIONING

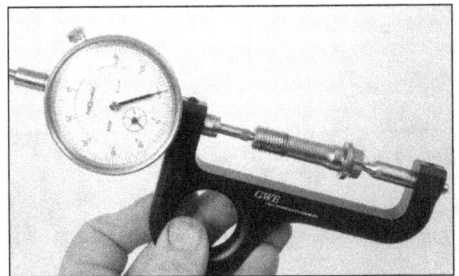

Aftermarket performance rods feature rod bolts with a dimple on each end. The bolt head has a dimple. This permits the use of a rod bolt stretch gauge. The shank tip of a rod bolt also has a centering dimple. A rod bolt stretch gauge engages both ends of the bolt. A rod bolt stretch gauge allows you to monitor the amount of stretch that the bolt experiences during torque tightening. First, engage the bolt onto the tool and zero the gauge in the bolt's relaxed state.

into recessed holes in the caps. It's common during rod cap removal to first loosen the rod bolts and to tap the bolt heads while holding the cap in your hand. However, using a rod splitter tool and rod vise is a secure method that avoids potential rod damage. A dedicated rod vise features a flat base and a moveable upper flat that allows clamping the rod big end. The tool jaws feature nylon or other heavy-duty plastic liners that prevent nicking or gouging the side of the rod big end. With the rod big end clamped in place, the rod bolts can be loosened or tightened without fear of rod damage. When removing caps, after the rod bolts are loosened and removed, the rod big end is placed onto a rod splitter tool. This tool features a two-piece round aluminum mandrel (mandrel sizes are available for various ranges of big end diameters). As the rod splitter handle is rotated, the two mandrel halves walk away from each other, smoothly

As torque is applied during bolt tightening, the stretch is monitored by installing the stretch gauge. The bolt in this example is specified to be tightened to a maximum of .0055 inch. After tightening with the specified torque value, you see that this bolt has stretched .0050 inch.

drawing the cap free of the rod. These two bench tools are very handy when removing or installing caps to rods, where the rod is not installed on the crankshaft rod journal.

Removing or installing rod bolts with the rod off the crankshaft is best done on a dedicated rod vise. This protects the rod from potential twist or burr damage.

I do not recommend the use of a vise to separate a cap from its rod when these specialty tools are not available. The rod bolts may be loosened by placing the rod big end into a bench vise, but the vise jaws *must* be padded with two clean pieces of wood, soft aluminum, or brass to hold the big end in place, avoiding direct contact between the rod big end and the surface of the vise jaws. Using a rag to insulate the rod may not suffice, as compression on the rag may allow the vise jaws to dig into the rod.

After the rod bolts have been cracked loose, do not remove the bolts. Instead, back them off about halfway. While holding the rod cap in one hand and with the rod held over a clean workbench that is padded with a towel, use a brass hammer to tap the rod bolt heads. This nudges the cap free from the slight interference fit.

Again, the use of a bench vise is not recommended. However, if you don't have access to the proper tools, rod caps may be tightened or loosened, but great care is required to avoid damaging the rod. Always maintain the correct cap orientation to the rod when installing the cap.

With the rod bolts loosened or removed, as the rod splitter's handle is turned, the two-piece mandrel smoothly separates the cap from the rod. A rod splitter tool offers an easy method of separating a cap from its rod without the need of a hammer.

AUTOMOTIVE MACHINING: A GUIDE TO BORING, DECKING, HONING AND MORE

CHAPTER 7

PUSHRODS AND LIFTERS

Never assume that a "stock" length pushrod is correct for any given build. A variety of alterations to the stock assembly can affect the required pushrod length, such as reducing block deck height, resurfacing the cylinder head deck, changing camshaft lift, changing rocker arm ratio, installing lifters that feature a different height, etc. Always measure to verify the pushrod length required for any given build. For example, by resurfacing the block decks, deck height might be reduced to a point at which a stock-length pushrod is too long for the application, resulting in the valves not closing fully.

Pushrods are available in three-piece and one-piece designs. A three-piece design features a tube with hardened lower and upper tips. A one-piece design features a hardened one-piece centerless-ground machined pushrod. Wall thickness of the tube varies depending on application, with most common performance thickness of .080, .083, .135, and .165 inch. Street and many race applications call for .080- to .083-inch wall, with thicker wall pushrods required for more extreme applications. Pushrod diameters vary, again depending on the application. Typical diameters include 5/16 and 3/8 inch, with larger diameters such as 11/16, 7/16, with extra-beefy 1/2 and 9/16 inch often required for race engines that feature very high valvespring rates. Smaller diameter pushrods are also available for applications requiring 3/16- and 1/4-inch diameters. Common tube materials, depending on application, include the use of 4130/4135 chrome-moly, as well as high-tensile tool steel. The larger the diameter and the thicker the wall, the less subject the pushrod is to deflection during high-RPM

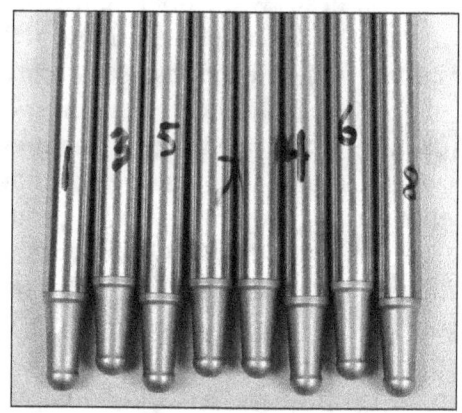

Some engine designs, where offset rocker arms are employed, may require varying pushrod lengths. For a recent 632-ci race engine, using a Jesel rocker system on Dart Big Chief II cylinder heads, the exhaust pushrods were 1/2 inch in diameter with a length of 11.124 inches, while intake pushrods were 7/16-inch diameter with lengths of both 10.953 and 10.805 inches, depending on location.

Never assume pushrod length based only on published specifications. Because of variations in a specific build such as block and head deck height rocker arm ratio, valve length, the size of your camshaft's base circle, thickness of the cylinder head gasket, etc., it's critical to take the time to determine the precise pushrod length(s) required. You should also take the time to measure for pushrod length at all intake and exhaust locations, or at least at the front and rear cylinders, in case your block decks are not perfectly parallel and equidistant from the crankshaft centerline.

PUSHRODS AND LIFTERS

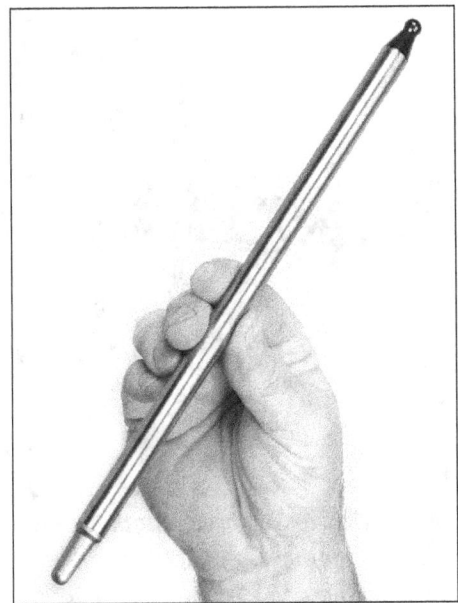

Hardened tips are needed at each end of the pushrod to withstand the frictional loads at the lifter and rocker arm. Note the taper at each upper and lower tip on this racing pushrod, to provide added clearance at the lifter and rocker, where the pushrod diameter is larger than the lifter cup and rocker arm cup as shown on this 1/2-inch diameter pushrod.

Performance aftermarket pushrods are often laser etched by the manufacturer for easy size reference. This pushrod is identified as having a wall thickness of .080 inch and a length of 9.000 inches.

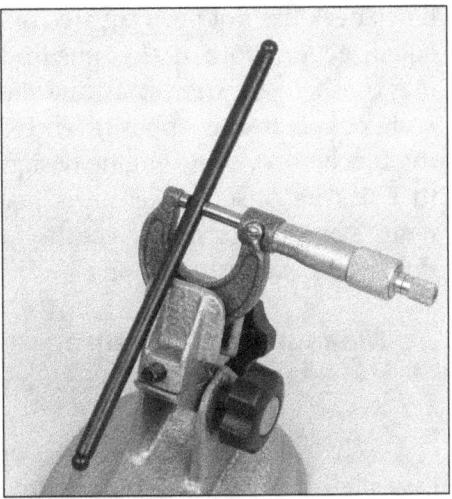

If necessary, use a micrometer to measure pushrod outer diameter.

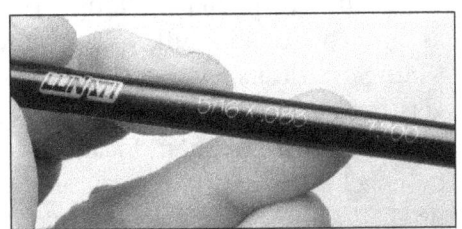

This pushrod has been laser etched to indicate diameter, wall thickness, and length. Not all pushrod manufacturers provide this easy-reference identification.

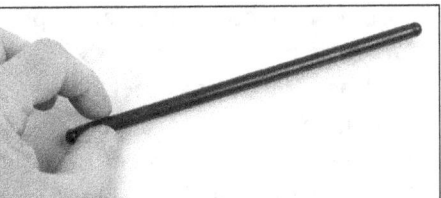

Checking a pushrod for straightness can be achieved by slowly rolling the pushrod on a plate of clean glass.

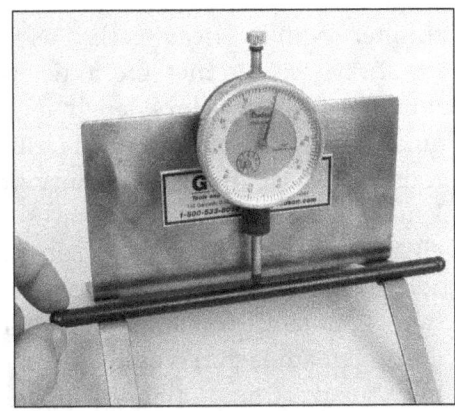

A dedicated pushrod concentricity checker makes verifying pushrod straightness easy and precise. The pushrod is positioned on the stand's cradles. The dial indicator plunger is positioned at the center of the pushrod. The gauge is zeroed, and the pushrod is slowly rotated to measure for any runout.

conditions. Bear in mind that larger diameters and thicker walls often translate into increased valvetrain weight. Space considerations determine diameter, with regard to pushrod passages in the cylinder head. Bigger and heavier isn't always better.

Although checking new pushrods for runout probably isn't necessary, it doesn't hurt just to make sure that none have been damaged during handling. Used pushrods should always be checked for runout. Pushrods can be checked easily for runout (bend) by placing the pushrod in a horizontal cradle (a dedicated pushrod checker stand is best). A dial indicator that is mounted to the stand is adjusted so that the indicator plunger contacts the pushrod at its center. The dial indicator is then adjusted so that the plunger is compressed against the pushrod to achieve a preload of about .050 inch. The indicator gauge is then adjusted to read zero on the gauge. The pushrod is then slowly rotated, noting the amount of runout. Generally speaking, a maximum allowable runout is about .001 to .0015 inch, with 0 to a maximum of .0005 inch preferred.

An alternative method for checking pushrod runout is to slowly roll a clean pushrod on a perfectly flat surface, such as a glass panel or a precision steel or granite platform. The pushrod should roll smoothly with no daylight visible between the flat surface and the center of the pushrod (any gap between the center of the pushrod and the flat surface can be measured with a feeler gauge). If runout is excessive, the pushrod

CHAPTER 7

must be replaced. Don't attempt to straighten it.

When building a stock engine to original specifications, a stock-length pushrod will likely suffice. However, given variables such as block deck height resurfacing, cylinder head deck resurfacing, valve length, a camshaft upgrade that features a different height base circle, use of a thicker or thinner cylinder head gasket, etc., it's always wise to measure to determine the correct pushrod length for a given application. Off-the-shelf pushrods are available in a wide range of lengths to suit any application, usually in increments of .050 inch. In addition, custom-length pushrods can be ordered from a number of pushrod manufacturers easily, including Trend, Comp Cams, Lunati, Crane, and others. Whereas the use of hydraulic lifters and/or adjustable rocker arms allow some leeway regarding length, pushrod length is especially critical when using solid lifters and/or nonadjustable rockers.

Always measure each pushrod location for length. Don't assume that the measured length for number-1 cylinder intake location suffices for all other locations. If the block deck has not been squared and equalized on both decks, pushrods may need to be shorter at one end and longer at the opposite end of the block. Also, some engine designs that feature offset rocker arms may require specific pushrod lengths for intake and exhaust locations.

Measuring for Pushrod Length

A checking pushrod provides an easy method of determining correct length. This is a temporary pushrod that is adjustable for length.

With the engine long-block assembled (crankshaft, camshaft, timing set, lifters, cylinder head gaskets, and heads), install a checking pushrod into the first location to be checked (for instance, number-1 intake location). Choose a checking pushrod that provides a length range that suits your engine. As an example, let's say that your engine "normally" requires a pushrod length of 7.500 inches. Choose a checking pushrod that provides a range of 7.000 to 8.000 inches.

Remove the number-1 intake valvespring and replace it with a light

Measuring for pushrod length is made easier with the use of light checking valvesprings. Use of these light springs maintains rocker arm geometry while checking, but doesn't cause unwanted resistance while trying to measure for required pushrod length.

checking spring. This makes it easier to rotate the engine and doesn't fight you as you check your measurement.

Rotate the crankshaft to place the camshaft lobe of the location to be checked on its base circle. In other words, the lifter must be on the base circle and not on the lobe ramp. This places the lifter as far down as it can be in its bore.

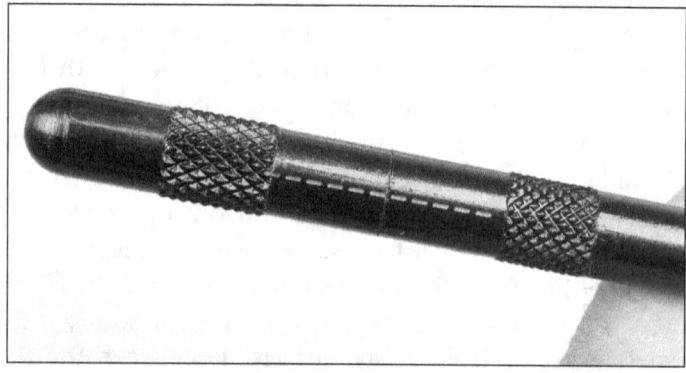

Some checking pushrods, such as this example from Comp Cams, feature a row of alignment marks. When the adjustment is fully collapsed as shown here and the two sections butt against each other, the length is as indicated on the body (for example, 7.000 inches).

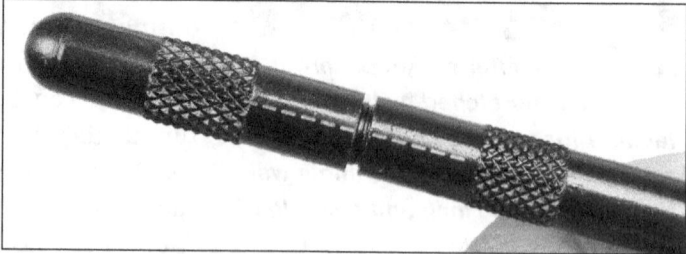

As the body is lengthened by rotating the sections, each full rotation indicates a change in length of .050 inch. In this example, a 7.000-inch minimum length checking pushrod has been rotated by one full revolution, with the index marks aligned. This now indicates a length of 7.050 inches. This "micrometer" design makes it easier to determine the adjusted length, especially if a long caliper is not available for measuring.

PUSHRODS AND LIFTERS

Wipe the valvestem tip clean to remove any oil. Using a marker pen, paint the valvestem tip. This provides a witness mark as the rocker tip travels across the valvestem tip.

Adjust the length of the checking pushrod to the theoretical length (again, if your engine normally calls for a 7.500-inch length, adjust the pushrod to that length).

Install the checking pushrod, making sure that the lower tip centers properly into the lifter.

Some checking pushrod designs are multipiece, allowing adjustments in body length and tip-to-body lengths. If the checking pushrod does not feature etched increment marks, it's best to place matchmarks on the body sections prior to removal from the engine. Then very carefully remove the checking pushrod to avoid accidental rotation, which alters length.

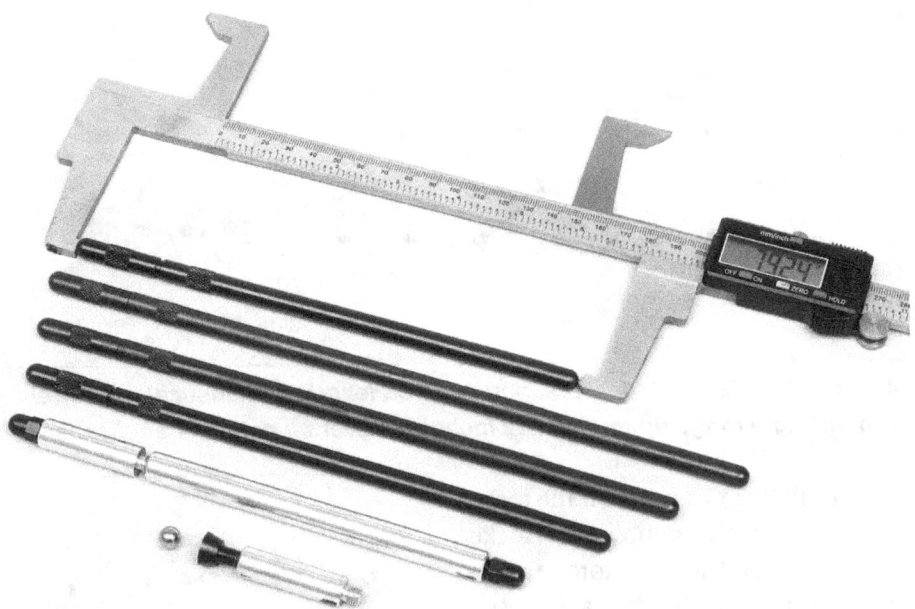

Checking pushrods are available in a variety of lengths and adjustment ranges. If you build a variety of engine types, it's best to keep a wide range of checking pushrods in your inventory to cover all potential builds.

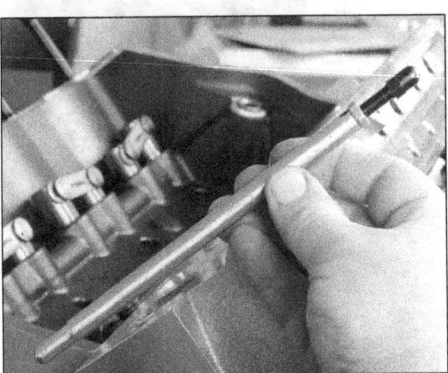

Adjustable pushrod checkers must be handled very carefully when removing from the engine following on-engine adjustment. Any rotation of the checking pushrod alters the measurement. It's a good idea to perform the adjustment and on-bench measurement several times to verify that the correct length has been achieved.

With camshaft and lifter installed, a light valvespring and rocker arm is put into place and an adjustable checking pushrod is installed. The cam has been rotated so that the lifter is on the lobe's base circle. The checking pushrod is carefully adjusted to accommodate the application. If solid lifters are being used, the checking pushrod is adjusted to achieve zero lash at the rocker-to-valve. If hydraulic lifters are used, a slight preload can be added to the measured length of the checking pushrod to suit the requirements of the specific lifters. This added length for lifter preload is in the range of .035 to .050 inch, depending on the recommendation of the lifter manufacturer.

CHAPTER 7

A long caliper is ideal for measuring pushrod length. Obtain a caliper capable of handling a range up to about 12 inches to cover all potential applications.

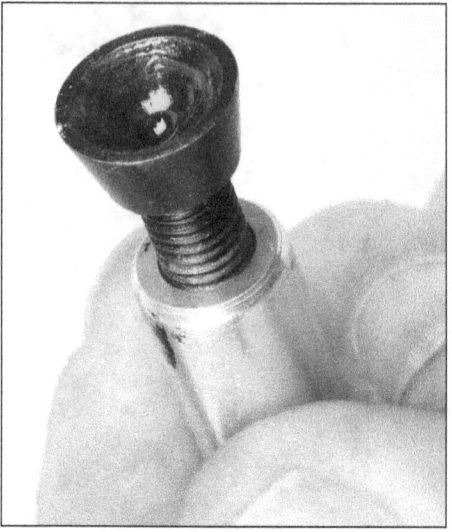

Certain valvetrain designs feature adjustable ball tips on the rocker arm pushrod ends and as a result require pushrods with upper cups. Although the rocker arm ball nestles into the cup during on-engine pushrod measurement, it is extremely difficult to measure the checking pushrod's cup with a caliper.

Install the rocker arm. If the rocker is nonadjustable, tighten the rocker arm bolt or nut to final torque value. If the rocker arm is adjustable, install at approximately the center of its adjustment.

Pushrod length is affected by the type of lifters being used. I delve into that aspect in Chapter 9. Rotate the crankshaft a full two revolutions (360 degrees).

Remove the rocker arm and inspect the witness rub mark on the valvestem tip. Ideally, the rub mark should be at the center of the valvestem tip. If the rub mark is off-center and closer to the intake side of the head, the pushrod is too short. If the rub mark is biased toward the exhaust side of the head, the pushrod is too long.

When the checking pushrod has been adjusted for proper length, carefully remove the pushrod, being extremely careful to avoid changing its length (if the checking pushrod does not feature index marks, place a matchmark that aligns the two

If the pushrod style requires an upper cup design, place a ball bearing into the checking pushrod's cup, but do this after the checking pushrod has been adjusted and removed from the engine. Otherwise, if you measure the checking pushrod by placing the caliper's anvil into the cup, you will have an incorrect measurement. Before measuring the checking pushrod with the ball in place, first measure the ball diameter. The ball diameter is subtracted from the overall measurement to obtain the correct length. The ball simply provides an easy way to make the measurement in terms of caliper contact.

With the upper cup clean, insert the ball.

86 AUTOMOTIVE MACHINING: A GUIDE TO BORING, DECKING, HONING AND MORE

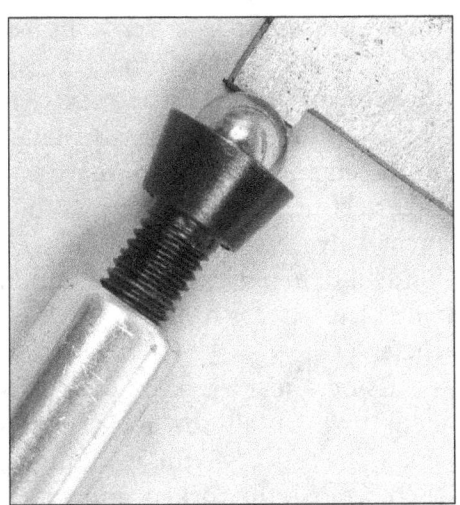

With the ball in place, allow the caliper to contact both the ball and the lower tip.

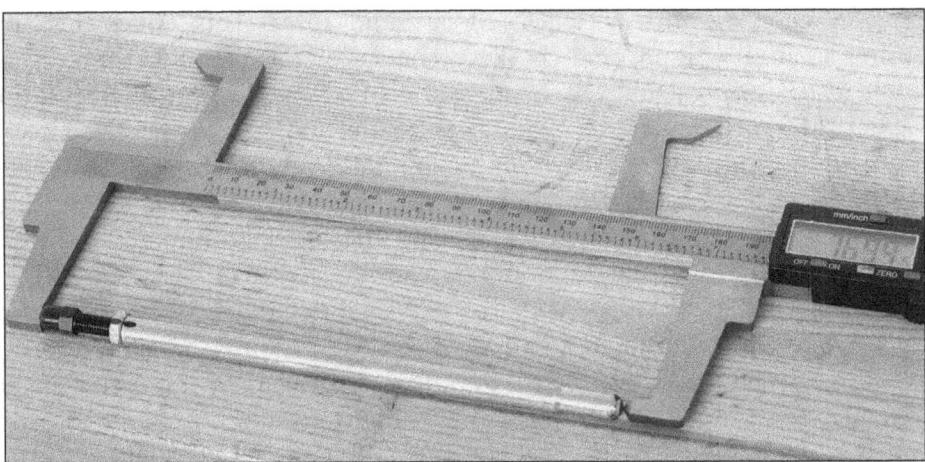

This pushrod, with a ball in the upper cup, measures an overall length of 7.6995 inches. Subtracting the ball diameter of .3125 inch, the ideal pushrod length is 7.3870 inches. Depending on the length offered by a pushrod maker, you could then order a length of 7.385 inches, with fine-tuning via valve-lash adjustment.

sections as a reference). Using a long caliper, carefully measure the pushrod. If you have hydraulic lifters, add to this length an appropriate amount to compensate for lifter preload, which may be in the range of .035 to .100 inch, depending on the specific style of lifter (check with the maker of the lifters for recommended preload).

If your pushrod design features a radius tip at each end, measure overall length. If your pushrod design features a cup at the upper end (for rockers that feature an adjustable ball), your measurement needs to include the distance from the lower tip to the inside of the cup. Do not attempt to measure the cup's seat in relation to the upper edge of the cup. Instead, use a 5/16-inch ball to insert into the cup. This provides a contact point for the caliper. After you measure the checking pushrod with the ball in place, subtract the ball diameter to obtain the actual length. For instance, if the overall measurement from the lower tip to the outside of the ball is 7.8125 inches and the ball measures .3125 inch in diameter, the final pushrod length is 7.500 inches.

When measuring a checking pushrod, most feature a fully radiused tip at each end, with no oil holes. If your style of desired pushrod does feature an oil passage, the missing end of the radius (due to the oil hole diameter and amount of chamfer at the oil hole) can lead to an imprecise measurement when using a caliper to measure length.

The theoretical length assumes that the pushrod has no oil hole in the end of it. Therefore, the radius at either end is complete, which lengthens the pushrod approximately .017 inch in the case of a 5/16-inch pushrod with .100-inch-diameter oil holes, minimally chamfered.

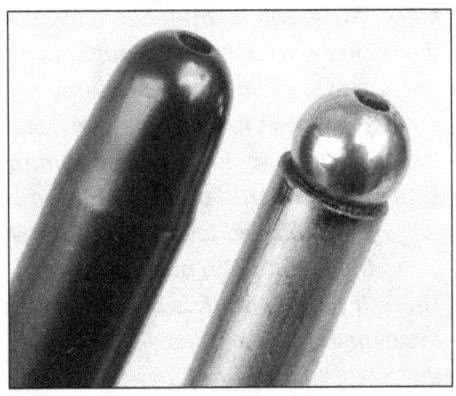

The actual length is what you measure if you had a caliper large enough to measure over the oil holes at each end of the pushrod. Unfortunately, this measurement is affected not only by the diameter of the oil holes but also by the entrance chamfer for each oil hole.

The gauge length is the most difficult to measure, as it requires a special-length checking gauge. This is because the oil holes and their chamfers are eliminated from the measurement. The only problem is that not all companies use the same gauge diameter. Leading makers such as Comp and Trend use a .140-inch gauge (which adds .017 inch at each

If the actual pushrod or pushrod checker features an oil hole, measuring with a caliper can be imprecise due to the caliper contacting the hole instead of the full radius. Using a gauged pushrod checker where you know that each full rotation of adjustment represents a distance of .050 inch avoids this variable. If the checking pushrod features no oil hole, caliper measuring can directly achieve the proper results.

end if measured with a caliper). If using a gauge-type pushrod checker that features no oil holes, the variable of the oil hole and its chamfer are eliminated, allowing you to use a caliper or to simply go by the number of full revolutions of the adjustable checker (with each full revolution equaling a distance of .050 inch).

Gauge-type adjustable pushrod checkers (such as those offered by Trend, Comp, and others) are marked with a standard length stamped in them. This is the length of the adjustable pushrod when the two halves are screwed together completely. As mentioned previously, extending the adjustable pushrod one full rotation lengthens the overall length by .050 inch. For example, a pushrod stamped 7.800 inches and screwed apart one rotation has a length of 7.850 inches (7.800 + .050). Therefore, you order the part number from the catalog that matches this gauge length because they are listed by gauge length.

The length of the required pushrod also depends on the type of lifter being used. If solid lifters are to be used, the rocker arms feature a lash adjustment. Therefore, with the lifter on the cam base circle, adjust the checking pushrod to the point where you achieve zero lash. Adjustment at the rocker arm then allows you to set the required valve lash.

If hydraulic lifters are to be used, you need to consider the plunge travel inside the lifter. If you are using a light checking valvespring, you can carefully adjust the checking pushrod until it just makes contact with the lifter, without compressing the lifter. An alternative is to use a spare lifter of exactly the same make, style, and part number, and tack-weld the plunger, effectively turning it into a solid lifter. This eliminates the chance of accidentally compressing the lifter during adjustment of the checking pushrod. After the checking pushrod has been adjusted to zero lash and measured for length, add the required amount to anticipate lifter preload (again, this compensation may be .03 to .050 inch or so, depending on the lifter specifications). Bear in mind that some hydraulic lifters are designed with very short travel distance (a sort of hybrid between a solid and hydraulic design). Check with the lifter maker for recommended lifter preload to consider when determining pushrod length.

After you've determined the correct pushrod length for your engine and have purchased the new push-

When checking for pushrod length, mark the valvestem tip with a black marker before installing the rocker arm. With the checking pushrod in place, the crank is rotated, causing the rocker arm to move through its entire sweep. With the rocker arm removed, check the witness mark on the valvestem tip. Ideally the rub mark should be centered on the tip. If the rub mark is biased toward the center of the engine, the pushrod is too short. If the rub mark is biased toward the exhaust side of the cylinder head, the pushrod is too long.

rods, always check to verify proper length. Test fit the pushrods, following the same procedure outlined here for determining length, as installed to the engine. Make sure that travel is correct, where you achieve a fully open valve condition without coil bind and a fully closed condition when the lifter is on the cam's base circle.

Using a marker, paint the valvestem tips, install the rockers, and rotate the crank two full revolutions, then remove the rockers and examine the witness rub marks. Again, if the rub mark is too far toward the intake side, the pushrod is too short. If the rub mark is too far toward the exhaust side, the pushrod is too long. If the rub mark is centered, the pushrod length is okay.

If you find that you have an incorrect length with the new pushrods, it means that you've likely made a mistake during your initial length check. Unless the new pushrods were custom ordered with a unique length, you should be able to return and reorder. Never blindly assume that the new pushrods are correct. Always double-check.

During pushrod length checking, verify that the rocker arm tip is relatively centered fore/aft on the valvestem tip.

CHAPTER 8

PISTONS

This chapter deals with measuring and understanding clearance issues relative to the piston and piston rings. Here I discuss clearances involving piston to bore, piston dome to head, valve to piston, and ring clearances, in addition to file-fitting rings.

Measuring Piston Skirts

Prior to boring and/or honing cylinder bores, the pistons that are intended for installation must first be measured for skirt diameter to determine the required bore diameter adequate for piston-to-wall oil clearance. Piston diameter dictates the final bore diameter.

Measuring piston diameter is not determined at the ring area; rather, the measurement must be taken at the skirt, but only in the specific height location specified by the piston maker. For example, the piston maker may specify that the diameter measurement be taken at a point exactly .500 inch from the bottom of the skirt. Measuring at the specific point recommended by the piston maker is necessary, since pistons are not the same diameter from top to bottom, by design. A very slight "cam ground" or barrel-shape profile at the skirt area is designed to reduce friction and to promote piston stability, which in turn optimizes ring seal. Both the cylinder block bores and pistons (hypereutectic or forged) must be measured at room temperature approximately 68 degrees F, because metals expand and contract with temperature variations. The measured piston skirt diameter dictates the required cylinder bore diameter to achieve the piston maker's specification for piston-to-bore clearance. Always measure skirt diameter at the point indicated by the piston maker.

Skirt diameter is measured using an outside micrometer. Considering the precise manufacturing techniques for today's aftermarket performance pistons, you should be able to measure only one piston from the set and assume that all remaining pistons have the same diameter. However, it never hurts to measure each piston just to be safe. Most of today's performance piston makers hold their tolerance to about .0005 inch at the gauge point.

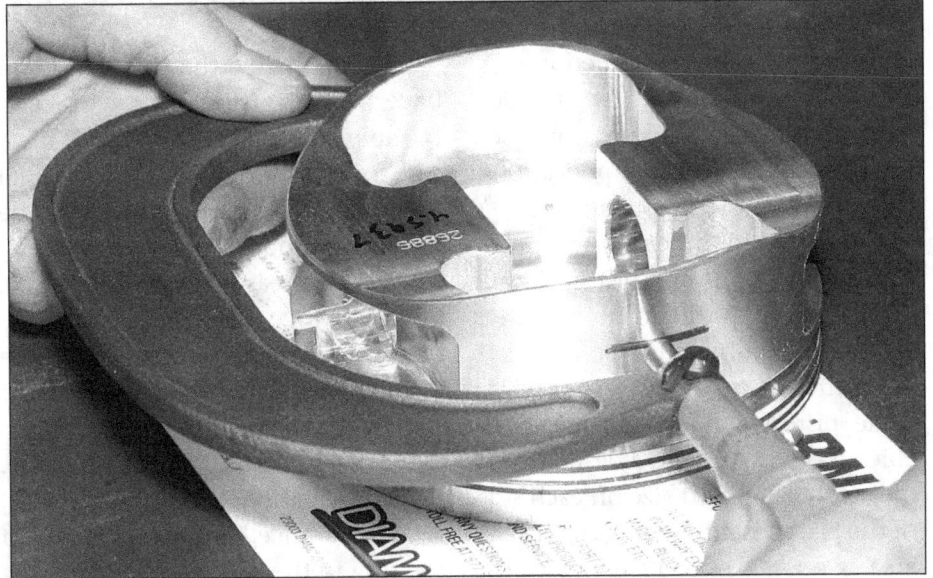
Before final-honing cylinder bores, the piston skirt must be measured at the exact skirt height location specified by the piston maker.

If pistons were sourced from an established manufacturer, such as JE, Wiseco, Ross, CP, Mahle, etc., it would be extremely rare to encounter a problem. Manufacturers such as JE normally hold to a very consistent tolerance of +/- .0005 inch, and even offer a "critical process" for custom piston orders held to even tighter tolerances.

Piston-to-wall clearance is specified by the piston maker. Hypereutectic pistons tend not to expand as much under operating temperature as forged pistons, so hyper pistons usually require a tighter piston-to-wall clearance. Always follow the piston-to-wall clearance that is recommended by the piston maker. As a general rule, given the same piston skirt measurement, a hypereutectic piston may require approximately .0015- to .0025-inch clearance, while a forged piston of the same size may require .0035 to .0055 inch for a naturally aspirated street application. Adding nitrous injection or forced induction may require an increased bore diameter of .0020 to .0035 inch for hyper pistons or .0045 to .0065 inch for forged pistons. Adding nitrous or forced induction may require an additional .001 to .002 inch of added clearance as opposed to naturally aspirated applications, depending on the piston maker's specs. Again, follow the piston maker's specifications for piston-to-wall clearance when the cylinder bores are being final-honed.

Although on the subject of skirts, some piston applications are available in an asymmetric design. This means that the skirt size on each side of the piston is different; a larger skirt area is on the piston's major thrust side (exhaust side of the right bank and intake side of the left bank) and a smaller skirt is on the minor thrust side, where friction and load are minimal. This saves weight and reduces bearing wear.

Asymmetrical pistons feature a larger skirt area for the major thrust side and a smaller skirt for the minor thrust side. The wider skirt accommodates the high stresses of the piston as it is pushed against the major thrust side of the cylinder. The exhaust side is located on the right bank and intake side on the left bank. Using a smaller skirt on the minor thrust side saves weight. These JE pistons (shown) for the LS engine platform feature a forged side relief design, and it provides added clearance to the reluctor wheel in stroker applications. Asymmetric pistons are labeled for bank location and front orientation.

Checking Ring-to-Piston Fit

Never assume that the rings you have fit your pistons correctly. Refer to the piston maker's specs and measure for ring side clearance and radial clearance. Insert a top ring into the top ring groove and use a feeler gauge to measure side clearance. With the ring seated against the floor of the groove, side clearance is the distance from the top surface of the ring to the roof of the groove. This is likely in the .001- to .002-inch range. Radial clearance, or back clearance, is the clearance behind the inside of the ring to the inside wall of the ring groove. This is likely in the .005-inch range. Perform this check prior to file fitting the rings to avoid wasting a bunch of time working on rings that don't fit the grooves.

Modifying Domes

If domes are to be modified, a dedicated, adjustable piston vise is a necessity. This fixture allows mounting the piston securely and is adjustable for valve angle. Before attempting to mill piston domes, pay particular attention to existing dome thickness, specifically the thinnest section of the dome. Depending on the piston material, the thinnest allowable area might be .150 or .200 inch, as examples. If in doubt, check with the piston maker for advice on this. If an area of the dome is too thin, the dome can sag under heat and pressure and potentially break through.

Depending on the combination of cylinder head design, piston

PISTONS

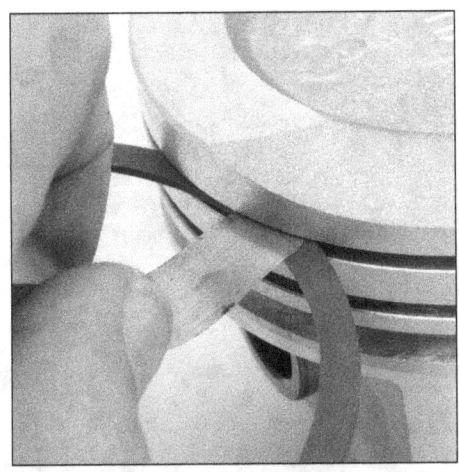

Checking piston ring side clearance with a feeler gauge. Follow the specification provided by the piston maker. Side clearance is usually about .001 to .002 inch.

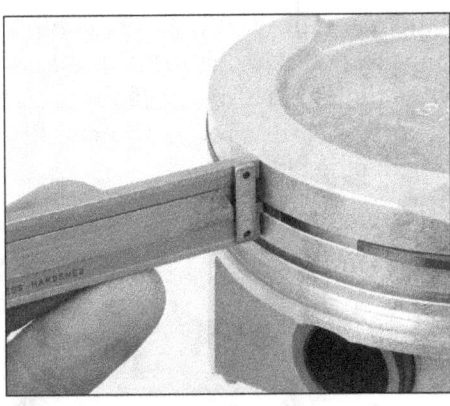

Ring back clearance is checked with the ring installed and pushed back to the inner groove wall. The distance from the face of the ring and the outer diameter of the piston surface is measured to determine back clearance. This is usually about .005 inch.

Before milling a piston dome, consider the thinnest section first to determine how much, if any, can safely be removed without compromising dome strength. The black mark on the cross section indicates the thinnest section of this piston dome.

design, piston compression distance, crank stroke, rod length, head gasket thickness, block deck height, and valve-to-piston clearance possibly due to camshaft profile and rocker arm ratio, it's possible to run into clearance issues. First, consider clearance between the piston dome and head, and between piston dome and the spark plug. The suggested absolute minimum clearance (with the head gasket in place and fully torqued) between the piston and head and/or spark plug is .040 to .050 inch for steel connecting rods and .055 to .060 inch for aluminum connecting rods (due to potentially greater expansion rate of alloy rods).

A common method of checking piston dome clearance relative to the head and spark plug is to apply modeling clay to a dry, clean piston dome; coat the chamber lightly with a thin oil to prevent the clay from sticking to the chamber. With a head gasket and head installed and fully torqued, but without pushrods, slowly rotate the crank to allow the piston to reach TDC. If you feel a dead stop, the piston may be in contact with the head, so don't try to force crank rotation. Remove the head and inspect and measure the clay for contact. If you did not experience a positive stop and rotation to TDC was achieved, examine and measure the clay areas that were compressed for thickness by carefully slicing a cross section of the

If the piston domes require modification by fly-cutting or making valve pockets deeper or larger, a dedicated piston pin vise allows the piston to be secured in the proper location and angle for the milling machine. This piston is being cut to obtain more valve radial clearance at Ross Racing Engines in Niles, Ohio.

clay with a razor and carefully measuring thickness with a small machinist's ruler or depth caliper. If you find tight spots that feature less than the recommended clearance, remove the clay and mark those areas on the dome.

Reapply clay, reinstall the head, this time with a spark plug installed, and repeat the process to determine spark plug clearance.

The piston dome is receiving a custom dome profile on a CNC lathe.

In preparation for piston dome machining, the combustion chambers are profiled digitally to obtain the required piston dimensions.

Examine the point between valve pockets. If this is very sharp, use a light abrasive to slightly soften this to minimize the potential for a hot spot that could contribute to detonation/pre-ignition.

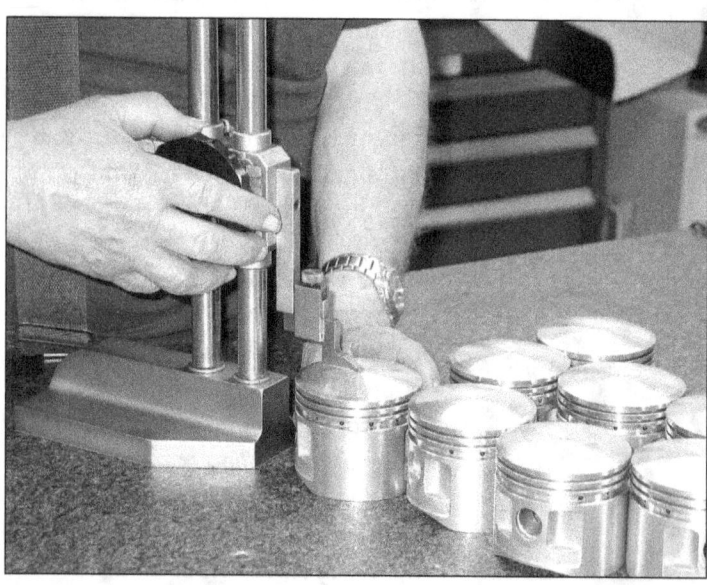

Prior to dome modifications, the initial dome heights are measured with a digital height gauge.

The sharp corner between valve pockets was relieved on this piston, eliminating a potential hotspot.

Dome Shapes

Piston domes are available in three basic types: positive dome, reverse dome (dished or bowl), and flat top. A positive dome features a rise above deck. A dished piston features a depression in the top below deck; a flat top has a smooth flat piston deck, with valve relief pockets where needed.

The additional piston volume provided by a raised dome increases compression ratio by reducing the volume of the piston-to-chamber area. Depending on the design of the cylinder head combustion chamber and the specific design of the piston dome, a high dome might help or detract from the efficiency of the ignited and burning air/fuel charge. One potential drawback with a high-dome piston is the possibility of increased piston rock as combustion pressure ramps over the dome projection. However, this can be impacted negatively or positively due to the variables involved in terms of dome shape and height, and chamber profile.

Reverse dish or bowl pistons reduce the dome height at the center area, providing an increase in piston-to-chamber volume, decreasing compression ratio depending on the volume of the chamber. Dished pistons are commonly used in forced induction applications to maintain combustion pressure under boost conditions to avoid detonation and excessive chamber pressure. The size of the dome volume (positive or negative) is matched to the volume of the combustion chamber to obtain the desired compression ratio. A flattop piston that features valve relief pockets is considered by many to be a preferred choice, again depending on the shape of the combustion chamber. Dome shape often boils down to a builder's preferences, past experience, and trial-and-error testing on the dyno or track.

An example of a flat-top piston with 5-cc valve reliefs to be installed in 4.125-inch bore with a 4.000-inch stroke. In combination with 64-cc cylinder head chambers, this piston provides a 12.2:1 compression ratio. With 68-cc chambers, this piston provides 11.6:1. With 70-cc chambers, you have an 11.4:1 compression ratio.

A flat-top piston with valve reliefs and an inverted dome. Note the double-cut intake valve relief. This piston fits either a standard small-block Ford (using the deeper pocket) or a "twisted wedge" application where the head chamber is tilted.

A domed "pop-up" piston featuring a healthy 44-cc dome. This 44-cc dome piston accommodates a big-block 124-cc open chamber head. The high dome is needed to maintain the high compression desired in combination with the large head chamber.

These pistons are sized for a 4.185-inch bore, feature a dome volume of 14.6 cc and are mated with 69-cc cylinder head chambers. The reverse dome increased volume allowed lowering compression ratio to a very streetable 10.54:1.

CHAPTER 8

Checking Valve-to-Piston Clearance

Check valve-to-piston clearance in both the vertical and radial planes. In the vertical plane, you're checking for the clearance between the valve face and the valve pocket. In the radial plane, you're checking for the radial clearance of the valve head to the radius of the valve pocket in the piston dome.

Although clay checking, as described earlier, is a common approach, this method poses variables such as the compression and possible spring-back of the clay, a potential separation of the clay from the piston, and clay sticking to the valve.

Using a degree wheel on the crank snout to check intake valve to piston vertical clearance, rotate the crank at least twice and then bring that piston to 10 degrees ATDC on the intake stroke, generally a position where the valve is closest to the piston. Be aware that two crank rotations are required to rotate the camshaft once.

Install a light checking valvespring onto the valve being checked. When checking valve-to-piston clearance, a solid lifter is required, because a hydraulic lifter may bleed down and provide a false reading. If the engine will be fitted with hydraulic lifters, locate a solid lifter of the same pushrod cup-to-tip length (a spare hydraulic lifter with the plunger tack welded to prevent plunging works).

With a lifter, pushrod, rocker, and light checking valvespring installed, adjust valve lash and set up a dial indicator onto the retainer and preload the gauge dial with enough travel to accommodate valve movement, and zero the gauge. With your finger or a small screwdriver, push the

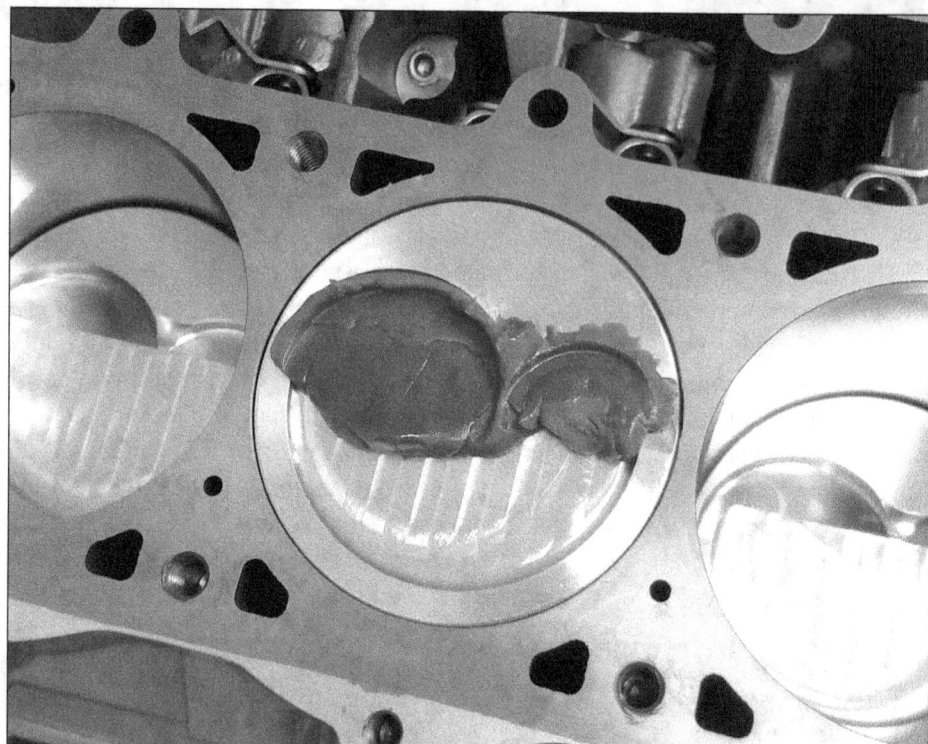

Clay was applied to both intake and exhaust valve reliefs. The piston dome must be dry prior to applying the clay to ensure that it sticks to the dome. A light coat of thin oil is applied to the combustion chamber and valve faces to prevent the clay from sticking to those surfaces.

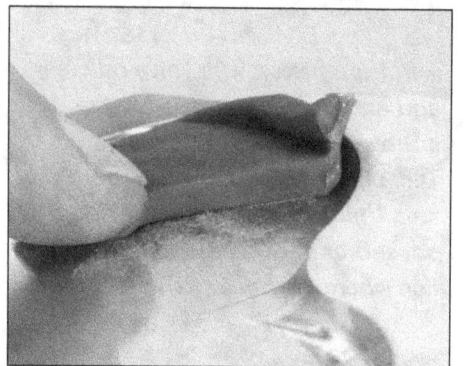

With clay applied to the piston valve pocket, the crank was rotated twice to rotate the cam one full turn. With the head removed, you see the valve impression in the clay. After cutting the clay with a razor, you see a cross section of the clay thickness, which is then measured. This intake valve shows about .200-inch valve-to-piston clearance. Minimum suggested intake valve clearance is .080 inch, while minimum exhaust valve clearance is .100 inch.

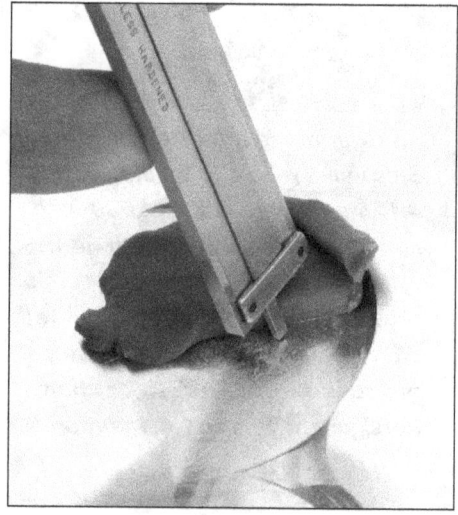

A dial caliper's depth tip can measure the clay thickness, or the clay section that was removed can be carefully measured with the caliper jaws. Due to the compressibility and potential spring-back of the clay, the clay method offers a rough estimate of clearance.

With a light checking valvespring installed in this intake valve, the crank is rotated to bring the piston 10 degrees ATDC. A dial indicator is set up, contacting the spring retainer. The dial is set to zero.

The spring is compressed until the valve contacts the piston. The gauge needle turns in a counterclockwise direction, showing this valve-to-piston clearance at .087 inch.

valve down until it touches the piston. The difference between the zero reference and piston contact indicates how much clearance the valve has to the piston. Generally speaking, for a naturally aspirated application, a minimum of about .080- to .090-inch intake clearance should be adequate. Follow the same procedure to check exhaust valve clearance, but with the piston located 10 degrees BTDC on the exhaust stroke. A generally accepted exhaust clearance is .100 to .110 inch.

For a blown (forced induction) application, valve-to-piston clearances need to be a bit greater, approximately .125 inch at the intake valve and about .175 inch at the exhaust valve.

Instead of checking with clay, a more accurate method of checking radial clearance is to remove a valve

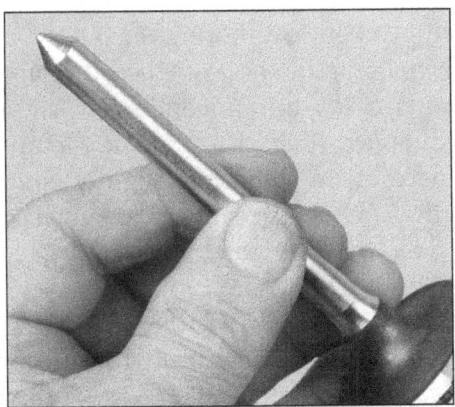

To check valve-to-piston valve relief radial clearance, instead of using clay, a spare valve can be cut and ground to a point to serve as a center-of-valve reference.

Measure the diameter of the valve head. After you measure the radius distance from the center mark, you factor one-half of the valve head diameter.

CHAPTER 8

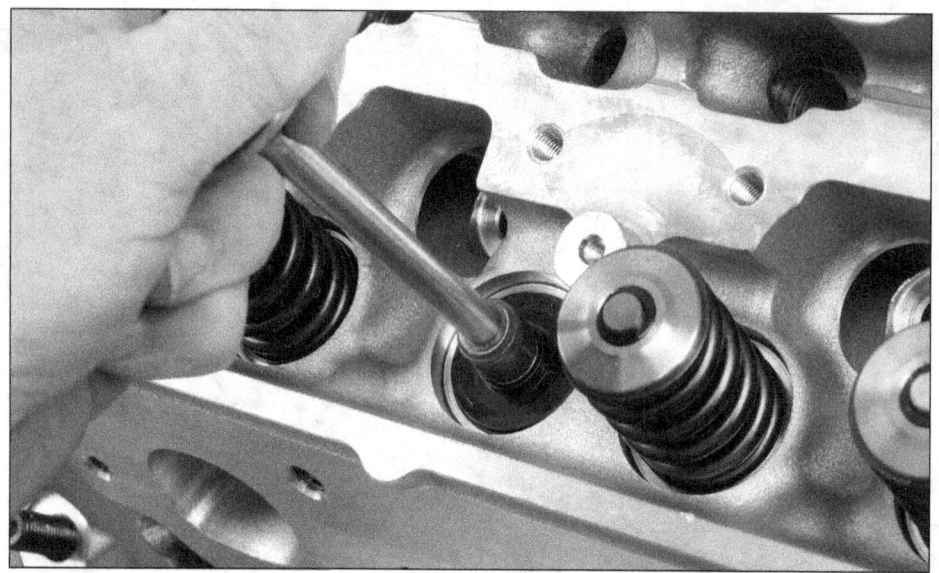

With the piston at 10 degrees ATDC to check the intake valve, the modified spare valve is inserted upside-down with the pointed end facing the piston. Using hand pressure, the pointed valvestem places a mark on the dome that indicates the centerline of the valve.

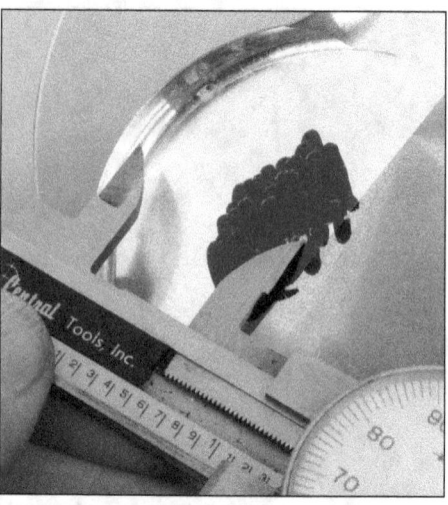

After removing the head, measure the distance from the center point to the edge of the valve relief. Using the radius of the already-measured valve head, you can determine how much radial clearance you have.

and grab a spark/junk valve of the same stem diameter. On a lathe, cut the tip off and grind it to a point. Color the piston dome valve pocket center area with a marker. Install the head gasket and head. Rotate the crank to bring the piston to TDC or about 10 degrees BTDC. Insert the ground, pointed valve upside-down into the valveguide and gently contact the piston, applying enough hand pressure to place a mark on the piston that provides a valve centerline mark. Remove the head.

Measure the diameter of the head of the valve that is to be final installed. Set your caliper to half of the valve head diameter. For example, if the valve head measures 2.080 inches in diameter, set the caliper at 1.040 inches. Place one end of the caliper jaw at the marked center valve mark and sweep across the edge of the valve relief to determine how much radial clearance you have. A suggested minimum clearance is about .085 to .100 inch.

If clearance is an issue, consider using a thicker head gasket (which of course decreases compression ratio). An alternative is to mill the piston dome at the contact area(s). This is done on a dedicated piston vise on a milling machine.

As noted earlier, be aware of existing dome thickness to avoid weakening the dome. Depending on the clearance area, the valve pockets may be cut deeper and/or larger in diameter, and/or the flat area of the dome can be milled to increase clearance.

If piston-to-head clearance is an issue and the pistons feature a center-domed profile with no valve pockets (such as found on a vintage flathead Ford, for example), the domes may be reduced on a CNC lathe. The pistons are first measured for dome height and profile, and the cylinder head chambers are digitally profiled for shape. The data is then programmed and fed to a CNC lathe that can cut the dome to precisely the height and shape required for clearance.

If more than about 4 grams of material is removed from the piston domes, the crankshaft should be rebalanced, considering the change of piston weight. For high-RPM racing applications, any change in piston weight should require the crank to be rebalanced.

File Fitting Rings

When overboring cylinders to repair or to increase bore displacement, it's not uncommon for the supplied ring set to include top and second rings that are slightly larger in diameter, to require custom file fitting to achieve the desired end gaps. This is not a compromise on the part of the ring maker. Rather, this allows the builder to establish the precise gaps recommended by the piston maker, based on how the engine is to be built and used.

A rule of thumb for ring end gap is .004 inch per inch of bore diameter. However, it is absolutely essential to follow the piston maker's specifications for ring end gap, as the recommendation may increase to as much as .006 inch per inch of bore diameter or more. The piston maker already knows how the specific piston material and construction is expected to grow in diameter during engine operation, so follow their specifications.

End gap is the clearance distance between the two ends of a ring when installed in the bore. Factors including forced induction (supercharging or turbocharging), the use of nitrous injection, and the operating environment (street, endurance racing, drag racing, etc.) all play a part in determining the optimum top and second ring end gaps.

File fitting top and second rings involves removing material from the ends with a fine file or, ideally, with a dedicated piston ring filing machine.

Rather than assuming that each cylinder requires the same final sizing, it's recommended to file-fit each ring for the specific cylinder. For example, instead of using cylinder number-1 as the reference to file-fit all rings, you should file-fit the top and second ring for cylinder 1, then file fit rings for cylinder 2, etc., keeping all rings organized for cylinder location. Slight variances in cylinder wall dimensions are possible, so for achieving optimal end gaps, custom fit rings to each cylinder.

Before file fitting rings, check each ring to its intended piston to verify proper ring groove side clearance and radial depth to make sure that the rings are compatible with the pistons.

Side clearance is the vertical clearance of the ring relative to the upper or lower base of the ring groove. With the ring placed into

Suggested Ring Gaps

To help illustrate how ring end gap recommendations can differ, depending on engine application, here's an example of suggested ring gaps, based on the use of JE 4032 high-silicon aluminum alloy pistons:

Application	Top Ring (inch)	Second Ring (inch)
High-Performance Street	Bore x .0045	Bore x .0050
Street Moderate Turbo/Nitrous	Bore x .0050	Bore x .0055
Late Model Stock	Bore x .0050	Bore x .0053
Circle Track/Drag Race	Bore x .0055	Bore x .0057
Nitrous Race Only	Bore x .0070	Bore x .0073
Blown Race Only	Bore x .0060	Bore x .0063

All oil ring rails with minimum gap of .015

With the above recommendations in mind, let's say that the finished cylinder bores feature a diameter of 4.125 inches. If the application involves a high-performance street engine, you multiply the bore size of 4.125 x a factor of .0045 to determine the proper end gap for the top ring. You multiply the bore size of 4.125 x a factor of .0050 to determine the end gap of the second ring. Second ring end gaps should always be slightly larger than top ring end gaps.

4.125 x .0045 = .0185 (top ring gap should be .018 to .0185 inch)
4.125 x .0050 = .0206 (second ring gap should be .020 to .0206 inch)

When you insert a ring into the cylinder for end gap checking, the ring must be set at an equal depth along the entire cylinder bore diameter. Using a ring-squaring tool makes this easy and quick. Insert the ring near the top of the bore and insert the squaring tool, which pushes the ring evenly down into the bore. Remove the tool and you're ready to check gap.

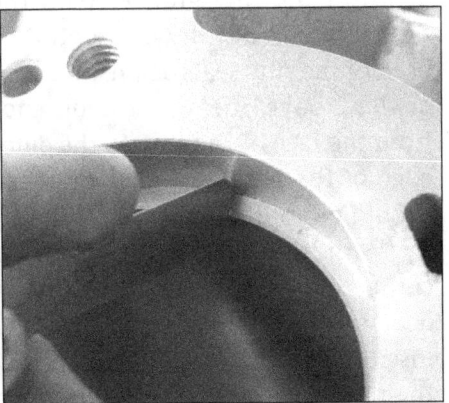

When checking ring fit to the cylinder, a feeler gauge is used to determine end gap. The ring must be squarely installed at the same depth around the entire perimeter of the ring relative to the deck. If the rings require file fitting, the end gap should be checked in stages between filing to avoid creating a too-large end gap.

Top and second rings that require file fitting may be filed with a small, flat, fine file, but a dedicated ring filer makes the job easier and more precise. Each end of the gap must be filed by the same amount. The filer features a diamond abrasive wheel that provides a nice square cut. By applying slight hand pressure to place the ring end against the wheel, count the number of handle rotations during each filing. After correctly filing a few rings, you get an idea of how many turns are needed to achieve your desired end gap. This makes filing the remaining rings a bit quicker. Always file by a few turns, clean the ring and check the gap in the cylinder. Filing in stages helps to prevent accidental overfiling.

its groove, push the ring down until the bottom of the ring is flush with the bottom land of the ring groove, then measure the clearance between the top ring surface and the roof of the ring groove with a feeler gauge. Side clearance should be .001 to .002 inch. Radial clearance is the inward/outward clearance of the ring within the groove. This is the difference between the outer diameter surface of the ring to the inner diameter surface of the ring, relative to the depth of the ring groove. With the ring pushed fully inward until the back of the ring seats against the wall of the groove, measure the distance from the face of the ring to the outer edge of the groove. Radial clearance should be approximately .005 inch.

With the cylinder bores wiped clean, compress the number-1 cylinder's top ring carefully by hand and insert it into the bore. Make sure that the ring is properly oriented. If a dot appears on one side, the side with the dot should face upward. Insert the ring about 1/2 to 1 inch into the bore, with the ring squared so that it is at the same depth along the entire circumference, relative to the deck. You can use a caliper or depth gauge or a small ruler to adjust this, or an easier and quicker way is to use a ring-squaring tool that automatically pushes the ring squarely into the bore. Check the existing end gap. In the case of file-to-fit rings, you may find zero gap or even an overlapping gap.

Remove the ring and file the ends, removing an equal amount of material from each end. Then insert the ring again and measure end gap using a feeler gauge. Perform the filing in small increments to avoid ending up with a gap that is too large. When the proper gap is achieved, remove the ring and *carefully* remove any burrs from the filed ends, using a small flat fine file. Wash the ring and store it on a clean workbench next to your number-1 cylinder's pistons and rod. Repeat this process for all top rings, and for all second rings, cylinder by cylinder, and keep all rings organized for cylinder location. Remember to orient all top and second rings properly, because, depending on the ring profile, they may have a dedicated top and bottom surface. If the top and/or second ring have a small dot mark, the mark must face upward when installed.

The supplied oil ring rails should provide a minimum of the specified end gap, so you should not need to file any of the oil ring rails. By the same token, if your pistons require support rails (due to a short piston compression distance where the wrist pin bore intersects with the oil ring groove), there is no need to perform any file fitting for the support rail. Its end gap is not critical; it only serves to provide oil ring package support over each end of the wrist pin bore and serves no sealing purpose.

If the piston wrist pin bore is raised due to the required compression distance, the pin bore can intersect the oil ring groove. In these cases, the piston maker provides a set of support rings that are installed to the floor of the oil ring groove, providing oil ring support at the voids at the top of the pin bore. The support rail features a small bump dot, which must be oriented at the center of the pin bore. This small protrusion prevents the support rail from accidentally rotating, keeping its end gap from moving over one of the pin bore voids.

CHAPTER 9

CYLINDER HEAD INSPECTION, SERVICE AND MACHINING

Before you can machine the head, you need to remove the valves and all related parts. This includes valves, valvesprings, retainers, and valve locks by compressing each valvespring with a valvespring compressor tool. In some cases, the valve locks/keepers may have seized onto the valves. Prior to compressing the valvesprings, place a hollow tube or a socket wrench onto the retainer and give it a whack with a hammer. This dislodges potentially stuck locks.

Although manual spring compressors are certainly available, they are usually cumbersome and time-consuming to use. The superior choice is a pneumatic valvespring compressor, which resembles a large C-clamp, with an air-powered valve. Simply locate the compressor's valve rest onto the face of the valve, engage the tool's cupped jaw onto the retainer, and activate the tool by pressing the valve's button. The spring compresses, allowing you to remove the valve locks. The use of a small pencil magnet makes it easier to remove the locks, eliminating the risk of dropping/losing the locks.

With the locks removed, release tool pressure and remove the tool. Remove the retainer and spring, and slide the valve out of its guide.

Aluminum cylinder heads feature valveguide inserts to prevent valvestems from wearing against the parent aluminum. To ease guide removal, it's best to heat the head to about 200 to 250 degrees F and apply penetrating oil. This allows the aluminum to expand slightly, making guide removal easier and safer. Removing an old guide can result in damaging the guide bore, which requires reaming the bore and then installing an oversize-O.D. guide. Bronze guides can deform easily when an impact hammer and driver are placed directly against the guide shoulder, which damages the bore surface. One trick is to partially thread a bolt into the guide and drive the guide out, applying force to the bolt head. Seat

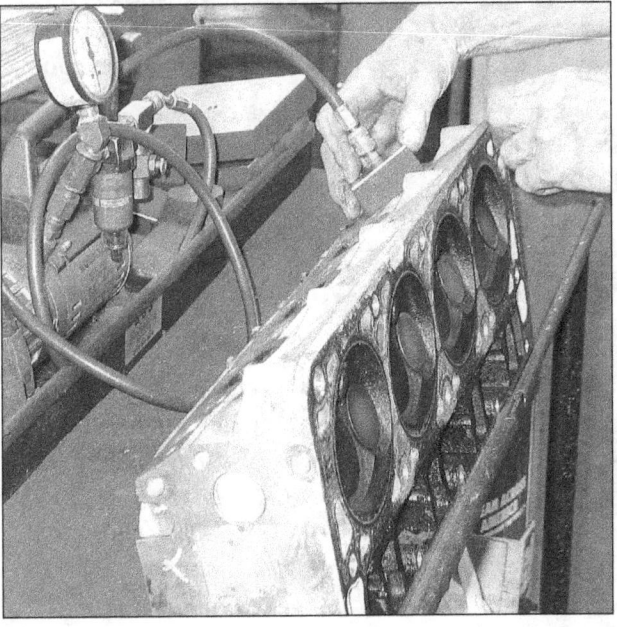

As a precheck before removing valves, a vacuum check may be performed to provide a reference regarding individual valves sealing against their seats.

CHAPTER 9

Remove rockers and pushrods, head bolts and heads from the block. If the head is stuck, do not pry with a screwdriver, which could damage the deck mating surfaces. If persuasion is needed, tap the head with a plastic or rubber mallet.

Using a pneumatic valvespring compressor, compress each valve far enough to remove the valve locks, then relax the spring and remove the spring and retainer. Be aware that aluminum heads feature a steel spring cup to prevent the spring from digging into the aluminum. Remove the cup.

Remove the valves. If valves are to be cleaned, reconditioned, and reused, store together in a box or tray.

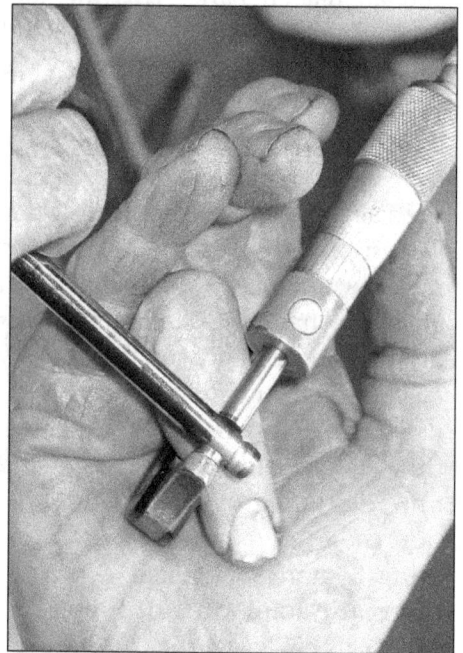

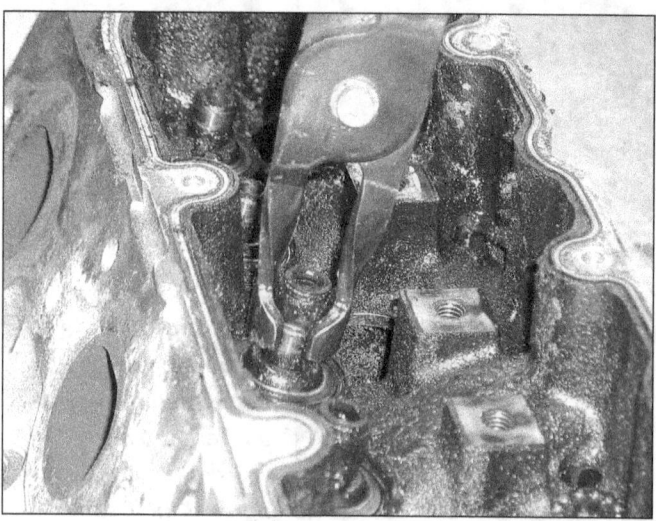

Using a valve seal puller, remove all valve seals from the guide bosses. If valves are to be reused, measure each valve's stem near the center of stem length.

Also measure each valvestem near the top, below the lock grooves. Record each valve's stem diameters and number each valve with a marker or organize them in a valve tray that features holes to store all valves and number each for location. For example, for cylinder number-1, label as "1 intake" and "1 exhaust."

CYLINDER HEAD INSPECTION, SERVICE AND MACHINING

When the decks are clean, inspect combustion decks for warp using a precision straightedge and feeler gauges. Here, a front-to-rear check is made.

Also check the deck in a diagonal path from the front intake corner to the rear exhaust corner.

Also measure for flatness in the opposite diagonal path, from front exhaust to rear intake corners.

and guide machines allow you to use a long stepped drill, often referred to as a core drill. The smaller diameter tip of the drill centers to the guide, while the larger diameter of the drill thins out the majority of the guide. This creates an internal step inside the guide. A stepped pilot can then be used to push the guide out.

Inspect the combustion deck and intake deck for flatness, using a precision machinist's straightedge and feeler gauges. Measure decks from front to rear, on the intake side of the combustion chambers. Then measure front to rear at the exhaust side of the chambers. Then measure diagonally (corner to opposing corners, in an X pattern). Then measure from the intake side to the exhaust side in the center and at each end of the deck.

Perform the same checks on the cylinder head's intake deck.

As a general rule, the maximum allowable warp from front to rear or diagonal paths on a cast-iron head is .004 inch or less. For an aluminum head, front-to-rear or diagonal allowable warp is .002 inch or less. Maximum allowable warp from the exhaust side to the intake side is about .001 inch. Any sudden or isolated warp of .001 inch or more along any 3-inch span is unacceptable.

Following cylinder head disassembly, any previously used head should be checked for flaws, including cracks and pinholes. Refer to the flaw detection chapter in this book.

Resurfacing the Deck

The head gasket deck surface of a cylinder head must be machined to a finish that is compatible with the intended type of head gasket. Surface finish is typically rated in RA (roughness average). The smaller the RA number is, the finer the surface's finish. Although older engine designs that feature composite head gaskets may function with a surface finish in the 50–100 RA range, today's MLS (multi-layer steel) head gaskets employed with aluminum heads and/or blocks require a smoother finish to compensate for the continuous expansion and contraction of aluminum as engine temperatures vary. The majority of today's aluminum heads require an RA in the 30 range, but some OEM specs for certain engines can require even finer finishes in the 20–30 RA range. If the finish is not smooth enough, excess "bite" can occur at the gasket, preventing the head from moving during thermal expansion and contraction, which can easily lead to gasket damage and subsequent coolant, oil, and/or combustion leaks.

To actually measure the RA of a surface, a special tool called a "profilometer" may be used. This tool features a moving stylus that runs across the surface and displays the RA in a digital screen. If a profilometer is not at hand, resurfacing milling machine manufacturers provide a chart of recommended feed rates and cutting speeds to achieve a specific RA finish.

Although cylinder head resurfacing may be accomplished with either a wet grinding station or a dry milling machine, milling is preferred, since it's faster, allows greater cutting depths per pass, and does a superior job of achieving a fine surface finish. Wet grinding is usually limited to removing .005 to .001 inch per pass. Milling (with cutters lightly lubricated to prevent aluminum from building up on the cutters) allows one deep-cut pass to eliminate warpage, followed by one light dressing pass to achieve the desired RA. However, to achieve the desired fine RA finish for aluminum heads and MLS gaskets, light cuts per pass and lower feed rates are recommended. Again, the resurfacing machine maker provides recommendations for traverse feed rate and cutting speeds. Cutter inserts are typically carbide or CBN (cubic boron nitride) for cast-iron heads and carbide or PCD (polycrystalline diamond) for aluminum heads. When milling aluminum heads for a fine RA finish, the rule of thumb is to increase the cutter RPM and slow down the feed rate (for example, a traverse feed rate of about 2 to 3 inches per minute).

Naturally, removing material from the cylinder head deck moves the combustion chambers closer to the pistons. And, in turn, there are potential issues of pushrod length, valvetrain geometry, increased compression ratio, potential valve-to-piston clearance, potential misalignment of intake manifold ports, etc. In general terms, resurfacing should be limited to no more than .010 inch of material removal. Keep in mind that these issues may be corrected by simply using a thicker head gasket. Various-thickness head gaskets are readily available for most popular engines, especially when dealing with MLS head gaskets, where thickness can be manipulated by the thickness or number of stainless steel support layers. Makers such as Fel-Pro, Mahle-Victor, and Cometic offer a variety of head gasket thicknesses.

Measuring Chamber Volume

When determining the compression ratio of the planned build, one of the primary factors involves the volume of the cylinder head combustion chambers. Today's high-quality performance aftermarket heads are either precision-cast or CNC milled to achieve a specific chamber volume, which is indicated on the cylinder head's instruction and/or specification information. Typically, cylinder heads made by the leading manufacturers feature chamber volumes exactly at, or extremely close to, the published volume specs. However, to know what volume each chamber actually provides, check each chamber with a graduated burette. This is especially important when dealing with an OEM head, where manufacturing tolerances can be fairly wide. Knowing, instead of assuming, chamber volume allows you to more precisely calculate compression ratio. In addition, if you plan to modify the chambers for maximizing flow and/or deburring/polishing, being able to measure chamber volume allows you to keep track of your progress. One of the objectives, when attempting to "blueprint" the heads, is to obtain an equal volume of all chambers.

To measure chamber volume, all valves must be installed and sealed with a light coat of grease. Place a clear plexiglass or acrylic plate over the chamber. The plate must feature a single hole that is slightly chamfered on the top side. Seal the plate onto the head with a film of grease. Tilt the head slightly on the bench so that the hole in the clear plate is at a high spot to allow air to escape. Using a graduated burette filled with a dye-colored water, note the level of the burette with the burette's valve closed. Place the tip of the burette into the plate hole and slowly open the valve, allowing liquid to fill the chamber. As soon as the chamber is full, with no trapped air, close the valve and note how much liquid drained from the burette. This indicates the volume in cubic centimeters (cc). Perform this task at each chamber, recording the measured volume of each chamber. If volume deviates from chamber to chamber, note the chamber that measured at

CYLINDER HEAD INSPECTION, SERVICE AND MACHINING

A valvespring height gauge is installed in place of the spring. This barrel-style micrometer is adjusted to draw the valve fully up into its closed position. The installed spring height measurement is then noted on the checker.

The rough surface texture of this cast cylinder head's combustion chamber is shown. Although ultra-polishing isn't necessary, smoothing out the surface may help to increase efficiency, but reducing the chance of carbon buildup is the major advantage.

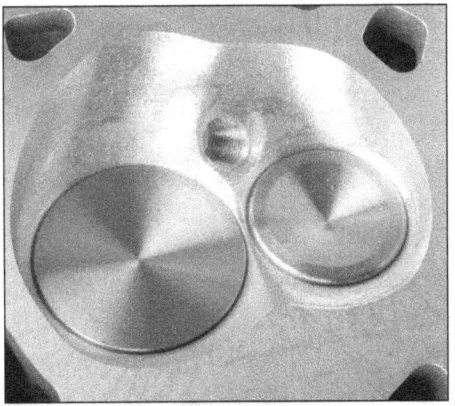

An example of a machined combustion chamber. Note how much smoother the surface finish is as compared to a rough-cast chamber. In addition to obtaining a smoother finish, a major advantage of CNC milling is achieving precision and equal combustion chamber volumes. The example shown here is a Trick Flow CNC-machined chamber.

the highest volume. This serves as the reference goal. Using the appropriate milling or grinding tooling, carefully remove material from smaller chambers to achieve the same volume at all chambers.

In addition to measuring chamber volume in an effort to achieve equal chamber volumes, the valve depths at the valveseats can be checked and corrected to further equalize the closed-valve chamber volume. With valves installed (and with each valve numbered with a marker for specific location), a horizontal fixture fitted with a dial indicator can be placed over the head deck, measuring from a fixed point on the fixture to the valve face. The valve at the greatest depth (the valve that is seated deepest in its seat) is marked as "zero" to create a reference point. As each remaining valve is measured, use a marker to note how much higher each valve is seated in relation to the deck. After all valves are marked, using a seat cutter, remaining valveseats may be cut to sink all valves to match the zero reference valve. This is part and parcel of "blueprinting" the head.

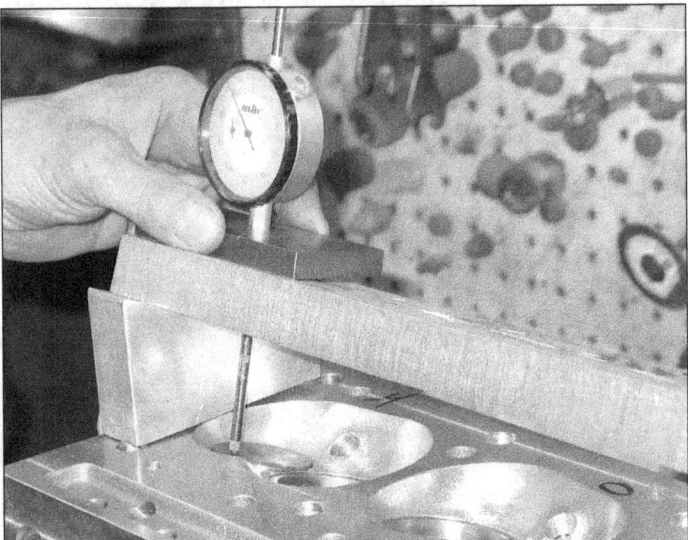

A checking fixture and a dial indicator allow you to check the seated depth of each valve.

The lowest valve in reference to the deck can be used as the "zero" reference. Other valve locations are marked for variations in depth, so you have to go back and dress other seats. By doing this, all valves reach an equal seated depth so that chamber volumes are as equal as possible. Although this is not necessary for daily drivers, this check is part of the blueprinting process in an effort to maximize performance.

CHAPTER 9

Installing New Guide Liners

Guide liners, such as those made of bronze, are available in a variety of common sizes for all popular valve-stem diameters. The guide bore is drilled to a diameter of about .025 inch smaller than the new guide liner O.D. The bore is then reamed to provide about a .0015-inch interference fit for the new guide liner.

If the cylinder head was previously fitted with bronze liners, a spiraled step-drill boring tool is preferred to remove the original guide. If the head features cast-iron liners, a straight-fluted boring bit is preferred.

Guide liners are to be installed from the top side of the head. When the liner is in place, a roller burnishing tool is used to finish the inside diameter of the liner.

The new liner is oiled and driven into its bore with a pneumatic hammer and appropriate size driver. Pay attention to the exposed height of the installed liner at the rocker side of the head. A seal cutter can be used to trim any extra length to the specified height. The valve-side of the guide can be trimmed flush using a stepped guide cutter bit, which features a smooth pilot tip that centers into the guide. After measuring the valvestem diameter, the guide may require a final expansion to provide the desired oil clearance. This is done either with a burnishing arbor or by driving a hardened carbide sizing ball of a diameter that's about .001 inch larger than the desired guide I.D., because bronze liners have a tendency to contract a bit after the inside walls have been forced to size. After valveseats have been finished, a guide brush is run through the guide liner to provide a crosshatch surface for oil retention. Generally speaking, a clearance of .001 to .0029 inch should be obtained between the finished guide inside diameter and the valvestem diameter, but always refer to the specifications listed for any specific engine. For example, a specific engine may call for an oil clearance of .001 inch for intake guides and .001- to .003-inch clearance for exhaust guides. Measure the valvestem with an outside micrometer and the valveguide inside diameter with a bore gauge. If the guide features excess clearance and/or taper, it must be replaced. Valvestem wear is certainly possible, but liners are softer and wear faster than the valvestems.

Refacing Valves and Seats

Valveseats are machined on a seat-and-guide machine. The cylinder head is secured to the traverse table with clamps. The table is then adjusted to accommodate the specific valvestem angle, to allow the seat cutter's pilot to align with the guide. Whenever guides have been serviced, the valveseats must be resurfaced because the freshly installed guide may have changed the concentricity of the valve relative to the seat. The fresh guide serves as the centered reference for the seat.

Valveseats may be machined using either tapered abrasive stones or by hardened cutters. Although either method can achieve functional results, the use of cutters is preferred for greater precision. The valve face is typically ground at a 45-degree angle. Although this matches the angle of the seat, some builders prefer to grind a 44-degree angle on the valve to obtain a slight interference fit. A matching angle of 45 degrees is most common, though. An interference angle is sometimes preferred to obtain a "quicker" seal between the seat and valve; the seat and valve eventually wear to a matching angle. Performance valves often also feature a slight angle cut at the throat side of the face and at the chamber side of the face to further improve flow.

The valve margin is the "straight" width area around the circumference of the valve head. If a valve is to be refaced, the margin must be maintained according to specifications for the particular engine. A too-narrow margin can absorb excess heat and

A valve refacing machine allows you to accurately regrind valve faces and valve tips if needed.

CYLINDER HEAD INSPECTION, SERVICE AND MACHINING

With the valve grinder adjusted to an angle of 45 degrees, the seating surface can be ground to obtain a fresh surface. If regrinding makes the valve margin too narrow, the valve must be replaced. Intake valve margins should be kept at approximately .050 inch and exhaust valve margins at about .080 inch or more. Always refer to specifications for the engine at hand.

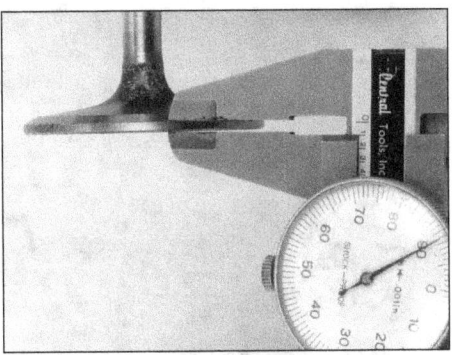

Valve margin must be retained at a sufficient width to avoid excessive heating of the valve. Always refer to engine specifications for minimum margin width. Typically, a minimum of about .050 inch on intake valves and .080 inch or more for exhaust valves is sufficient.

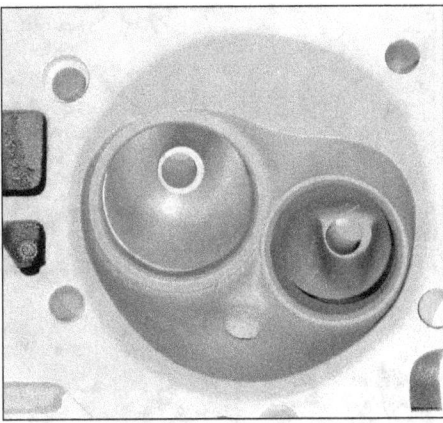

Some builders prefer to have the combustion chambers and exhaust throats coated with a thermal barrier coating. This type of coating contains combustion heat, reducing the heat that would otherwise be transferred to the head. This is often done with engines that use forced induction. If the chambers are to be coated, valve-seats must then be cut afterward to remove the coating from the seats.

can lead to pre-ignition and overheating of the valve. A typical valve margin is in the area of .040 to .060 inch in width for intake valves and .060 to .090 inch or greater for exhaust valves. Again, always check valve margin specifications. If regrinding a valve results in a too-narrow margin, the valve must be replaced.

The mating of the valve-to-seat width is typically established at .060 to .080 inch in width. A narrower mating surface may slightly improve airflow but is less durable. Typically the mating contact area is in the center of the face; some builders prefer to obtain the mating a bit closer to the combustion chamber side of the valve, but be aware that a mating surface that's placed too close to the combustion chamber side can result in a burned valve.

The seat is typically cut to create a three-angle profile, with about a 60-degree angle at the seat throat, 45 degrees at the seat face, and 30 degrees at the outer edge of the seat. This three-angle profile improves flow efficiency. The depth of the seat cut must be monitored on the seat and guide machine during cutting to establish the valve-to-seat mating approximately at the center of the valve face.

The seat cutting is typically performed in the following order: The 30-degree angle at the outer edge of the seat is followed by the 45-degree seat face. The valveseat is then painted with machinist dye (Prussian blue) and the valve is then installed and lightly tapped up/down to create a witness mark on the seat. After removing the valve, the witness mark on the seat is inspected to verify that the mating is occurring at the center of the valve face. The 60-degree throat cut is then made. Seat cutters are available that are adjusted for each angle operation and that allow cutting all three angles at the same time.

The cylinder head is checked and leveled left to right while observing a bubble level.

The head is also leveled inboard/outboard. Leveling is necessary to align the machine's power head and tooling to the plane of the valveguides.

AUTOMOTIVE MACHINING: A GUIDE TO BORING, DECKING, HONING AND MORE

CHAPTER 9

This cast-iron head's exhaust seat has been pounded down as a result of running cheap unleaded fuel, requiring the installation of a hardened valveseat.

When setting the head up on the seat and guide machine, the head is positioned at an angle that places the valveguides in a vertical plane. The head is rigidly clamped to the machine's traverse table.

The seat insert's pocket cutter fits onto the pilot.

This two-tipped cutter was used to create the insert's seat pocket.

The appropriate-diameter mandrel is fitted to the guide. This serves as the pilot to accept the seat cutter.

The new seat insert is indexed to the seat and guide machine to set the cutting depth. After this depth is set, the operator can cut to the stopping limit without fear of cutting too deep.

CYLINDER HEAD INSPECTION, SERVICE AND MACHINING

After selecting the proper cutting tool that bores out the existing seat, the seat pocket is cut, creating a flat base and vertical walls to accept the interference-fit seat insert.

The seat insert pocket is cut and ready to accept the insert.

The insert is positioned onto the pocket.

Valveseats may be ground with an abrasive stone or cut with seat cutters. Cutters provide a more precise finish.

An appropriate-size driver is placed onto the insert. The insert is then pushed or tapped into the pocket.

The new seat insert is installed, ready for three-angle cutting.

AUTOMOTIVE MACHINING: A GUIDE TO BORING, DECKING, HONING AND MORE 107

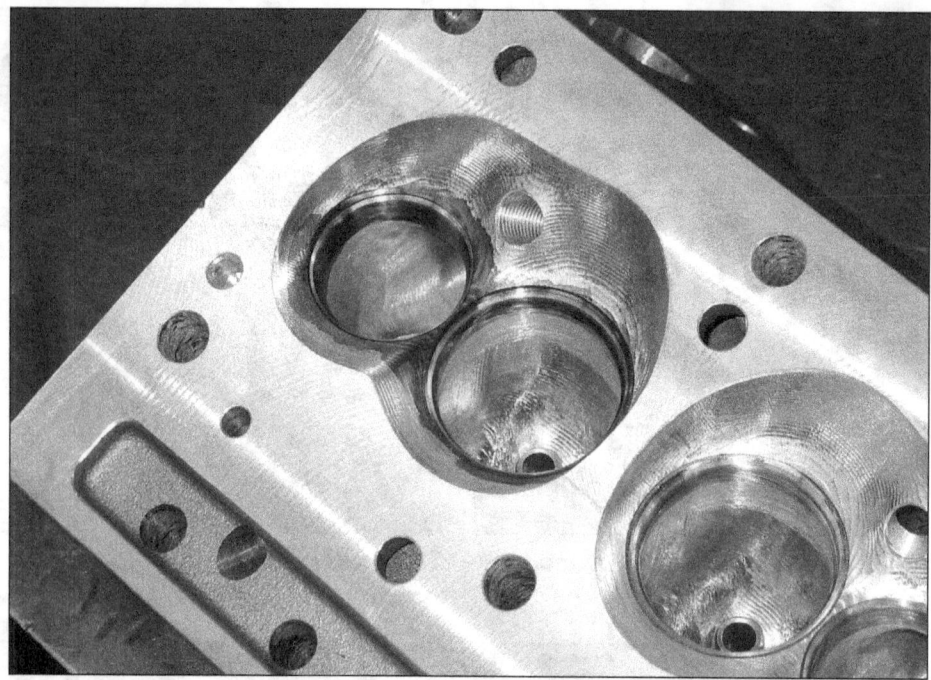

After a seat has been cut, applying machinist dye to the seats, followed by test fitting the valves, provides witness marks to see where the valve faces contact the seats.

Cutting the new seat insert is handled by this single cutter that creates all three seat angles in one operation.

Valveseat grinding stones are available in specific angle degree designs, allowing creation of one angle at a time.

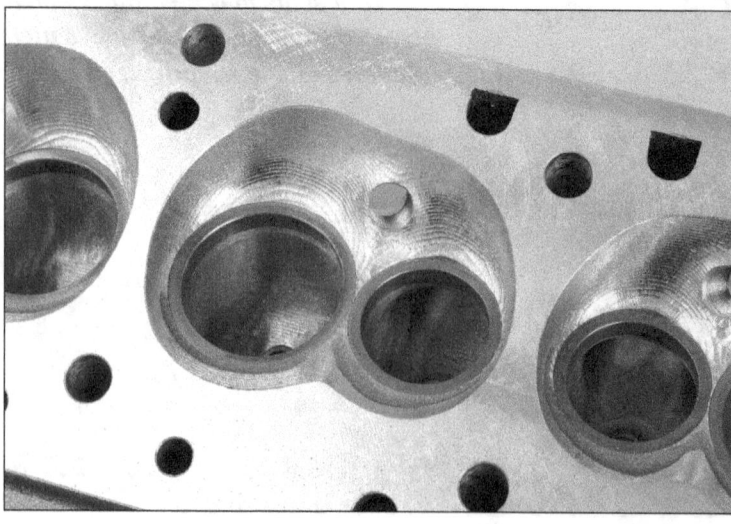

Hardened seats installed in an aluminum head, ready for angle cutting.

High-performance valves often feature a chamfer cut of about 30 degrees above the 45-degree mating face angle for improved flow.

After each seat is cut, or at least after all seats have been cut, a vacuum check should be performed with valves in place to verify valve-to-seat sealing.

If a cast-iron head features integral seats cut into the parent cast-iron and the seat has been damaged or worn, or if an aluminum head requires new seats, a seat insert may be installed. First, the existing seat is machined out, using a piloted cutter on the seat and guide machine. The new seat insert is first indexed on the machine so that the cut matches the thickness of the seat insert. The cut is made to accommodate the seat with an interference fit of generally .005 to .007 inch, but check the specification provided by the seat insert maker. The new seat insert is then interference fit into the cutout using either pressure using the seat and guide machine or with a mandrel and a hammer. The seat insert may then be cut to accommodate the valve, using a three-angle seat cutter (30/45/60 degree).

Measuring Valvespring Height

Using a barrel-type micrometer, measure the installed valvestem height from the spring seat to the stem tip and note each valve's height. Install the micrometer with the retainer and locks that you intend to use. Rotate the micrometer barrel until it eliminates all play and the valve is pulled fully into its installed position. Read the adjusted height on the valvespring height micrometer, and refer to the recommended installed height of your new springs.

If valveseats have been resurfaced and/or valves have been refaced, the valves now sink lower into the seats.

Use a height checker caliper to measure the installed valvestem height. This check is important when you're measuring a nonadjustable rocker setup. Tips that are too high may be resurfaced to equal the installed height of all valvestems. Depending on the hardness of the stem tips, some valves may require the addition of hardened caps after resurfacing the tips.

This can affect the installed valvespring height. In order to regain/restore valvespring installed height to specification, a shim(s) may be placed under the springs. Shims are available in a variety of thicknesses to compensate. Aluminum heads already require a steel shim/spring seat between the head and spring to prevent the spring from digging into the softer aluminum. Make sure that the steel spring seat is in place when measuring installed spring height. Only use shims appropriate to restore the recommended spring height. If you install too thick of a shim, it can compress the spring and may lead to coil bind that can increase spring pressure, which can then lead to excessive loads on the pushrods and lifters.

Measuring Valvestem Height

Valvestem height is a different issue when compared to spring height. Valvestem height refers to the distance from the spring seat to the tip of the valvestem. If this changes due to sinking the valves deeper into the seats, or with the use of longer or shorter valves, this adversely affects pushrod length, if the valvetrain is nonadjustable as a result of using nonadjustable rockers. Using a caliper of dedicated stem height gauge, measure the distance from the spring seat to the valvestem tip and refer to installed stem height specifications. If the installed stem heights differ, lay a precision straightedge across the furthest front and furthest rear

CHAPTER 9

Used or new valvesprings should be checked for rated pressure at both closed/installed height and open positions on a valvespring checking stand.

valvestem tips and note the differences in height of the remaining valvestem tips. To make all valvestem heights identical, taller valves may be refaced on a valve grinder. Shorter stems might be extended to match the others with the addition of hardened valvestem caps, which are available in various thicknesses. If the rockers are adjustable, this isn't as critical, since minute differences may be compensated for during valve lash adjustment.

Checking Spring Pressure

Check all valvesprings on a bench spring height/pressure gauge. Compress each spring to its recommended installed height; note and record the spring pressure displayed on the gauge. Compress the spring further to its open height and note the pressure. Compare your findings to the camshaft maker's specifications for open and closed spring pressure. Open and closed spring pressures and installed height specs should be found on the new camshaft's specification card.

Porting Cylinder Heads

Efficient intake and exhaust ports cannot have severe restrictions and excessive turbulence. Today's outstanding selection of performance aftermarket cylinder heads pretty much eliminates the need to perform any further port modifications. Many performance head makers offer two basic versions: as-cast and CNC ported. As-cast heads feature port shapes that have been developed by extensive research and are pretty much good to go. By spending a few more bucks, CNC-machined heads are available that bring all dimensions and shapes to a tighter tolerance, including combustion chambers, and intake and exhaust ports.

If you're dealing with OEM heads and want to improve breathing efficiency, the only reliable approach is to take advantage of a cylinder head flow bench that allows you to measure flow and efficiency as is and during port modifications. Although a shiny and polished surface inside the ports may look trick, the smoothness of the surfaces is less important than the shape of the ports. Basically, you want to eliminate any obtrusive restrictions to flow by smoothing out any sharp bends or ledges in the airflow paths.

But hand-porting heads with a rotary tool and Roloc pads is something of an art and science. If you do not possess the skill or experience to port your own heads, there is no shame bringing the heads to a professional porter. If you port your heads yourself, don't get carried away by knocking down everything in the port to please your eyes. Also, by removing too much material, you can end up with port walls that are too thin and may be susceptible to pinholes or cracking. Just because one port may allow you to remove X amount of material, don't assume that the remaining ports will allow the same removal because casting core shifts can be present that make some walls thinner than others. Cylinder head porting, monitored on a flow bench, is the sensible approach, but this requires a specialized shop that understands the nature of certain engine designs (Ford, Chevy, Mopar, etc.).

If you're planning to use a quality performance aftermarket head made by one of the leading manufacturers such as Trick Flow, AFR, Edelbrock, etc., these firms have already done the research and development to provide superior-flowing heads.

The valveseat area is critical to flow. A good baseline for seat angles is 30, 45, and 60 degrees. New aftermarket heads already feature these angles.

Final Assembly

In preparation of final assembly, the head, valves, springs, retainers, and locks must be perfectly clean and organized on a clean workbench surface. Be sure to scrub all valveguides and verify that they're clean.

Install the new valveguides to their bosses, as described earlier under "Installing New Guide Liners." Lubricate the valve faces and seats, and lube the valvestems. Carefully insert the valvestems into the guides and through the seals, being careful not to tear or damage the seals. Install the necessary spring seats and/or shims. Install the spring and its retainer. Using a pneumatic valvespring compressor, carefully compress the spring just far enough to allow installation of the valve locks. Applying a bit of assembly lube to the inside of the locks helps to hold them in place during installation. Make sure that the locks engage the lock groove on the valvestem. While monitoring the location of the locks, decompress the spring, making sure that the locks remain engaged. With the spring compressor removed, use a clean plastic hammer to tap the valvestem tip. This helps to ensure that the locks and retainer are properly secured.

To prevent scratches or nicks on the cylinder head deck surface, make sure that the head is always resting on a clean cylinder head stand or resting on a clean rag or towel.

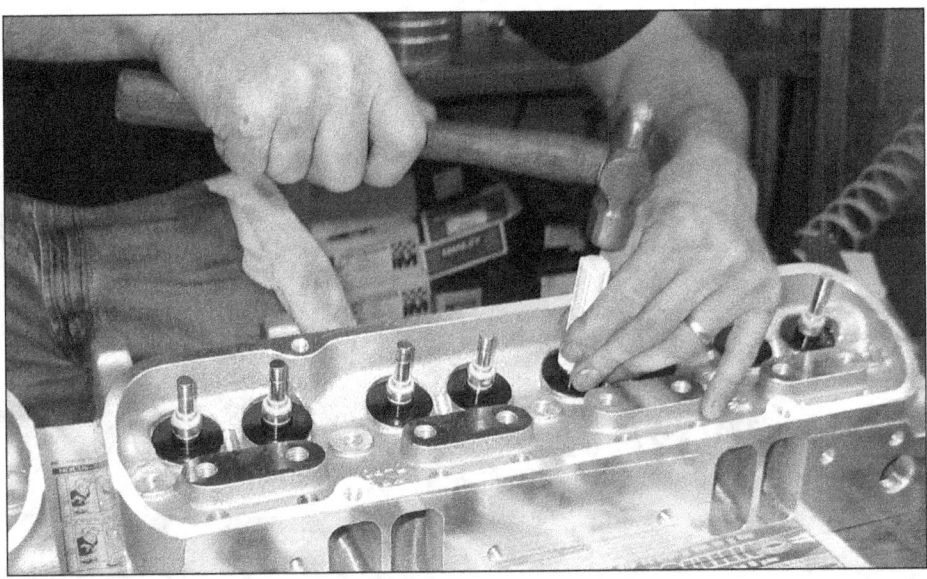
Positive-lock valve seals are interference-fit onto guide bosses.

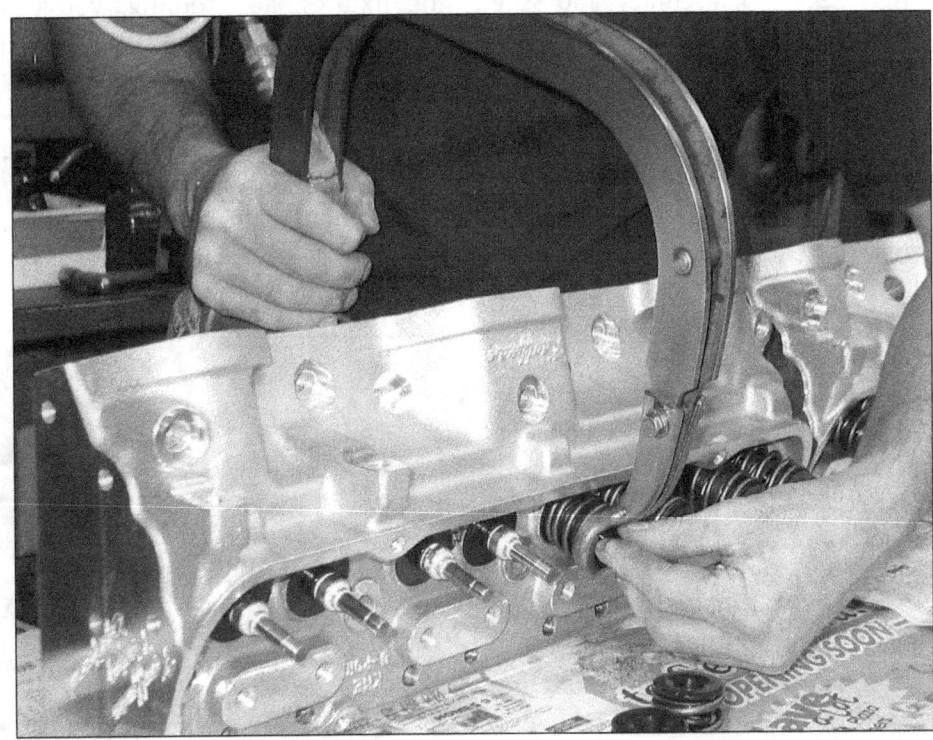
When installing valves and springs, compress the springs just far enough to allow installation of the valve locks.

CHAPTER 10

ENGINE BLOCK CNC MACHINING

CNC (Computerized Numerical Control) machining offers both a high degree of accuracy and speed for engine block machining, in addition to prototyping, fabrication, manufacturing, and modifications to existing components.

CNC machines are expensive, and many people are intimidated by what they assume to be a steep learning curve for machining operations. The expense is only justified by the amount of work your shop plans to do to make the machine pay for itself. To address these concerns, I visited Gressman Powersports in Fremont, Ohio, to follow the CNC machining of a single engine block, from start to finish.

Using a CNC machine means that the job can be performed faster (as opposed to moving the block from machine to machine and taking the required setup time). If speed is not an issue, and if work time is the only concern, then you don't need a CNC. However, if you want to obtain accuracy without the need for an array of cumbersome specialty accurizing fixtures, a CNC fulfills that need.

One aspect of owning a versatile CNC machine is the fact that you can take advantage of its capabilities beyond block or head work. Given the machine's programmability, clamping fixtures, and tooling, you can extend your work (and profitability) by fabricating specialty pieces from scratch (making your own valvecovers from billet stock, milling custom engine accessory brackets, making engine mounting plates for race cars, and making spacer plates, bushings, etc.). Having this capability expands the services that you offer to your customers. Plus, you can pursue fabrication jobs from local industries beyond the automotive scene. If this is what you have in mind, research the machine(s) carefully that you're considering to make sure they can handle all of the work that you currently have, plus any additional work with which you may become involved down the road.

CNC machines capable of block work are available in various sizes, axis capabilities, and tooling options.

ENGINE BLOCK CNC MACHINING

> ## Axis Primer
>
> Whenever you discuss CNC machining, you need to think in terms of the axis of approach that the tooling follows. Depending on the model, a CNC milling machine may operate on one or more axes.
>
> X axis: The tooling moves left to right (horizontal travel).
> Y axis: The tooling moves in-out (fore/aft).
> Z axis: The tooling moves up-down (vertical travel).
> A axis: The axis of rotation is parallel to the X axis; his allows the block to rotate in relation to the tooling head.
> B axis: The work piece rotates perpendicular to the A axis (if viewed overhead, the work piece rotates clockwise/counterclockwise).

The beauty of a CNC machine is that, compared to using an array of specialty truing fixtures where the block must potentially be moved between different machines, with a CNC, you change tools instead of changing machines. If the CNC machine is equipped with a built-in tool changer, a tooling change can take as little as 2.5 seconds.

The examples in this chapter involve an RMC V-40 CNC and the sample block is a Dart small-block Chevy iron unit. My intent is not to favor any single brand. Rather, I'm simply using this machine as an illustrative example.

Milling the Block

Start the machine and allow the machine's computer to fully boot. During this warmup, everything moves to a "known" plane.

A precision mounting plate is installed to the rear of the block, so the block is accurately located in the machine's base fixture. This helps ensure that the block is machined with the utmost precision.

The first step is to install a centering bar in the main bore to accurately locate the block to the machine's base fixture. A series of bushing adapters are needed to precisely fit the bar to the specific main bore diameter. A precision mounting plate is installed to the rear of the block, which accurately locates the block to the CNC machine's base fixture. A camshaft tunnel centering bar helps the machine to locate the block. This bar features expandable locators that center the bar into the cam tunnel.

A centering bar is inserted through the main bores.

AUTOMOTIVE MACHINING: A GUIDE TO BORING, DECKING, HONING AND MORE

CHAPTER 10

Block in place. Notice the cam bore centering bar.

A precision centering bar is installed through the camshaft bore. The cam bore bar features expandable locators that precisely center the bar into the bore. The CNC machine's digital probe reads this bar position that factors in true bore center. This provides the machine's computer with information regarding precise location of the cam bore in relation to the main bore centerline.

Before installing the block into the machine, the main bore must be at its final diameter and alignment, so perform align honing first if you plan to align hone the block.

Depending on what you plan to cut, install the appropriate tooling head and cutter tip. CNC machine designs differ, depending on make and model. Some machines offer a tool changer, which stores all of the tooling you plan to use, and automatically changes tools at the touch of a button.

The machine must be able to precisely reference the block's crankshaft/main bore centerline. A fixture/locating bar is inserted through the main bore. This requires using precision spacers to locate the bar, based on your main bore diameter. Using the machine's digitizing probe, touch the probe off the top of the fixture bar. This calculates the bar diameter and, therefore, determines the centerline of the main bore. Zero the machine.

Install a cam bore centering fixture into the cam tunnel. This bar features adjustable fingers that self-center the bar within the tunnel. The bar protrudes out of the front of the block to provide a reference surface for the probe.

At this point, you need to let the machine know where the block itself is located. Using the machine's auto

Although training in the use of a CNC machine is mandatory, most control panels are fairly easy to read and understand (the sample shown here is on an RMC machine). A fairly short learning curve is required. The display screen features prompts that guide the operator through each step. When initially learning how to use the machine, the use of noncritical, spare "scrap" blocks is highly recommended. Learning and potentially making mistakes on spare blocks is far better than making a mistake on a customer's block.

Here you see an example of a CNC machine's menu screen that allows you to choose the type of block to be serviced. A CNC machine that has been designed to machine engine blocks features software that contains programmed specifications for specific types of blocks, so a knowledge of complex computer programming is certainly a plus, but really isn't needed.

AUTOMOTIVE MACHINING: A GUIDE TO BORING, DECKING, HONING AND MORE

ENGINE BLOCK CNC MACHINING

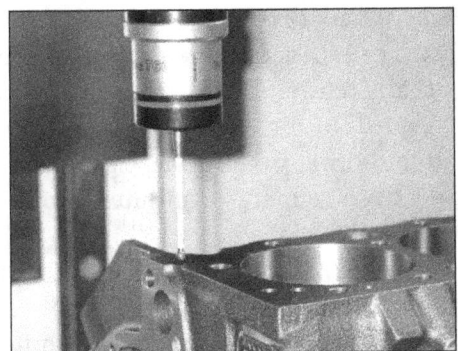

The machine's digital probe reads the block deck surfaces at six points on each deck. This provides existing deck height and existing deck angle information to the computer. This data, stored in the computer memory, is then referenced to resurface the decks to achieve equal bank deck height, correct deck angles, and parallelism to the main bore centerline.

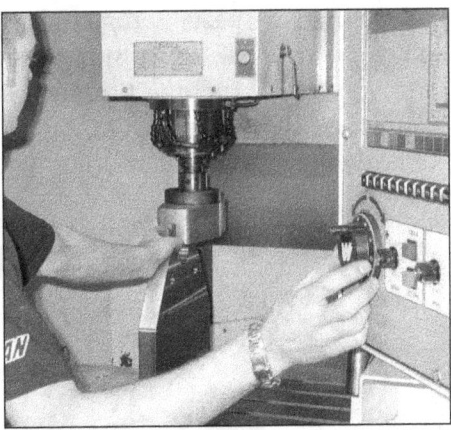

The deck surfacing cutter tool is zeroed to the main bore bar's resting plate, which serves as an initial depth reference.

setup program, the probe contacts the cam bar, referencing the X, Y, and A axis. This provides coordinates that tell the machine exactly where the block is positioned.

The machine control display allows you to select a block from a menu of block designs. Various styles of Chevy, Ford, Mopar, etc., block programs are already loaded in the software for the block designs listed in the menu. You can now allow the machine to reference OEM blueprint dimensions, or, if the machine provides a "conversational" feature, you can override any known dimension to change the desired deck height, bore diameter, etc. The machine automatically assumes blueprint data unless you input your own custom data.

A milling head is installed, fitted with either a CBN cutter (for cast-iron) or a carbide cutter (for aluminum), and cutter height is adjusted.

The first operation involves cutting the block decks. This allows you to create the desired deck height and ensures both decks are "square" and parallel to the crank centerline, at the correct bank angle, and that decks are identical, bank to bank. Zero out the X axis for crank centerline. The probe touches the main fixture bar to locate crank centerline as discussed earlier.

Next, the digital probe touches the front of the block (the timing cover mating deck). The machine now knows where the X axis travel starts. The machine already knows to machine to blueprint specifications (for example, based on a stock GM block. GM bases their dimensions from the dowel pinhole in the right front corner). However, don't assume that your specific block is correct. Let the probe find the existing cylinder bore centerlines (the probe touches at two points in the X axis and two points in the Y axis, and automatically knows the existing bore centerline).

The probe then touches six points on the deck to determine existing deck height. As an example, let's say that the operator wants to achieve a deck height of 9.010 inches. At the touch of a button, the program is called up, and the display prompts you to input the desired deck height. Enter the desired deck height, and then enter the existing deck height, and tell the machine how many passes you want to run to accomplish this.

Although the machine head is cutting the deck, the display constantly shows what's taking place in terms of how much material is being removed, cutter location on the deck, which pass is currently running, etc. With an iron block and selected cutter, you're able to take as much as a .008-inch cut per pass. When the first deck has been cut, the machine automatically rotates the block and cuts the opposite deck. After the second deck has been cut, the milling head automatically pulls away from the block and the machine stops. The result is a perfect deck relationship: both decks are perfectly parallel to the mains and (in this case) at a perfect bank degree angle relative to the centerline, and both decks are perfectly parallel to each other.

Now it's time to bore the cylinders. Set up the CBN cutter on the cylinder boring fixture to the desired bore diameter. Look at the computer display screen. As a result of the previous probe-check of the bores, the machine knows how far off (from centerline) each bore is located. For example, on the sample block, cylinder number-2 was off about .004 inch in the X axis and about .002 inch off in the Y axis. At this point you need to make a decision: do you want to follow blueprint specs or are you going to follow the existing bore centerline?

At this point, the machine already knows where the existing deck height is located, in order for the machine to know when to begin the cut. However, it wants to know the bore depth, so that it knows when to stop cutting. Here, you have an option: let it run down to the bottom of the bore, or let it perform an offset cut at the bottom to gain web clearance. No special programming skills are needed. The display asks, and you follow the question/answer format. With the boring head chosen, the machine can cut up to .040 inch on a single pass.

When boring, you should bore one cylinder, and then check to see if any cutter depth adjustment is needed. In the example shown here, total boring time for all eight cylinders was a mere 4 minutes and 40 seconds.

When all of the holes are bored, change to a chamfering cutter to create a perfect (and identical) chamfer

When commanded to cut the block decks, the automatic tool change quickly selects the multi-bit deck cutter tool head, which is fitted with the appropriate CBN or carbide cutter, depending on block material.

Because the machine already has the main bore centerline and orientation in memory, the decks are trued for perfect parallelism and angle. As with other operations, everything is referenced from the main bore centerline. The operator can easily choose the desired block deck height.

The machine's cylinder bore cutting tool allows speedy and accurate cylinder boring. Depending on the amount of material to be removed, the bores can usually be cut in one pass. The user-friendly display/control center allows simple and clear communication with the operator. A typical high-nickel block's 8-cylinder bores can typically be machined in about four minutes. After the cutter has been programmed for the cut diameter and depth, the machine automatically moves the boring cutter from bore to bore, achieving identical boring operation to each cylinder. The CNC machine automatically rotates the block (bank to bank) during the operation.

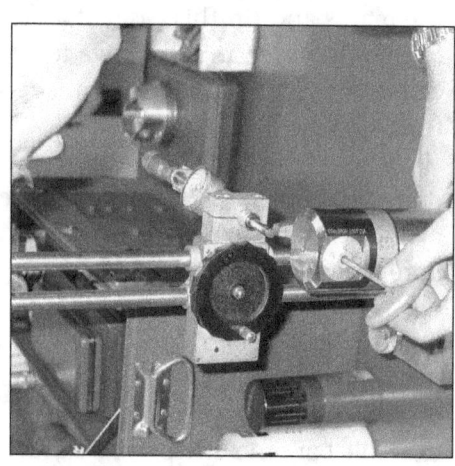

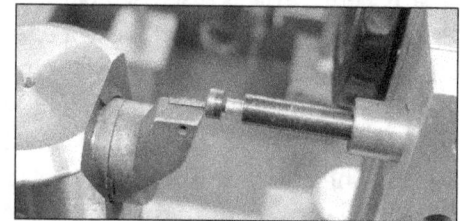

This close-up shows the dial indicator probe in contact with the cutter tip.

The cylinder bore cutter tool is set up on a remote fixture to adjust the cutter for the desired bore diameter.

The CNC machine's digital probe creates a reference of cylinder bores, in terms of bore centerline location, as the probe indexes to several points along each bore's circumference. Using information already stored in the computer relative to rod journal location, this allows a precise creation of an extremely accurate and ideal bore centerline during boring procedures. This is useful when accurizing an OEM block or when boring a raw aftermarket block to achieve desired cylinder bore diameter. The probe runs in/out of each cylinder bore wall to determine existing wall locations relative to the Y axis, then runs side to side to determine the X axis.

at the top of each cylinder. Creating a chamfer eliminates the sharp top edge of the cylinder and eases piston ring entry when installing pistons and rings. The program brings the fixture to bore center. You then enter manual mode on the controller and choose the desired chamfer.

In the example, all eight bores were chamfered in a total time of 1 minute and 9 seconds.

As with the boring operation, chamfering (like boring) is done automatically, with the cutter lifting, moving to each successive cylinder, lowering, cutting, etc. After the computer has been programmed for bore location, diameter, and the chamfer depth, the process runs automatically, with no need for the operator to manually relocate the cutter.

Whenever the CNC machining center is performing an operation, a real-time display constantly shows cutting location, amount of material removal, axis travel, and cutting results, making it easy for the operator to monitor the work in progress.

If lifter bore corrections are needed, the computer is already programmed for lifter centerline. Simply adjust the cutter diameter and run. Machining 16 lifter bores takes about 10 to 12 minutes (depending on depth of your lifter bores). Machining lifter bores with a cutter provides a more accurate lifter bore with a finer finish for oil retention, as opposed to honing the lifter bores.

CNC Terminology

A complete glossary of technical terms that relate to CNC processes

After the decks have been cut and the cylinders bored to size, an angled cutter creates an identical chamfer at the top of each bore. When the amount of desired chamfer is programmed, the machine automatically moves from bore to bore, creating identical chamfers at all bores. At this point, the cylinders are ready to be final-honed in a honing machine.

After the first bore is cut, it's a good idea to verify bore size, in case further cutter tip adjustment is needed.

would take dozens of pages. Here are a few terms that you should be familiar with.

Closed Loop System

A positioning system that can use either step motors or servo motors with an added optical encoder attachment. The motors receive movement commands from the machine's computer. The optical encoder sends this movement information back to the computer to verify that the correct movement was executed. This allows the computer to create an instant record of tool positioning and movement. A closed-loop system can achieve much higher positioning speeds as compared to an open-loop system.

This sample block's eight bores were machined to size in a total of 4 minutes and 40 seconds.

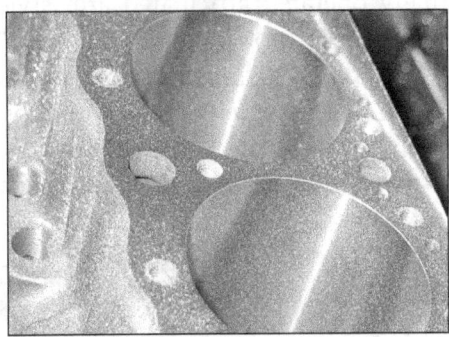

CNC operation results in a finished block that features identical banks (decks and bores).

CHAPTER 10

Machine Time: Typical, Small-Block Chevy	
Auto program setup	1 minute and 20 seconds
Cutting block decks (2 decks)	4 minutes and 30 seconds
Probe 8 cylinder bores to determine bore centerline	3 minutes and 50 seconds
Cylinder boring (8 cylinders)	4 minutes and 40 seconds
Cylinder bore edge chamfer (8 cylinders)	1 minute and 9 seconds
Bore lifter bores (16)	10 to 12 minutes

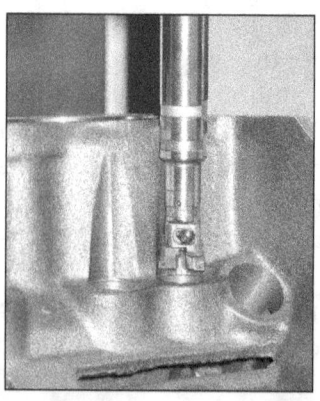

OEM blocks often feature lifter bores that are slightly off-center or incorrectly angled, due to casting core shifts when the block was cast, and as a result of seasoned use. Although lifter bore correction may not be a high-priority issue with a common street engine, lifter bore correction is one of the key elements in blueprinting/accurizing a block for performance use. Lifter bores can be checked and corrected for centerline and angle (if needed) without the need for add-on specialty fixtures. The machine's computer is already programmed (using software provided for a variety of block types) for "blueprint" specifications. Depending on the lifter diameter and oil clearance desired, the operator can quickly select the appropriate data. When the machine is activated to run, it cuts all lifter bores in quick succession. Naturally, if oversizing is required for correction of lifter bores, simple program selection directs the machine to create the required parent bore that will later accept bronze inserts. If inserts are installed, the CNC machine can be used to final-size the insert inside diameter and to trim off any excess that protrudes above the casting.

Here's a Dart billet LS1 block undergoing CNC machining in one of Dart's machining centers. The entire block, from billet to finish-machined block, is handled on a single CNC machine.

Using special software, CNC capabilities also allow precision weight removal from the block's exterior and/or lifter valley. When a block type has been digitally mapped, a program can be written to remove a desired amount of material in specific areas of the block exterior. This provides not only a method of reducing block weight, but achieving a weight reduction in a very precise and repeatable manner.

CMM

Sometimes called a computer modeling machine, the proper name is a coordinate-measuring machine. Available as a stand-alone machine with an automated probe or as manually operated articulated arm style probe, the probe is used to "read" X, Y, and Z axes points to create a 3-D image profile (with information sent to and stored on a computer). An example of application is using a CMM to create a profile of a combustion chamber in preparation of CNC machining a custom piston.

DXF File

The DXF (Drawing eXchange Format) file allows you to translate two and three dimensional drawings between different CAD programs. DXF represents the vectors (x, y, and z coordinates).

G-Code

The G-Code is the standard universal machine tool language. These codes represent x, y, and z (and a, b, and c) coordinates. This is the "language" that the machine uses to create and execute movements.

M-Code

These are movement codes that are used to switch systems on/off, such as coolant, spindle, or other accessories. They can also be used for G-Code program control such as repeating a program.

Operating a Vertical Milling Machine

A vertical milling machine features a power head with built-in controls and a worktable on which the part being milled is secured. Depending on the model of machine, the head may be fixed in a vertical position or it may be adjustable for various off-vertical angles. The worktable features left-to-right traverse and in-out traverse. Some machines will also feature a worktable that is adjustable for various angles.

A typical vertical milling machine, such as a Bridgeport Series 1 model, for instance, features a high- and low-range selector, depending on the speed that is required. A low-range selection allows speeds of 60 to 500 rpm, and a high-range setting allows for speeds of 500 and higher rpm. A vertical milling machine may be used for drilling, in which case the spindle handle allows for up-and-down movement of the spindle. However, for milling operation, the machine's quill (this secures the milling bit) needs to be locked out and the manual handle needs to be left in the full upright position. This provides increased stability for milling operations.

A speed wheel-dial (usually on the right side of the head) is rotated to set the spindle speed. To adjust speed, the spindle must be running in the "on" position while adjusting the speed wheel. To select the machine's high or low speed range, the spindle must be *off*. Rotate the high/low selector handle to the desired high or low position, then turn the spindle by hand until the selector lever clicks fully into the high or low setting.

A three-position switch (usually on the left side of the head) then allows you to turn the spindle on (up for high speed, down for low speed, or in the middle position to turn the spindle off). Depending on the model, the machine may feature a digital control that allows you to program cutting depth and travel in one or more axis. This is a very basic overview of machine setup. Always read the operating manual thoroughly for any given machine to become familiar with the operation. ■

Vertical milling machines are available with a variety of features. Standard angle capabilities include the ability to mill in X, Y, and Z angles (X: left-to-right; Y: in/out; Z: up/down). A rotating head allows milling in a range of vertical angles away from 90 degrees.

Open Loop System

A positioning system that generally uses step motors and receives signals from the computer that execute command movements. This information is not transmitted back to the computer to verify that the movement was correct. In other words, if the movement was not correct (if the positioning system stops unexpectedly), the computer loses track of the mechanism position.

Repeatability

The smallest distance that can be repeated by a machine movement. For instance, if the repeatability is specified as .001 inch and a movement from X-coordinate .000 to .001 inch and back to .000 inch, the position is within .001 inch of .000 inch.

Servo Motor

A motor that is typically a brush or brushless DC type with an optical encoder. It is used in what is called a Servo Loop system, where positioning information is constantly tracked by minimizing the error between the command and real position.

Step Motor

A motor that derives its motion by receiving input signals in a very specific sequence. The most common type is one that rotates 1.8 degrees for each input pulse. This provides a very simple way of controlling motion very precisely with the use of common digital logic circuitry.

STL File

A StereoLithography File (normally associated with stereolithography prototyping machines) can also be used to represent 3D surfaces for CNC tool path programs.

Tool Path

A series of vector coordinate positions that define a cutting path. The cutting path can be a simple two-dimensional or more complicated three- or four-dimensional path.

Vector

A line that has both length and direction. This refers to the line that is created from the starting point to the end of an axis line (x, y, z).

CHAPTER 11

Port Machining

Over the decades, the casting and forging process for heads, intake manifolds, and other engine parts has improved. However, traditional manufacturing tolerances have not been extremely precise, and often components do not correctly align. And this imprecision and oftentimes imbalance in these engine components has hindered performance. To extract ultimate performance from an engine, you need to make sure that each port meets the intended specification, or if you're modifying your heads, intake, or exhaust, you must make sure that it meets your requirements and is compatible with your engine package.

Ports and Runners

The flow of air and fuel from the manifold to the cylinder head's intake port needs to be smooth, with no immediate obstructions as the mixture moves from the intake manifold port to the cylinder head's intake port, to promote a full flow. Common intake ports are either somewhat "oval" in shape or somewhat "rectangular" in shape. In reality, the oval ports are usually not perfect ovals and rectangular ports are not perfect rectangles; these are simply terms to describe the "type" of port shape.

As runner volume increases, so does the amount of air/fuel that can pass through. However, as runner volume increases, this larger area can also slow the air/fuel velocity, which reduces throttle response. Smaller runners promote more velocity and crisper throttle response.

The speed at which the air/fuel mixture can pass through, known as velocity, is critical. The air/fuel mixture must be able to travel fast enough to keep the mixture in suspension. Otherwise, fuel droplets can fall out of suspension and won't burn as part of the mixture, resulting in a rich condition. Ideally, you want the fuel/air mixture to travel through as more of a "fog" instead of as fat raindrops.

The primary advantage of CNC porting is a high degree of precision and repeatability, in addition to job speed. This cross-sectional view of a prototype cylinder head shows the intricate porting work that was accomplished on a five-axis CNC cylinder head porting machine. This eliminates variables that would otherwise exist with hand porting, in terms of material removal, location of removal, shape, and runner volume. (Photo Courtesy Centroid)

PORT MACHINING

A smooth surface finish in the combustion chamber reduces the potential for pre-ignition hot spots and carbon buildup. (Photo Courtesy Centroid)

In a fuel injection setup, the flow is mostly a "dry flow" of air until it reaches the back of the intake valve, when fuel is introduced.

As engine displacement is increased as a result of boring cylinders to larger diameters and/or increasing crankshaft stroke, the engine requires additional intake runner volume. However, if the runners are too large in volume for the engine to take advantage of, the power may increase, but at a higher RPM range. Smaller runner volume is generally better for the street, while larger volume is generally better for top-end at the track. With that said, you still have other variables, depending on the specific engine, bore/stroke, cam profile, etc. There's no such thing as "one size fits all" when talking about intake runner volume. Like other aspects of the engine, runner volume needs to be matched to the specific application. That's where you rely on the recommendations of the major performance cylinder head manufacturers. The exhaust port shape and size is important but less critical than the intake path. The exhaust primary tubes should not be notably larger than the cylinder head's exhaust ports though, because this can have a detrimental effect on exhaust scavenging.

Many potential buyers today tend to focus strictly on the port/runner volume numbers (again assuming that more is better). In reality, port length and cross-sectional area tells a more accurate story. A shorter runner length that features a larger cross-sectional area can actually flow better than a long runner. Again, this depends on the specific head design and other variables in the engine combo.

Porting and Runner Reshaping

A common mistake is to go overboard when attempting to remove material from the inside of the intake runners. I cannot describe every particular porting operation for a particular head and intake combination and, in fact, entire books are dedicated to the subject. Although smoothing out the runners and eliminating all of the rough casting surfaces and any lumps and bumps inside the runners may look nice, keep in mind that the cylinder head manufacturer may intentionally leave some surfaces slightly rough to keep the air/fuel mixture atomized. In other cases, a head can benefit from a smooth, uninterrupted finish. The head design may have also included a small hump with a drop-off inside the runner to promote swirl. Not everything in the runner that might appear objectionable to the eye is necessarily detrimental.

With that said, a couple of mods are always good to make, including port matching and volume equalization. Always match the intake manifold outlet port to the intake port on the head (this holds true for the intake manifold gasket as well). Make sure that the gasket has enough of a footprint to seal without overhanging into the intake path, which creates a restriction. If the cylinder head maker recommends a specific intake gasket, it's best to listen to him.

Each runner (and port) volume also should be equal in each port and runner location.

Although many performance aftermarket heads already feature efficient shapes and surface finishes as a result of extensive in-house research, to extract maximum efficiency from an OEM head, the need for modifications is common. This is a job best left to a skilled pro. If you are not already intimately familiar with a specific head design and its performance characteristics and/or you don't have access to a flow bench to accurately measure and monitor runner volume and velocity, don't touch them. Chances are you'll do more harm than good.

CNC-Ported Cylinder Heads

Rather than hand-porting cylinder heads or intake manifolds, the use of CNC machines and programmed software enables the builder to not only obtain the exact port and runner profiles and surface finish that's desired, but also enables you to precisely match each port and runner with exacting repeatability. This enables you to obtain the same runner volume in each intake runner, eliminating the human error factor from hand-porting intake runners. In the past several years, and with enhancements in manufacturing technology, CNC-ported cylinder

---

AUTOMOTIVE MACHINING: A GUIDE TO BORING, DECKING, HONING AND MORE

CHAPTER 11

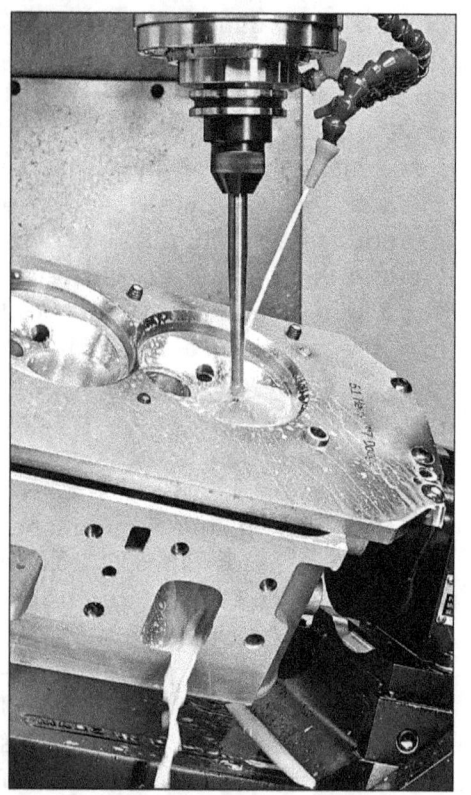

A CNC machine that features five-axis capability features both a moving machine head and a moving work piece base as well. This allows virtually unlimited machining angles. (Photo Courtesy Centroid)

heads have become a viable option for popular engine applications. CNC porting in general terms is a more exact form of hand-porting cylinder heads, with an unlimited ability to exactly duplicate an original shape many times over.

Advantages of CNC Porting

- Consistency of port volume, cross-sectional area, combustion chamber volume, and shape
- Valveseats and ports can be blended seamlessly
- Surface finish can be manipulated by electronic machining
- Cylinder head performance and flow characteristics can be duplicated engine to engine
- No casting core shift; all features are precisely machined

Verifying and Monitoring with a Flow Bench

Rather than making assumptions regarding modifications to a cylinder head or intake manifold runners and ports, a flow bench allows you to obtain measurable data and verify the advantage or disadvantage of existing or modified port and runner combinations. The flow bench allows you to run and monitor airflow at a constant test pressure. The pressure drop is measured across the port/chamber area, determining the ratio of the pressure drop across the calibration. Readings are then monitored through the range of valve lift, from the moment of opening to max lift, and especially just before the valve closes. Pressure is readjusted to calibration test pressure before each check (at 10 percent of valve

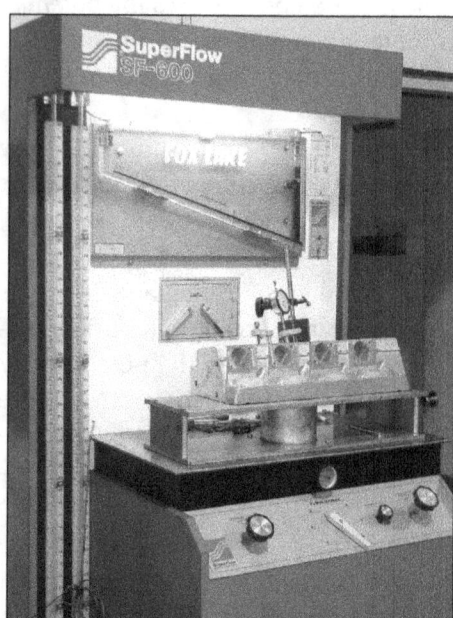

Shown here is a Superflow SF-600 flow bench. Flow bench measurements allow measuring intake and exhaust port airflow, at various stages of valve lift to max lift. This allows verifying/recording original flow and allows the head specialist to verify the results of porting modifications. Without a flow bench, modifying ports is a guessing game. Note the two levers on the lower wall of the unit. This allows pressure to be diverted to either the intake or exhaust paths.

A multi-axis CNC machine is ideal for cylinder head and intake manifold port work, such as this Centroid A560-XL unit. (Photo Courtesy Centroid)

movement, 20 percent, etc.). Controls on the flow bench allow the operator to switch from sucking air through intakes and blowing air through exhausts.

An airflow bench measures this airflow in relation to an applied pressure differential, measured in inches of water column.

Wet flow testing uses a solvent that is similar to fuel in terms of specific gravity. Wet flow testing allows you to not only measure airflow, but how fuel/air is distributed within the port as the valve operates. A special pressure differential valve, called a P-D valve, is a special valve that features a hollow stem where the stem passage connects with orifices in the P-D valve's face. This allows you to determine not only how much volume (in cc's) exists in the port but also where the fuel/air is being distributed, and in relation to valve movement, based on the amount of valve lift. Gaining this qualified data removes the guesswork.

Adding additional axis abilities to CNC systems allows additional angles of attack. A five-axis CNC offers articulation suitable for machining cylinder heads and intake manifolds. An example is Centroid's A560 XL five-axis head porting machine. This provides the ability to port/modify a wide range of heads (V-12, V-10, V-8, V-6, and inline heads). After the port (or combustion chamber) has been digitized and the program written, a five-axis machine has the ability to modify intake ports, exhaust ports, and chambers with complete precision and repeatability from head to head.

Porting intake manifolds (4-barrel carbureted, for example) is also easy because both the machining head and the work piece platform are free to move independently in five different axes. The only time-consuming aspect involves writing the program. Luckily, machine manufacturers offer training, and in some cases as much as 10 days of training is included with the purchase of a machine. In other cases, manufacturer training is available as an option at additional cost. When you purchase a CNC machine, you're not left to figure it out on your own. Training is available.

Port Matching

Port matching refers to achieving a proper alignment and shape between the intake manifold's intake ports and the cylinder head intake ports. Depending on the cylinder head and manifold selections, a slight mismatch can occur, resulting in an airflow interruption or "tumble" as the charge leaves the manifold runner and enters the cylinder head port. Although this may not be critical on a street-driven engine, port matching is one of the factors that help to extract maximum engine efficiency.

Depending on the manifold-to-head combination, it may be necessary to remove material from either the manifold or the head. Carefully measure the cylinder head's intake ports and the intake manifold's ports. If the intake manifold's ports are wider (for example) than the intake ports on the head, first grind to widen the head's ports to match the same width. Then grind the intake manifold's roof and floor areas to match the head. The goal is to have the same size port at manifold and head, and to have them align with no steps/interruptions. However, it's common to size the intake manifold ports just a tad smaller (by about .015 inch or so) to accommodate any play/slop in the manifold bolt holes.

Establishing the same size of the intake and head intake ports is only part of the job. The ports must align. The objective is to obtain a smooth port-to-port transition. Before you start grinding, you need to establish the fixed reference points: use the block that you intend to use, with deck height finished. Install the heads either with the exact type of head gaskets that will be used during final assembly, or shim the heads to mimic the head gasket thickness. You also need to shim the space between the manifold and heads with the same thickness of the crushed intake gaskets (it's best not to use actual intake gaskets as these may interfere with precise outline scribing). Place

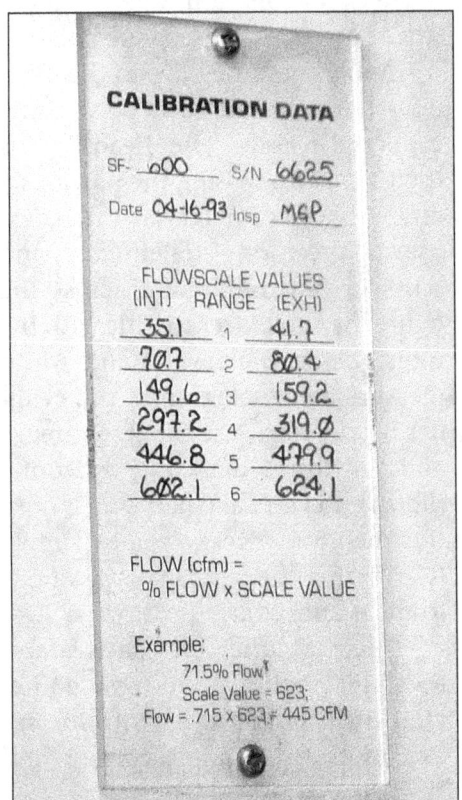

The flow data on the flow bench is checked in small increments (stage 1 through stage 5) to gain precise flow data.

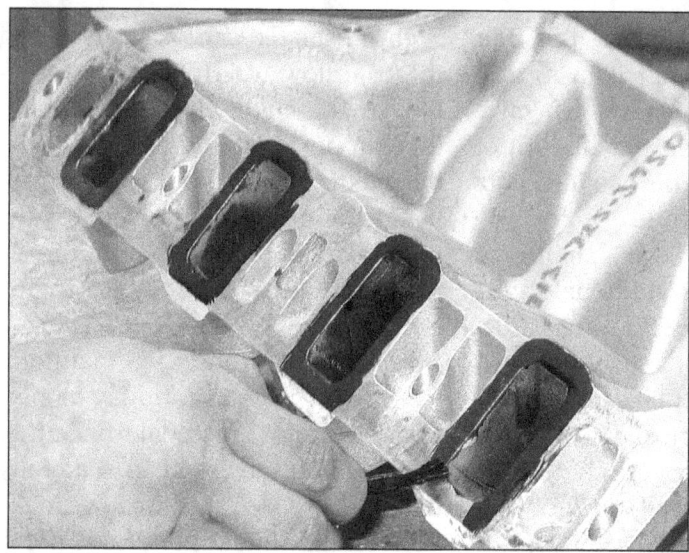

Machinist dye is applied to the port areas prior to checking port alignment. This allows you to easily see the scribe lines that you scratch onto the surface.

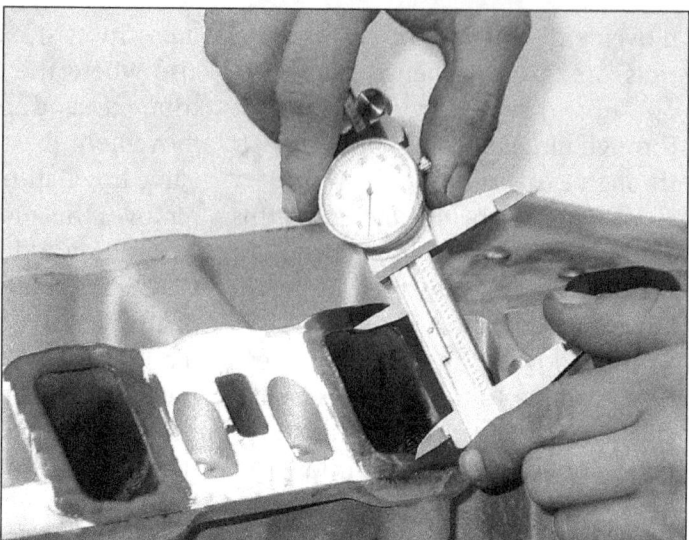

After the port roofs are established as the reference points, and after measuring the cylinder head ports, the dimensions are transferred to the intake manifold.

the manifold onto the block and heads and tap it down to make sure it's fully seated.

Check to see if either the floor or roof of the ports aligns with the head ports. It's best to establish roof alignment/match-up. You can change to different shims to raise or lower the manifold to achieve roof alignment (just remember to use intake gaskets of the same thickness during final assembly). Slide the manifold fore/aft to check for common-wall alignment (the thin walls that separate ports).

Apply machinist dye to the manifold deck around each port. Using calipers, measure the head's ports (height, width). Using the previously established roof height as the index, use a precision straightedge and scribe a horizontal line across the entire manifold deck, in line with the roofs. Using the height and width measurements taken from the cylinder head's ports, use the straightedge and a scribe to mark the horizontal (floor) and vertical (wall) guides onto the manifold decks (you're simply transferring the head's port locations to the manifold).

Select a cutter bit that features the same radius as the port corner radii (if in doubt, apply machinist's dye to the head port corners and

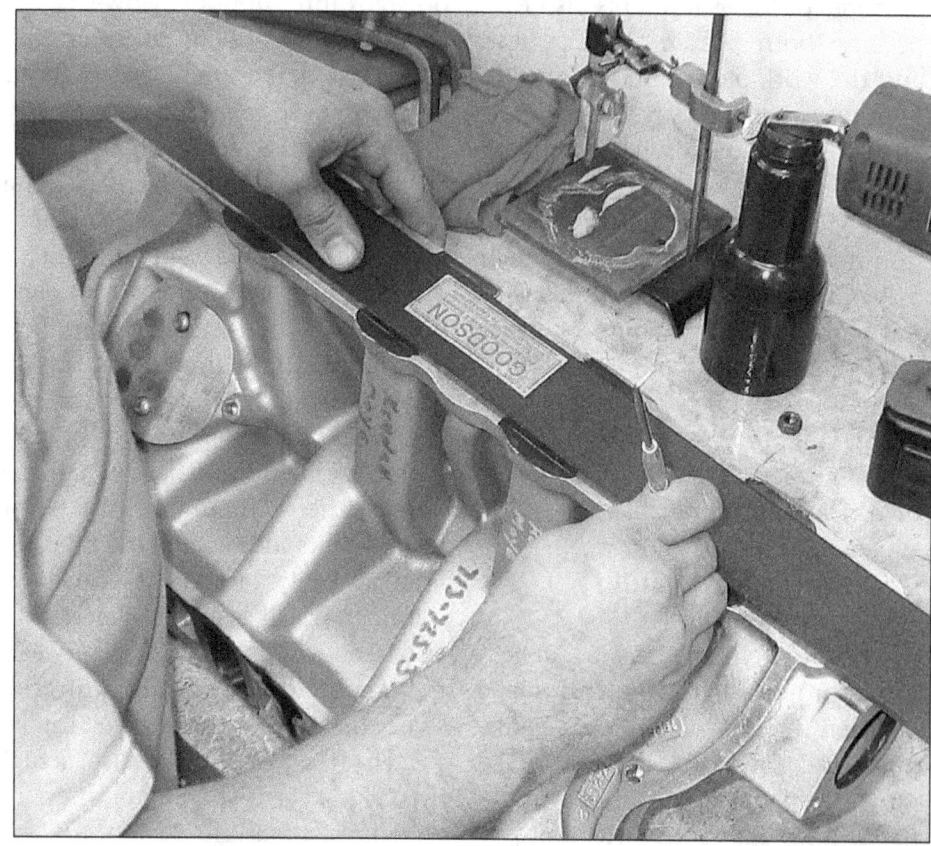

Using a machinists' precision straightedge as a guide, parallel and aligned scribe lines are made at the floors, across the entire bank of ports.

PORT MACHINING

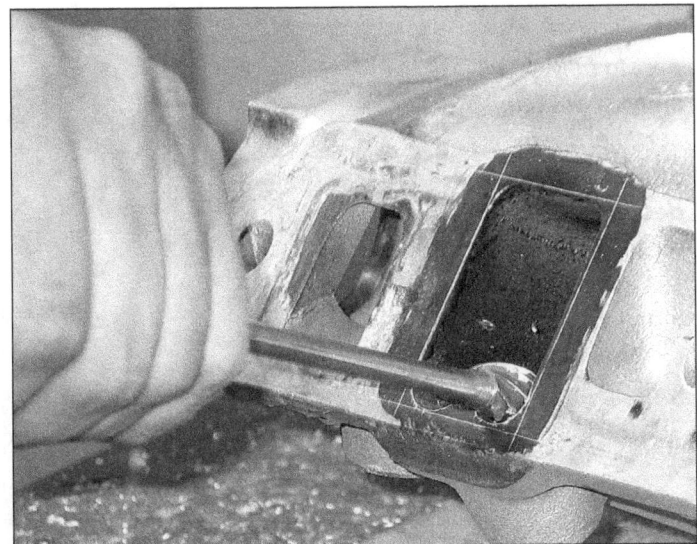

A cutting bit with large flutes is necessary when cutting aluminum material. Check to make sure that the cutter radius matches the corner radius of the ports before cutting.

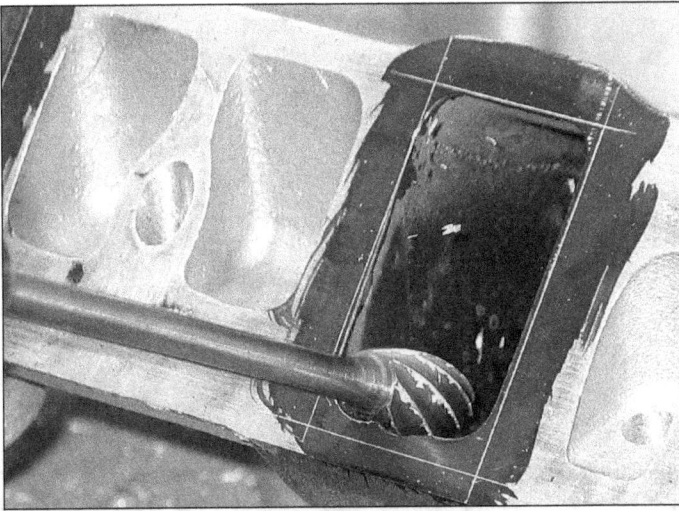

Care must be taken to avoid removing material beyond the scribe lines.

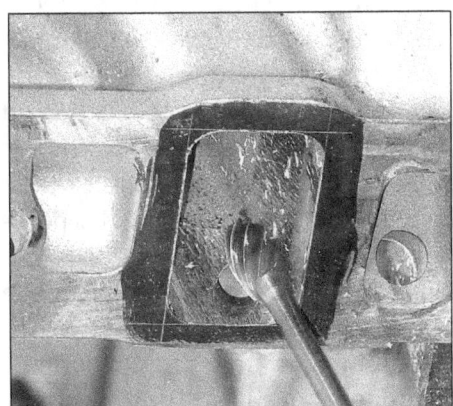

Taper-blend the cut inside the runner at a depth of about 1 inch after you've removed material around the port edges.

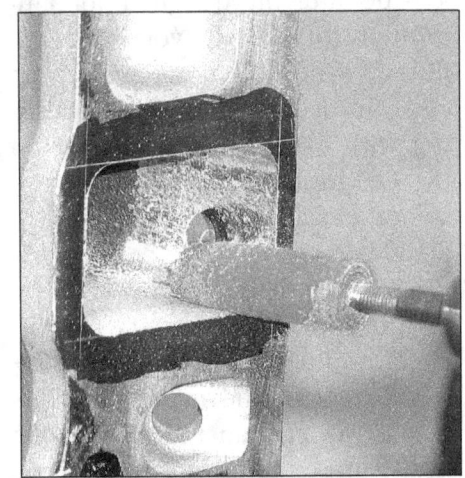

Smooth out all cut surfaces using a 60-grit abrasive stone or roll.

General Rules for Port Alignment of Blocks, Heads and Intakes

- If a cylinder head is angle milled, the intake face on the cylinder head must be adjusted at the same angle, with minimal material removed. It then may be necessary to increase the diameter or create slotted bolt holes in the intake manifold for attachment to the cylinder heads.
- For 90-degree V-8 engine blocks, for each .010 inch removed from the head or block deck, the intake port opening is lowered by .007 inch. To bring the port alignment back into position, the intake manifold needs .005-inch material removed from each side to effectively make the manifold seat lower on the heads.

Do the Math
- Small-block Ford example (intake face 45 degree from vertical mounted on block)

    (Mill off intake face) = (Tan [45-degree vertical intake face angle] x [.010 block deck]) x .5 = .005 amount to be milled off intake flanges

- Small-block Chevy example (intake face 35 degree from vertical mounted on block)

    (Mill off intake face) = (Tan [35-degree vertical intake face angle] x [.010 block deck]) x .5 = .004 amount to be milled off intake flanges

In most instances, you can just divide the total amount of decking on 1 bank by 1/2 to figure intake manifold adjustment.

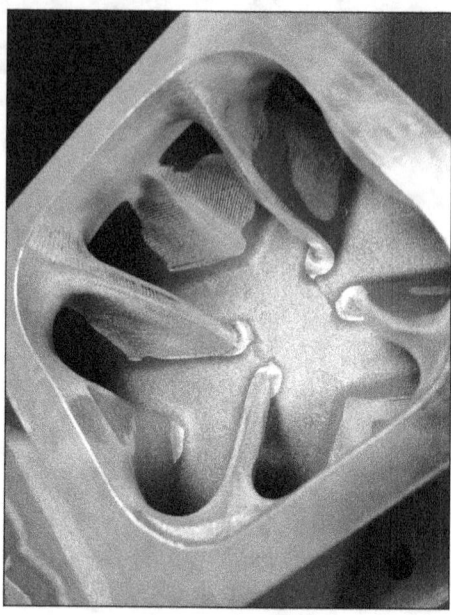

Blend into the port to fully smooth out the surface, again, at about a 1-inch depth. If you prefer a smoother surface (more of a polish), then go over the surfaces with 80 grit.

This is a good example of an intake manifold's plenum runner dividers that have been CNC contour-shaped to perfection, in a matter of a few minutes. (Photo Courtesy Centroid)

hand-roll the cutter in the corner to see if the cutter makes full contact with the corner radius).

Using a radius-nosed cutter bit on a controllable-speed electric die grinder (more controllable than pneumatic), begin to cut the port's edges exactly to the scribed outlines. When each edge is cut open to the scribe line (and straight), blend the grinding into the port at a depth of about 1 inch or so (possibly shorter, depending on the manifold design). DO NOT grind beyond your scribe marks. Keep in mind that for aluminum cutting, you must use a wide-flute bit designed for aluminum (otherwise, you clog the flutes). When all ports have been cut, finish by smoothing/polishing with a 60-grit abrasive roll on the die grinder tool. If you want a smoother finish, follow this up with an 80-grit roll.

You can also take advantage of intake manifold gaskets in your attempt to port match. For instance, if the floor of the manifold's ports is a bit lower than the floor of the head's intake ports, you could move to a thicker intake gasket to move the manifold up slightly. For popular engines, manifold gaskets are usually available in a variety of thicknesses. Consider this before you start hacking away at either the manifold or head.

If using different intake gasket thicknesses doesn't solve the initial

This example shows a 4-barrel single plane intake manifold is mounted via a fixture plate, ready to be custom ported. Machining at a variety of angles is possible, since both the head and base move in various axes, achieving intricate cuts at varying angles. (Photo Courtesy Centroid)

alignment (in terms of manifold installed height), it may be necessary to remove material from the intake manifold mounting flanges to achieve good port alignment and sealing surfaces.

Intake Manifold Plenums

For a carbureted manifold (or a carb-style manifold that uses an air throttle body), take a look at the plenum divider walls. Remove any imperfections (excess casting bumps, flashings, etc.). To aid in airflow or fuel/air flow, smooth out the end of the dividers. Depending on the specific manifold, the dividers may feature rough or almost-squared-off edges. Using a grinder or abrasive roll, radius these edges to a bull-nose shape, avoiding creating a sharp knife-edge. The goal is to remove sharp edges and/or abrupt surfaces that could create excess turbulence.

If you plan to use a carburetor spacer (to increase plenum volume for more top end), apply machinist dye to the manifold's carb mounting pad and install the spacer. If any manifold pad material extends beyond the inside walls of the spacer, scribe a line using the inside of the spacer as the template. Remove any exposed material from the carb pad to remove any obstructions to flow (match the manifold's plenum opening to the spacer). Gently blend into the plenum opening, eliminating any "steps" that might disrupt flow.

Intake Port Surface

An ultra-smooth mirror-like finish isn't really necessary in the intake ports. Finishing with an 80-grit abrasive roll is adequate where polishing is desired. Polishing work is more important to soften and reduce any sharp turns or immediate changes in the flow path, which is where flow speeds are the highest. The shorter the turn, the more need for smoothing. The advantage of polishing can vary, depending in part on the size of the manifold runners. Smaller runners can benefit more from surface polishing than larger port runners. The reason is that smaller-volume runners may be more sensitive to turbulence factors that can result from casting surface boundary layers.

Extrusion Honing

Extrusion honing involves running an abrasive-permeated putty through the ports under pressure in a specialized machine. An example is Kennemetal Extrude Hone, located in Irwin, Pennsylvania (just east of Pittsburgh), that offers a honing process designed to smooth out cylinder head ports, intake manifold runners, exhaust manifold runners, and fuel-injected upper intake plenum boxes . . . all of those hard-to-reach applications that might take days to polish by hand. As far as upper plenums are concerned, such as those used on Ford 302 H.O. motors, extrusion honing is the only option, avoiding the need to cut the plenum apart, and then polish and weld it back together.

Extrusion honing involves the use of a specially designed hydraulic extrusion press that forces a polymer abrasive "putty" through the ports of the work piece. The special polymer is embedded with abrasive material, and the exact compound is a tightly guarded secret. A wide range of polymer densities and abrasive grades are available, depending on the specific application (in terms of how much material is to be removed or how smooth the finish needs to be). As you would expect, a finer abrasive is used for aluminum and ultra-smooth finishes, while a coarser abrasive is used for cast-iron.

Because the abrasive-impregnated polymer is pushed through the ports at high pressure, material removal within the port is extremely uniform. As a result, the primary purpose of this process is to smooth the surface finish in the port walls, as opposed to material removal. Granted, the abrasive action removes material, but this is minimal. As far as changing port shape is concerned (let's say you want to knock off a lip or ledge in an exhaust or intake port), this process doesn't accomplish that objective, so port "modification" still has to be done by hand or on CNC. The main advantage of the extrusion process is to be able to uniformly smooth the port walls. And toward that end, this process does a fantastic job!

The work piece is mounted onto a fixture to isolate the porting area. The fixture has steel plates with special polymer seals that seat against the deck surfaces to allow the abrasive polymer to extrude through only the target port. The machine cycles the abrasive-impregnated polymer through the port, first on a downstroke, then on an upstroke. Depending on the specific work piece, the machine may cycle as many as 400 times, at about 20 seconds per cycle stroke. When you factor in routine monitoring checks and possible abrasive changes, the job may take all day. Before and after the honing process, an airflow check is performed on a SuperFlow air bench to quantify the results. The final result is incredibly smooth, with no telltale machining marks at all.

CHAPTER 12

ENGINE BALANCING

A properly balanced engine operates more smoothly and with less dynamic strain. The results can include slightly better fuel economy, smoother operation throughout the RPM band, and most important, less life-draining and power-robbing harmonic vibration and avoidable stresses. In other words, a properly balanced engine lasts longer and has the potential to create more horsepower.

A slow-revving big-displacement V-8 may perform fine for common street driving while in a slight state of imbalance. However, today's smaller V-6 and 4-cylinder inline engines are much more reactive to balance condition. Whether an engine machine shop builds street motors or race motors, or a combination of the two, it's becoming increasingly important to provide a balancing service to properly recondition both low-RPM street motors and high-revving competition motors. Balancing is not for racers only!

For high-performance and racing engine applications, achieving proper crankshaft balance is an absolute must. For engines that experience high engine speeds and sustained high RPM, out-of-balance dynamic forces not only rob horsepower but can also play havoc on components such as main bearings, the crankshaft, rod bearings, rods, and pistons.

The purpose of balancing, in a nutshell, is to match the crank's geometric centerline axis to the mass centerline axis. The geometric centerline is an unchanging point of reference. This is the static center of rotation of the crank's main journals. The mass centerline is the axis that can change, as rotating and reciprocating forces act on the centerline under dynamic conditions.

If the crank's mass centerline (created by the force of imbalance) is too far out of alignment from the geometric centerline, these two centerlines constantly fight each other. In other words, the crank's mains are forced to rotate in an eccentric path. This ongoing creation of an offset

Everything that attaches to the crankshaft has an effect on dynamic balance. This includes connecting rods, pistons, piston pins, piston rings, rod bearings, pin locks, and estimated engine oil that will cling to crankshaft counterweights, rods, and pistons.

pressure point can squeeze the oil film out from between bearings and journals. Naturally, the result of a severe imbalance is eventual bearing failure. Don't think that an engine has to vibrate wildly for this to be a problem. Even small forces, though possibly not felt by the driver, can magnify and, over time, can lead to shortened engine life. Balancing optimizes the operational conditions and is a prime factor in obtaining maximum engine life.

To remedy this serious condition, the crankshaft must be balanced. In the process, the entire rotating assembly must be considered, because of the dynamic effects placed on the crankshaft by the rotating and reciprocating weight (mass) that is moved by the crankshaft. This includes connecting rods, rod bearings, pistons, piston rings, piston pins, and piston pin locks (where applicable). You also need to consider the anticipated weight of oil that clings to the crankshaft counterweights, rods, and pistons.

Rotating weight, or mass, includes the crankshaft and the connecting rod "big" end and the rod's big end bearings. Reciprocating weight includes pistons, rings, piston pins, pin locks (for full-floating pins), and the "small" end of the connecting rods. By equalizing the weight experienced by the crankshaft, you reduce or eliminate unbalanced reciprocating forces as the crankshaft rotates through its cycles. Engine balancing isn't required for race engines only. Any engine must be properly balanced to obtain both performance and durability. Performance engines simply require a greater degree of precision balancing to minimize imbalance conditions as much as possible. Consider an imbalance condition

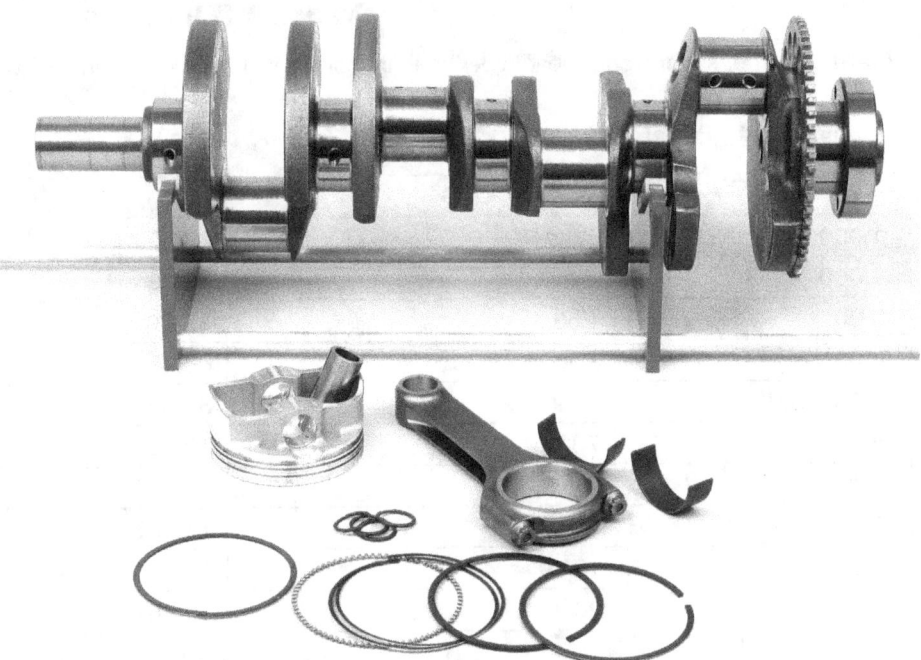

This is what you need to create your bobweights prior to balancing an internally balanced V-8 crankshaft: the crankshaft, one connecting rod, one piston, one piston pin, one piston's ring package (including an oil ring support rail, if required for your pistons), pin locks for full-floating pins, and one rod's pair of bearing shells. This assumes that you've already weighed and weight-matched all pistons and weighed and matched all rods. If the crank is externally balanced, you need to add the front dampener/harmonic balancer and the flywheel.

of 56 grams (which equals about 2 ounces). At an engine speed of about 4,000 rpm, this results in a force of about 56 pounds of crankshaft deflection. At 8,000 rpm, that force climbs to a scary 224 pounds of imbalance force. The goal is to minimize imbalance as close to zero as practical. It's important to note that chasing absolute zero is both difficult and unnecessary. Considering the clinging and slinging nature of engine oil, even if you were able to zero balance the crank, it's not going to run at zero during engine operation. Realistically, balancing a non-high-performance street crank to within less than 4 grams and a performance and/or racing crank to within less than 1 gram is acceptable and practical to achieve with today's computer balancers.

Out-of-Balance Forces on the Crank

An imbalance condition can place stresses on the crankshaft during engine operation. A few sample charts illustrate these forces. In the first example, I consider an imbalance condition of 1 gram at a radius of 3.25 inches (radius referring to the distance of imbalance from the crank centerline). This helps to understand how imbalance in grams results in pound imbalance during engine operation. Impacts per second and impacts per hour refer to the number of times this force impacts the crankshaft per RPM increases. It's easy to understand how an imbalance condition can cause the crankshaft to deflect at higher RPM, which

CHAPTER 12

Crankshaft Imbalance

The impacts per second and impacts per hour are constants based on engine RPM.

Imbalance of 1 gram at 3.25-inch radius

RPM	Imbalance (pounds)	Impact Per Second	Impact Per Hour
1,000	.20	16.67	60,012
2,000	.81	33.33	108,000
3,000	1.83	50.00	180,000
4,000	3.26	66.67	240,012
5,000	5.09	83.33	299,988
6,000	7.33	100.00	360,000
7,000	9.98	116.67	420,012
8,000	13.03	133.33	479,988
9,000	16.49	150.00	540,000
10,000	20.36	166.67	600,000

Imbalance of 9 grams at 3.25-inch radius

RPM	Imbalance (pounds)
1,000	1.83
2,000	7.33
3,000	16.49
4,000	29.32
5,000	45.81
6,000	65.97
7,000	89.79
8,000	107.27
9,000	148.42
10,000	183.24

Imbalance of 56 grams at 1-inch radius

RPM	Imbalance (pounds)
1,000	3.57
2,000	14.03
3,000	31.57
4,000	56.13
5,000	87.70
6,000	126.29
7,000	171.90
8,000	224.52
9,000	284.16
10,000	350.81

can cause main bearing oil clearance to diminish, eventually destroying the bearings, with subsequent damage to main journals. This also places undue stress on block main saddles and main caps. The transfer of energy caused by the imbalance can also impact rod-bearing clearances, with accompanying stresses placed on piston pins and piston pin bosses.

It's important to note that not only are you concerned with the imbalance value in grams, but the radius as well. The radius refers to the distance from the crank center-

line where the imbalance occurs or is corrected. The greater the radius (the farther the imbalance is away from the crank centerline), the greater the force that the crank is subjected to.

If the crankshaft requires a reluctor wheel (for monitoring by a crankshaft position sensor), the reluctor, also called a tone wheel, must already be installed prior to spin balancing the crank.

Connecting Rods

The first order of business involves weighing all rods and pistons. Each connecting rod is weighed on a dedicated and extremely sensitive scale along with an adjustable rod scale stand. Connecting rods are weighed in three steps: big-end weight, small-end weight, and overall weight. On a rod-to-rod basis, weights should be within a maximum variance of 1 gram. Always weigh rods with caps installed and rod bolts tightened to spec. If you plan to upgrade to stronger rod bolts, the bolts that you plan to use must be installed before you start weighing rods.

High-precision digital scales can be extremely sensitive, often influenced by a slight movement of air. The digital scale should be located in an area away from open doors or

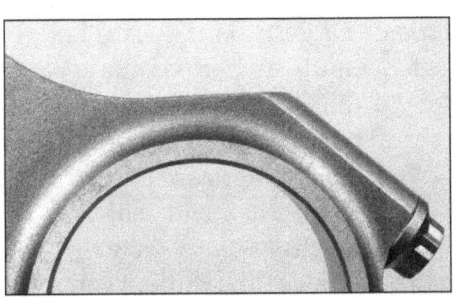

Performance connecting rods are designed with maximum strength while eliminating unnecessary mass. As a result, there isn't much material available for weight removal.

This side view of a Scat LS rod big end's rod bolt area shows how little material is present in terms of potential weight removal. As mentioned earlier, today's rods are designed with maximum strength while minimizing mass. Having no excess material in this area presents a problem on a rod that required weight reduction, but considering how well today's performance rods are manufactured and pre-weight-matched, this simply isn't an issue.

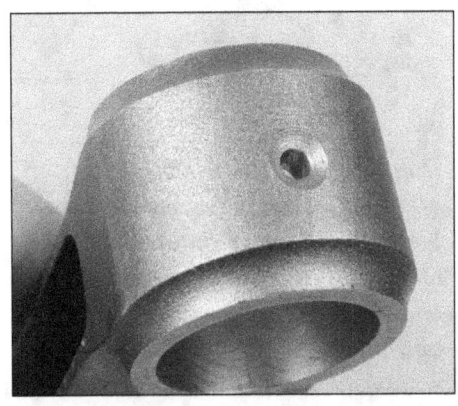

Here's the small end (piston pin end) of a performance rod. Even if you needed to remove a bit of weight from the small end to obtain a matched set of rods where the pin ends weigh the same, you'd only be able to remove very little material. If by chance you do "kiss" this area for weight removal, make sure that the oil hole is not burred or obstructed.

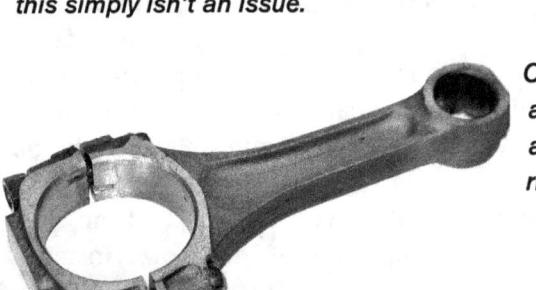

Old-school OEM rods feature balance weight pads at both the small and big ends. This provides material removal for weight matching.

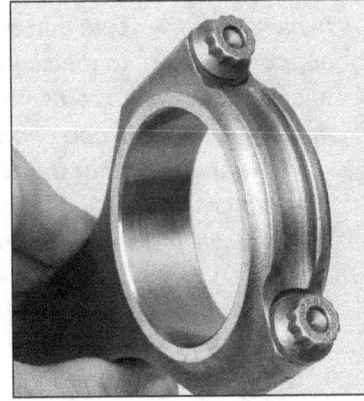

Notice the raised ribs on this rod's cap. These are part of the design to provide big end strength and are not considered "weight pads."

Performance aftermarket rods feature laser-etched number identification at each side of the cap parting line. This unique number allows you to keep rods and their caps organized. If you're dealing with rods that are not marked, use either an ink marker or a light-duty electric etching gun to create marks. Never use number or letter stamps and a hammer, since you could very possibly distort the rod big end.

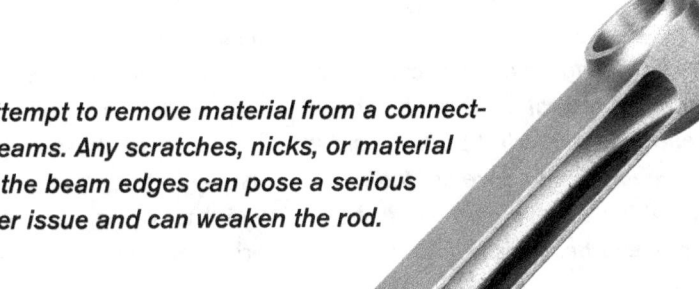

Never attempt to remove material from a connecting rod's beams. Any scratches, nicks, or material removal from the beam edges can pose a serious stress riser issue and can weaken the rod.

windows. Stand very still and allow the scale reading to settle down. Then tare the scale to confirm that it's reading zero weight. When weighing a component, stand still to avoid air movement and allow the reading to settle. Some scales are so sensitive that even slight body movement (waving your arm, moving toward or away from the scale) can cause the reading to fluctuate.

The rod big end is weighed using a precision scale that is specifically designed for engine balancing. You support the big end on a specialty stand that rests on the scale, and the small end is supported on a separate stand that is positioned next to the scale. When properly set up, the rod is positioned horizontally with the big end and small end centers at the same height. Before weighing the rod, first place the rod big end stand on the scale and press the "tare" button. This negates the weight of the stand, zeroing the scale with the stand in place. This prevents the weight of the stand from influencing the weight reading. Then mount the rod with both ends supported on the individual stands. After the scale is zeroed, record the weight of the big end in grams.

Remove the rod from the stands and, if necessary, install a smaller-diameter bushing on the stand (some scale stands feature two different bushings, one for big ends and one for small ends). If you change the bushing on the stand that rests on the scale, install that bushing and once again tare the weight to zero the scale. Next, install the rod with the small end on the scale stand and the big end supported by the adjacent stand. Adjust the rod so that the small and big end bore centers are on the same horizontal plane (level). Note the weight of the small end and record this in grams.

Perform these steps for each rod, using a felt marker to record the weights on each rod (or carefully organize the rods on a large sheet of

This side view of a performance aftermarket rod clearly shows that there is no "extra" material available for weight removal at the rod's small end. As mentioned earlier, today's performance rods manufactured by established makers are so well weight matched out of the box that no weight corrections should be needed.

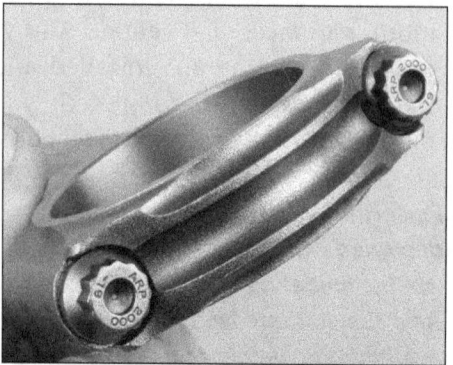

High-performance rods are already equipped with high-strength rod bolts. If you're dealing with OEM rods or used aftermarket rods and plan to install new rod bolts, do this prior to balancing, as different rod bolt brands/types could differ in weight as compared to the original bolts.

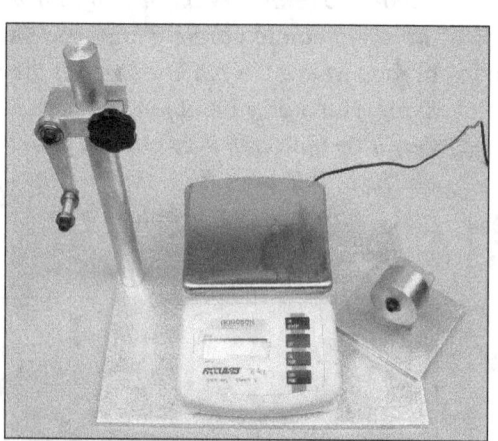

Precision digital weighing scales are offered by several manufacturers, in varying levels of sensitivity. In addition to the scale, you must also have a rod support stand that is placed on the scale and a rod support adjacent to the scale. This allows you to weigh rod small ends and big ends while one end of the rod is supported off of the scale. Shown here is a scale set offered by Goodson Tools & Shop Supplies.

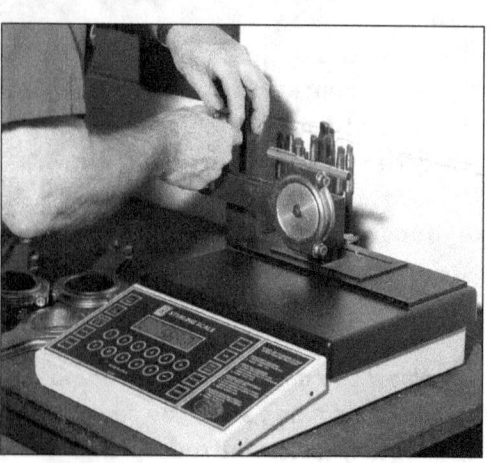

When setting up a connecting rod on a digital scale, it must be suspended level so that both the small end and big end bore centerlines are at the same height. Here the small end height is adjusted.

ENGINE BALANCING

A small bubble level aids in adjusting the rod's state of level.

All weigh scales accomplish the same task. Shown here is a model that features an off-scale support stand where the unweighed end of the rod is suspended by an adjustable chain.

The off-scale support is adjustable to allow leveling the rod when weighing either end.

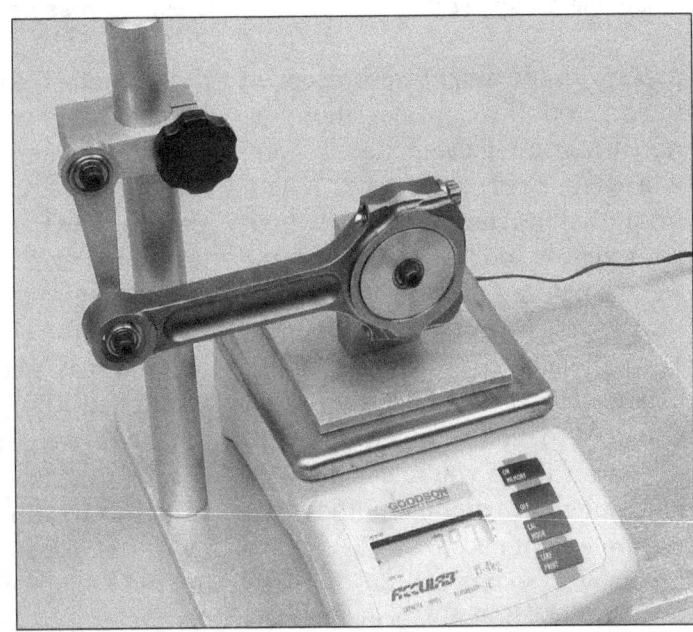

An example of weighing a rod big end. A support stand is placed onto the scale platform and zeroed out (by pressing the tare button). The big end is then placed on that stand, while the small end of the rod is suspended on a stand that is not on the scale. The remote support stand is adjustable for height to level the rod centers.

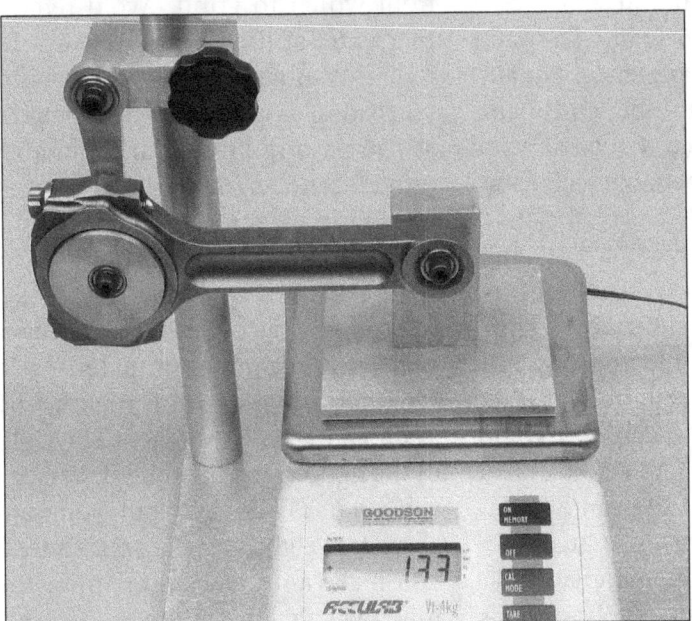

This photo shows the rod's small end being weighed. Again, the on-scale stand has been zeroed so as not to include the weight of the stand. The small end is placed on the stand, while the big end is supported off-scale. The support bushing that engages into the big end bore is simply swapped onto either stand as needed.

CHAPTER 12

Old-design OEM connecting rods likely require weight matching by removing material from all but the lightest rod big ends and small ends. When grinding a rod, follow the "grain" of the metal. Here the sides of a rod big end are being ground to remove a few grams, in the area where the cap meets the rod. Notice that the grinding wheel is contacting the rod in a vertical orientation. If you grind perpendicular to the rod, you can create unwanted stress risers. Even after grinding in the correct plane, be sure to bead blast and polish the ground surfaces to eliminate potential stress risers.

paper with the weights recorded next to each rod. If weight deviations are noted that are greater than 1 gram, you may need to remove weight from the heaviest ends to lighten ends that are too heavy, to match the weight of the lightest rod. In practical terms, weight variations under 1 gram are certainly acceptable. Chances are, the only instance that you need to remove weight to equalize rods is when you're dealing with older original equipment rods that feature weight pads.

Again, considering today's high-quality performance aftermarket rods, it is extremely rare to find a set of rods that are not already weight matched. The objective is to obtain a set of rods that are weight matched. When using OEM production rods, although today's mass production rods are much more accurately matched by weight than in previous decades, it's not uncommon to run into a set of rods in which a few are under- or overweight. Considering that many OEM rods are made in a mold using a pressure-cast "powdered metal" construction, it may be difficult to weight-match rods by removing material from rods that are too heavy, because there may not be enough material removal availability without weakening the rods. In those cases where you are forced to use OEM rods, to achieve a matched-weight set, you may need to obtain several additional rods, weighing each, to achieve a weight-matched set. The goal is to have all rod small ends match to within .5 gram. The same holds true for rod big ends. Equalizing the weight of rod big ends benefits rotating balance. Equalizing rod small end weight benefits reciprocating balance.

In the "old days," it was common practice to correct connecting rod and piston weights by removing material from the rod big ends and small ends (most rods featured a "weight" boss at each end where material could be removed on a grinding wheel. By the same token, pistons could be weight matched by carefully removing material from the underside of the pin boss areas.

Thankfully, because of the precision manufacturing techniques of CNC, today's performance aftermarket rods and pistons rarely require modifications to achieve rod-to-rod or piston-to-piston weight matching.

If you do need to remove weight from rods, this should be done on a grinding wheel. If you're removing material from a weight boss on the bottom of the cap, or from a weight boss at the top of the small end, you can lay the rod flat on the feed table of a bench disc sander or grinder, and use the flat side of the wheel during material removal.

If you're removing material from the bolt sides of the rod, the grinding wheel should make contact parallel to the surface (making the grinding scratches run in a direction from the top of the bolt toward the bottom of the bolt area). Don't grind perpendicular/90 degrees from the length of the rod, as this can create stress risers. After grinding, any disturbed surfaces should be glass bead blasted and polished to remove any scratches. Depending on the design of the rod, you may not have enough material from which to grind. Avoid removing material that could weaken the rod. If removing material from the bolt sides, avoid removing material at the parting line. If the shoulders provide enough material, you may be able to carefully remove material from the upper shoulders.

Again, you want to avoid reducing rod strength. Carefully remove a very minute amount of material and reweigh, repeating until the big end and/or small end matches the weight of the lightest rod in your set. You can easily remove weight but you cannot add weight, so take your time. If you make a mistake and remove too much weight, that rod now becomes

ENGINE BALANCING

Rod bearings from the same set match in weight, so there's no need to scale weigh all bearings. Simply weigh one rod's pair of bearing shells when making up the bobweight card.

One rod's bearings are weighed. This weight is recorded on the bobweight card.

High-quality, high-performance forged pistons are often CNC machined to provide maximum strength while removing unnecessary weight to reduce mass. Pistons, such as those made by JE as shown here, optimize strength-to-weight ratio and leave little if any material for removal. Because these pistons are designed to a high degree of precision, they are already weight matched out of the box, with no need to perform any weight corrections.

your lightest, making it necessary to match the remaining rods to that lightest rod. Grinding any surface of a rod creates scratches, which can result in stress risers. After grinding, you should bead-blast the ground surfaces and/or polish to remove or reduce these scratches.

When grinding material from a rod big end, always keep the rod cap in place and fully torqued to spec. Today's performance aftermarket rods are designed with minimal material while maximizing strength. As a result, there probably isn't much material available at either end to remove without weakening the rod. Because quality performance rods are made to such exacting tolerances, as I mentioned earlier, a set of rods is so closely matched in weight that you likely don't need to touch them.

Performance aftermarket rods are always laser etched with matching numbers on the rod and its cap. Never mix rods and caps. If your rods are not marked, use an etching pen on one side of the rod big end, above and below the cap parting line (for example, 1, 2, 3, 4, etc.). Avoid stamping numbers onto rods with a number stamp and a hammer. It's too easy to potentially distort a rod. Always etch numbers, if necessary, onto one side of the big end, parallel with the rod bolt. Never stamp or etch onto the rod beam, and don't use a file to cut notches onto the rod. File cuts can result in potential stress risers.

Also, if you plan to run original/stock rods and plan to upgrade the rods with stronger aftermarket high-performance rod bolts, install the new bolts first before weighing the big ends. Just remember that prior to final weighing the individual components and making the bobweights, all modifications to rods and/or pistons must be performed first. Changing the weight of these components after balancing affects crank balance for the worse. Pistons and rods must be in a ready-to-install state before you make the bobweights.

Pistons

When weighing pistons, there's no need for a special stand. Make sure that the scale surface is clean and tare the scale before placing a piston onto the scale pad. Each piston and its pin may be weighed together as a

CHAPTER 12

It's always a good idea to weigh each piston to verify weight, but if a set of new forged pistons from any of the leading performance piston makers is selected, you shouldn't need to make any modifications.

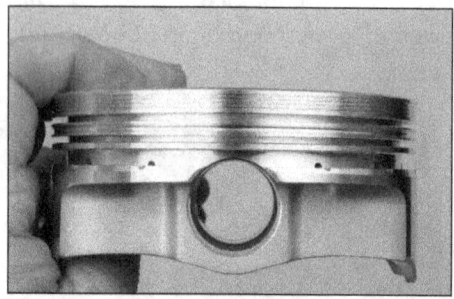

If the pistons feature a short compression height that results in the pin bore intersecting the oil ring groove, a support rail is required at the bottom of the ring groove to provide oil ring support in the void areas that are open to the pin bore. When weighing your ring package, be sure to include a support rail when making up the bobweight card.

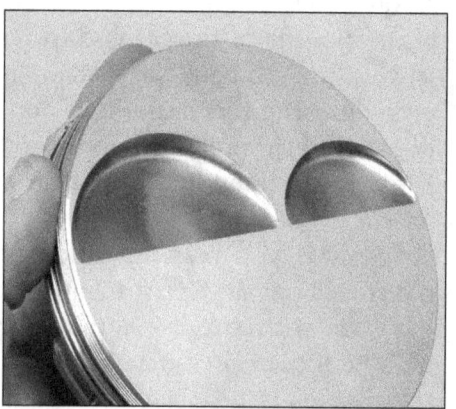

Before balancing, it's a good idea to verify valve-to-piston clearance during test fitting, just in case any valve reliefs need to be enlarged or deepened. If you later discover a need for increased relief, you will likely want to rebalance the crank.

OEM pistons, you may very well find differences in weight. When you're dealing with a set of pistons, always use the lightest piston as the reference goal. Weight can then be removed from heavier pistons to obtain a set that is weight matched. If weight does need to be removed, only remove material from the underside of the pin boss. This can be done by carefully drilling one or more shallow holes in the boss. Don't get carried away. Start with a relatively small drill bit, perhaps 1/8 inch in diameter, and drill to a maximum depth of about 1/8 inch, and reweigh the piston. This gives you an idea of how much weight removal that specific relief provided. Continue as needed by moving to a larger-diameter drill bit and performing small-increment material removal, weighing after each step until that piston's weight matches the lightest piston.

An alternative is to chuck the piston in a dedicated piston vice and carefully mill material from the underside of the pin bosses. Remember: it's easy to remove material, but it is impossible to replace weight. As I mentioned earlier, with today's high-quality aftermarket performance pistons as offered by leading piston makers such as JE, Mahle, Ross, Icon, Diamond, CP, etc., you don't need to correct for weight. Ideally, all piston and pin combinations should weigh exactly the same; as long as weight variations are within a range of less than 1 gram, you're good to go.

If you are unable to equalize rod small end weight and piston weight, experiment by matching heavier pistons to lighter rod small ends, or heavier rod small ends to lighter pistons. If this provides satisfactory weight matching, you need to label

package or individually. Weighing each piston along with its pin is more convenient. If minor weight differences are found, mixing and matching pins to pistons may be necessary to obtain equal weight-matched piston and pin combinations. As stated earlier, when you're dealing with today's high-quality performance aftermarket pistons, chances are that each piston in a set weighs the same, as does the piston pins that are included with the piston package. However, it's best to weigh each and every piston and pin simply to verify weight match, rather than assuming that all pistons and all pins weigh the same. After weighing each piston, mark the dome or boss with a felt-tip marker to note its weight.

If you're dealing with budget-priced pistons or older-generation

ENGINE BALANCING

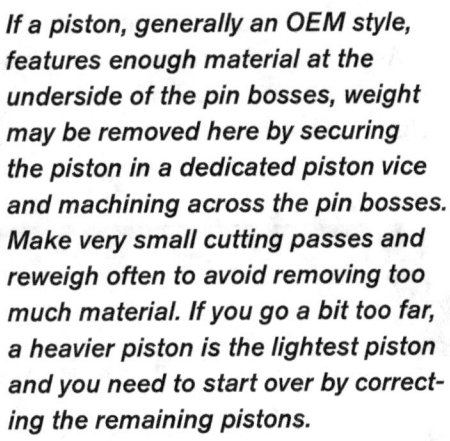

If a piston, generally an OEM style, features enough material at the underside of the pin bosses, weight may be removed here by securing the piston in a dedicated piston vice and machining across the pin bosses. Make very small cutting passes and reweigh often to avoid removing too much material. If you go a bit too far, a heavier piston is the lightest piston and you need to start over by correcting the remaining pistons.

Pistons can be weighed separately, without the pin and/or locks. If you choose, each piston can be weighed in combination with its pin and pin locks. If this is done, make sure to keep that pin with that piston. If the piston and rod assembly uses a free-floating pin, where both the piston and rod are free to rotate on the pin, pin locks or buttons are required to secure the pin in place during engine operation. If locks are required, they must be weighed and factored into the bobweight data.

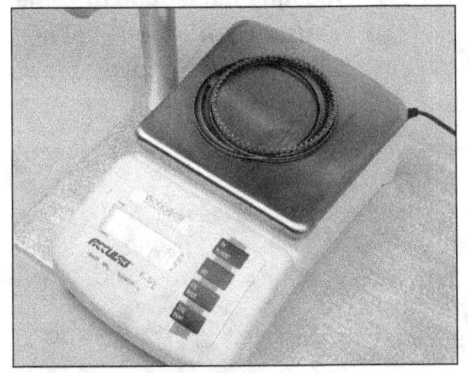

Weigh one piston's ring package. If the piston requires a support rail, make sure to include the support rail as part of the ring package.

each piston and its matching rod so that they stay together during final assembly.

If rod pins do not weight match, use the lightest pin as the reference. Before attempting to remove any material from the pins, first try mixing and matching pins to pistons, for example, pairing the lightest pin to the heaviest piston, etc. You may be able to establish a combination for all piston and pin pairs that allows you to create matching-weight piston/pin combinations without the need to remove material from either pistons or pins. If necessary, material may be removed from heavier pins by *carefully* chucking the pins in a lathe and lightly kiss-chamfer-cutting material from the ends of the inside diameter. Again, if you're dealing with current-day high-performance aftermarket pistons and pins, this isn't necessary due to the extremely close tolerances employed during manufacturing. In the past 20 years or so, I've never run into a set of pistons or pins made by leading manufacturers such as JE, Diamond, Mahle, Ross, Keith Black, Icon, etc., that are not already weight matched.

Don't weigh the piston rings straight out of the box. After the block cylinders have been honed to final size, check ring clearance of all top and second rings. If the rings need to be file-fit to obtain correct ring end gap, the rings must be filed first before weighing them. Granted, the amount of weight removed by filing may be minuscule, but just make sure that the rings are in the condition of properly fitting the cylinders before weighing them, in case any file fitting is involved.

Also, keep in mind that pistons may or may not feature specialty coatings, such as ceramic thermal barrier coating on domes and antifriction coatings on skirts. If the pistons are already coated, they're ready to be weighed. If the pistons are not currently coated, but you plan to send them out to be coated, wait until they're coated and then weigh them. These coatings don't increase weight dramatically, but it just doesn't make sense to weigh them while bare when you know that these coatings will be added later.

One point that I'm trying to make is that, although high-quality aftermarket performance rods and pistons are likely already weight matched, don't assume anything. Just to be safe, take the time to weigh each rod and each piston. You'll probably be wasting your time, but you'll feel better after you verify this.

Engine Styles

Not all engine balancing requires the use of bobweights. Engines that operate the crankshafts in a single plane such as inline

CHAPTER 12

4- and inline 6-cylinder engines, or opposing-cylinder engines (as found in Porsches), have opposing rod throws that run in only one plane. Balancing these engines simply involves balancing the crank by itself, and then weight-matching rods and pistons/pins, with no need to factor in the weight of the reciprocating assembly when balancing the crank. V-style engines involve multiple planes of force, requiring counterweights to compensate for the reciprocating weight of the rods, pistons, pins, rings, and rod bearings. These engines require the use of bobweights to represent the mass of the rods, pistons, etc., during crank balancing.

Bobweights

To balance a crankshaft, you need to create "bobweights" that attach to each of the crank's rod journals, to simulate the weight that the crank experiences in operation.

In order to create these bobweights, you first need to create a bobweight card. The card lists the weight (in grams) of the components that will be installed onto the crankshaft during assembly. As noted, this includes connecting rods, rod bearings, pistons, wrist pins, piston rings, piston pin locks, along with the estimated weight of engine oil that will cling to these surfaces. As each component is weighed on a digital balancing scale, you record the weights on the reference, or bobweight, card.

There is no need to weigh each piston ring set or each rod bearing, because these components are always closely matched in weight. Any difference is so negligible that it doesn't affect balance. That's why it's only necessary to weigh one piston's set of rings and only one rod's bearings.

After the rods, pistons, and pins have been weighed and recorded, weigh one rod's pair of bearings and record this on your bobweight card.

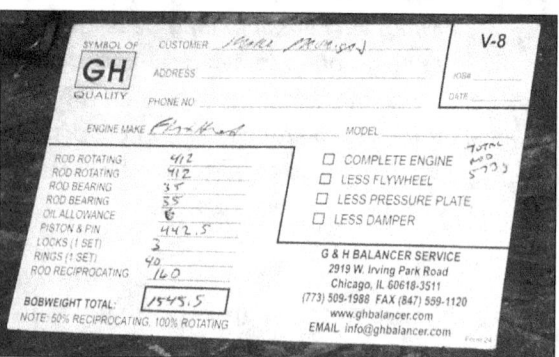

Weigh one piston's pin locks (if featured) and record. Weigh one piston's set of rings, which includes the top ring, second ring, and oil ring set. If your pistons feature a fairly

A sample bobweight card. You include 100 percent of the rotating mass (both rod big ends and both rod bearings that share one journal) and 50 percent of the reciprocating mass (one rod small end, one piston, one set of rings, one set of pins, one set of pin locks).

When both bobweight halves are verified for weight, weigh the pair and verify that it meets your total bobweight requirement.

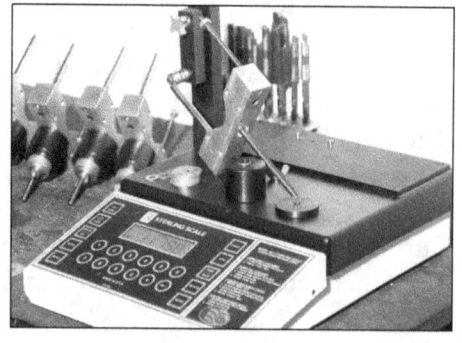

Both sides of a bobweight must be of equal weight. If, for example, total bobweight needs to be 2,000 grams, each half of the bobweight must weigh 1,000 grams. Assemble each bobweight half to the appropriate half-weight and weigh each half of the bobweight.

ENGINE BALANCING

short compression distance where the pin bore intersects with the oil ring groove, you also have an oil ring support ring for each piston. Weigh the entire set of rings for one piston and record this weight.

The bobweights are composed of two-piece aluminum plates that each feature a "V" notch that attaches to the crank rod journals. These plates accept the bobweight that simulates the weight of the rods, pistons, pins, rings, rod bearings, and anticipated oil-cling that the crank deals with during operation. There are two basic types of bobweight designs, one featuring hollow tubes that are filled with lead or steel shot, and another style that features weighted shim discs that slip over the bobweight studs.

To create a bobweight on a V-8 or 90-degree V-6, you consider 100 percent of the rod throw's rotating weight (the big end of the rod and the rod bearing) and 50 percent of the reciprocating weight, which includes a piston, rod small end, rings, wrist pin, and locks. For other engine configurations, different percentages of the reciprocating weight may be required for use. The manufacturer of the balancing equipment usually provides a reference chart or has this information programmed into its computer software.

When the total bobweight is determined, the weights are assembled to duplicate the real-life reciprocating mass.

Installing Bobweights

The bobweight must be installed perpendicular to its rod pin. In other words, install the bobweight to simulate an opposing pair of rods 90 degrees from TDC of the rod throw. With the specific rod journal positioned upright at TDC while on the balancing machine's V-blocks, position a bubble level on the top surface of the bobweight clamp flat surface and adjust the bobweight to level before fully tightening it onto the journal.

Bobweights attach to the crankshaft's rod journals with aluminum V-block clamps that align together on sliding pins. Because aluminum is softer than the crankshaft's surface, this does not damage the journal bearing surfaces. Naturally, both the clamps and the journals must be clean prior to installing the bobweights.

Bobweight Card

This sample is for a 90-degree V-8.

Component	Reciprocating Weight
Piston	694.0 g
Piston	+ 195.0 g
Pin locks	+ -0-
Piston rings (one piston set)	+ 63.5 g
Rod (small end)	+ 293.0 g
Total	= 1,245.5 g
Times number of pistons per throw	x 2
Reciprocating weight per throw	= 2,491.0 g
50 percent reciprocating factor	= 1,245.5 g

Component	Rotating Weight
Rod (big end)	609.5 g
Rod bearing	+ 46.0 g
Total	= 655.5 g
Times number of rods per throw	x 2
Total	= 1,311.0 g
Oil (anticipated oil weight on big end)	+ 4.0 g
Total rotating weight per crank throw	= 1,315.0 g

Reciprocating Plus Rotating
Total bobweight (1,315.0 + 1,245.5) = 2,560.5 g

In this sample V-8 situation, each bobweight is assembled to weigh exactly 2,560.5 grams. Because each bobweight consists of two halves, each half of the bobweight must be assembled with equal weight. In the example above, each half of the bobweight must weigh half of the total bobweight, which in this case is 1,280.25 grams.

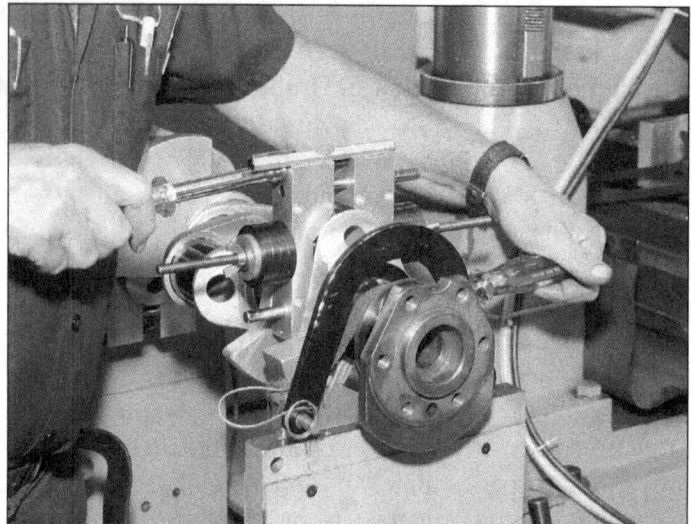

Bobweights must be installed to the crankshaft perpendicular to each of the crankshaft's rod throws. With a rod throw positioned at twelve o'clock, a bubble level is placed on the bobweight clamp to assist in obtaining a 90-degree location.

An easy and quick way to center the bobweight onto the journal is to temporarily install an aluminum spacer that takes up half of the total width difference between the bobweight clamp and the journal width. Note the spacer installed here. This allows you to sandwich the spacer between the end of the journal and the clamp. After the bobweight clamp is secure, the spacer is removed.

Each bobweight must be centered, front to rear, on each rod journal. Installing bobweights too far forward or rearward affects balance and provides a false reading.

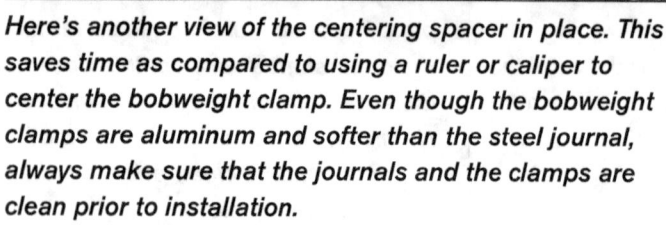

Here's another view of the centering spacer in place. This saves time as compared to using a ruler or caliper to center the bobweight clamp. Even though the bobweight clamps are aluminum and softer than the steel journal, always make sure that the journals and the clamps are clean prior to installation.

Some balancers feature a strobe light to monitor crank angle. Note the small timing wheel.

ENGINE BALANCING

Also, and this is often overlooked, the bobweight must be centered on the crank's rod journal, with equal distance between the front of the bobweight clamp to the adjacent crankshaft face and the rear of the bobweight clamp to its adjacent crank face. An easy way to do this is to make a centering shim that you can slip onto the journal, between one side of the bobweight clamp and the adjacent counterweight. As an example, if the distance between a journal's boss faces is 1.90 inches, and the bobweight clamp is 1-inch thick, insert a U-shaped shim that is .45-inch thick onto the journal, on either side of the bobweight clamp. Sandwich the bobweight clamp and spacer together and tighten the bobweight clamp to the journal, then remove the shim. Instead of spending time by measuring, a premade shim (for the specific rod pin length of the crank) makes it easy and quick to obtain a centered location for the bobweight. By not centering the bobweight on a journal, you could end up with a difference of a few grams from front to rear of the crank. If the bobweights are installed toward the rear of the journals, you end up overbalancing the rear of the crank and underbalancing the front. The difference may or may not be harmful, but centering the bobweight eliminates this variable.

4-Cylinder Inline Engines

When balancing a 4-cylinder inline engine, you have opposing strokes (two up and two down), so the forces cancel each other out; you don't need to create bobweights. Simply weight match the reciprocating parts (rods, pistons, etc.). Then spin and balance the crank without adding bobweights. Weigh the pistons and pins separately. You can then match pistons to pins to "even out" the piston/pin set weights, thereby reducing the time needed to machine weight from pistons (match the lightest piston with the heaviest pin, etc.).

Crankshaft

The crank can't be final-balanced alone. Performing a static balance of the crank means that only the weight is distributed evenly around the center of rotation. The crank must be dynamically balanced to compensate for the rotating force of the rod big ends and the reciprocating forces by the rods, pistons, rings, etc., to correct for centripetal force.

Centripetal force (not to be confused with centrifugal force) is created by crankshaft imbalance, where the imbalance force tries to deflect the crank back and forth during operation. This back-and-forth stress can result in main bearing damage or even crankshaft fracturing. By dynamically balancing the crank,

Some crankshaft balancers feature a safety bar (note the black loop next to this crank's rear flange). This does not contact the crank. It simply provides a fail-safe to prevent the crank from jumping off the balancer in the unlikely event of a severe crankshaft wobble.

Crankshafts are spun via a belt driven by the balancing machine's electric motor. Always wear safety glasses during spin balancing to protect your eyes from potential airborne particles. If you have drilled the outer edge of a counterweight and have added a slug of heavy metal, spinning the crank before welding the slug presents a possible danger if the slug accidentally leaves the crank. If weight was added to a counterweight outer edge, don't stand in front of the crank during spinning until the slug is secured with a weld. Some machinists use temporary sticky putty on the counterweight (creating a specific weight on the digital scale) to perform a test spin. Because the putty can sling off, this is another reason to avoid standing directly alongside the crank during the spin.

you lighten the heavy side or add weight to the lifter side to eliminate centripetal force.

A dynamic balance involves balancing the crankshaft in two planes (as opposed to static balance in a single plane). A dual-plane balance involves both ends of the crankshaft, where balance correction at one end

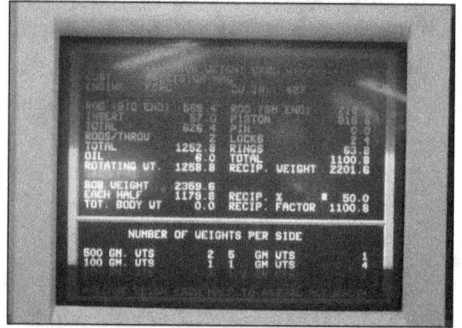

A computer balancer, depending on design, can be used to record individual weights from the bobweight card data and display final bobweight requirements.

If the specific balancing machine does not provide a drill press, the bobweights must be removed and the crank then placed on a V-block fixture at an overhead drill press for weight removal. This is followed by moving the crank back to the balancing machine and reinstalling the bobweights to recheck the dynamic balance.

Weight Removal Table

The following table illustrates the amount of weight that is theoretically removed from a crankshaft counterweight, based on the diameter and depth of a given drilled hole. This helps to eliminate guesswork when the need to remove weight from a crankshaft's counterweights is required.

When weight needs to be removed from a crankshaft counterweight, material may be removed by either drilling into the outer face of the counterweight or by removing outer face material by turning the crankshaft on a precision lathe. By drilling the outer face of a counterweight, you create a potential windage drag. The advantage of using a lathe is that you can remove weight and obtain a smooth surface, theoretically reducing potential windage drag. If weight addition is required, you have two choices: either drill a counterweight outer face and insert a tungsten slug, or by cross-drilling a hole through the front to rear of the counterweight and press-fitting a tungsten slug. If a heavy-metal slug is installed on the outer face, even if a press-fit is achieved, the weight must be welded to the counterweight to ensure that it doesn't sling out during engine operation. Installing heavy metal weights through a counterweight eliminates the potential for the slug to be accidentally thrown out by centrifugal force. ■

Diameter (inch)							
	1/4	3/8	1/2	5/8	3/4	7/8	1
Depth (inch)	Weight (grams)						
1/8	.8	1.8	3.1	4.9	7.1	9.6	13
1/4	1.6	2.5	6.3	9.8	14.0	19	25
3/8	2.4	5.3	9.4	15.0	21.0	29	38
1/2	3.1	7.0	13.0	2.0	28.0	38	50
5/8	3.9	8.8	16.0	24.0	35.0	48	63
3/4	4.7	11.0	19.0	29.0	42.0	58	75
7/8	5.5	12.0	22.0	34.0	49.0	67	88
1	6.3	14.0	25.0	39.0	56.0	77	100

ENGINE BALANCING

A balancing machine that incorporates a built-in drill press provides convenience and saves time, avoiding the need to relocate the crankshaft to a separate drill press.

Handy reference charts are available that tell you what diameter and depth of hole is needed to remove a specific amount of weight, pretty much eliminating guesswork. The balancer tells you how much weight needs to be removed and at what location on a counterweight.

Whenever drilling a counterweight edge to remove weight, always place a clean shop rag on the adjacent journals to prevent contamination.

Depending on where weight removal is most appropriate, instead of drilling to remove all or part of the weight required, the outer faces of the counterweights can be machined on a precision lathe. If the balancing machine indicates that weight should be removed from a larger radius, lathe cutting can save some time.

Here an aftermarket crank for a big-block Mopar application is "kissed" on a lathe. The alternative is to drill a series of shallow holes along the edge of the counterweight.

AUTOMOTIVE MACHINING: A GUIDE TO BORING, DECKING, HONING AND MORE   143

CHAPTER 12

Most crankshaft dynamic balancing machines spin the crankshaft at about 750 to 1,000 rpm, at a speed that is sufficient to obtain imbalance data.

If you're chasing dynamic balance and trying to get picky, there are times when only a very small amount of material removal is desired, which can be handled by hand grinding an area of a counterweight. If using a handheld grinder, cover the adjacent journal with a clean shop rag, and be very careful. One slip could nick the journal.

directly affects balance at the opposite end.

The crankshaft is typically spun at a speed of approximately 750 to 1,000 rpm, sufficient to develop forces that are measurable.

Setting up the crankshaft on the spin balancer involves entering the radius from the crank's centerline to the outer radius of the counterweights, as well as the distance between the centerline of counterweights. A computer balancing machine then determines the balance condition at each front and rear counterweight and provides the operator with the necessary information regarding the amount of weight that needs to be added or removed, and the location of that modification.

Heavy Metal

When weight must be added to a crankshaft, a special "heavy metal" slug is used. This material is also referred to as "Mallory" metal. In essence, this material is composed of a heavy tungsten alloy, which is a little more than twice the weight of steel of the same dimensions. Because this material is heavier than steel, it allows you to use a smaller-dimension slug

In this case, the rear counterweight required a heavy weight placed close to the crank centerline at a small radius. To drill the hole, a hole was required at the rear flange to access the counterweight. This was done with the crank anchored vertically on a drill press.

Here a slug of heavy metal is carefully interference fit into a counterweight. The pass-through hole, required for drilling the affected counterweight and to install the heavy slug, is then filled or another hole drilled to offset this first hole.

A close-up view of the installed slug of heavy metal. Installing tungsten through a counterweight enables you to work closer to the crank centerline and eliminates the potential for the weight slug to sling off of the crank during engine operation. If a tight interference fit isn't possible, the weight is then tack welded to the crank to make sure that it doesn't dislodge.

Heavy Metal Plug Weight

The following chart (courtesy of ABS Products) illustrates the theoretical weight gain of a heavy metal plug based on diameter and length of the plug. The weight gain represents how much weight is added after removing the same volume of steel. For example, if a 1/2-inch hole is drilled in a steel counterweight at a depth of .750 (3/4 inch), a tungsten heavy metal plug of the same size achieves a weight gain of 24 grams. The size of that hole removes 19 grams of steel, but the tungsten heavy metal plug weighs 43 grams, so by removing 19 grams of steel to make way for the heavy metal plug, you end up adding 24 grams of weight. ∎

Diameter (inches)	Length (inches)	Weight Gain (grams)
7/16	.875	21
1/2	.750	24
1/2	1.000	32
1/2	1.200	35
1/2	1.250	41
5/8	1.000	52
5/8	1.200	62
5/8	1.250	65
3/4	1.000	66
3/4	1.200	80
3/4	1.250	92
7/8	.500	48
7/8	.700	63
7/8	.750	70
7/8	1.000	92
7/8	1.100	101
7/8	1.200	105

Diameter (inches)	Length (inches)	Weight Gain (grams)
7/8	1.250	114
1	.500	61
1	.700	83
1	.750	89
1	.850	102
1	1.000	127
1	1.100	133
1	1.200	145
1	1.250	150
1-1/8	1.000	155
1-1/8	1.200	172
1-1/8	1.250	190
1-1/4	1.000	189
1-1/4	1.200	229
1-1/4	1.250	249
1-3/8	.750	180
1-3/8	1.250	290

During the dynamic balancing procedure, this crank was in need of weight reduction by 8.8 grams at the front at 30 degrees of angle, and the rear required weight reduction of 4.8 grams at a 1-degree angle.

Some computer balancing machines provide a radial location view of front/rear imbalance, showing not only how much weight needs to be removed or added, but where on the clock position and radial distance.

After correction, the same crank's balance was improved to an acceptable –0.7 grams at front at 16 degrees of angle and –0.4 grams at a 5-degree angle. That's certainly close enough. Considering dynamic forces and the variable of clinging and slinging oil expected during engine operation, there's really no point in spending excess time to chase down a few tenths of a gram.

to provide the needed weight. Unlike lead, tungsten is weldable, environmentally friendly, and withstands shocks and heat.

When you select an aftermarket performance crankshaft, you need to know the "target" bobweight. This is the approximate bobweight that the particular crank likely requires. If the target weight isn't included on a spec sheet with the crank, consider calling the maker and asking. If your required bobweight is heavier than the crank's target weight, you likely need to add a bit of a heavy metal. In that case, make sure that you have slugs of tungsten on hand. If your bobweight is the same or lighter than the crank's target weight, you likely only need to remove material to balance the crank.

Under- versus Overbalancing

For various racing applications, a common balancing "trick" is to underbalance or overbalance the crankshaft to best suit a specific engine RPM range. Although not suitable for a street performance application, where engine balance needs to provide suitable state of reduced harmonics from idle through occasional high-speed operation, under- or overbalancing allows the machinist to minimize harmonics in a predetermined engine RPM range. This is applicable for engines that typically run only within a specific RPM range (for example, due to the nature of the racing series, the engine may operate only within 6,000 to 8,000 rpm). A slight vibration or harmonic at idle or low-RPM is acceptable, since the vehicle doesn't run at these lower engine speeds on the track.

Under- or overbalancing may or may not be beneficial on all race engines built for the same purpose, due to variations in valvespring stiffness, timing chain, or timing gear harmonics, etc. Basically, in the case of certain race engine applications, you simply don't care about vibrations at engine speeds that aren't used on the track, as long as you can dial-in the balance to optimize engine operation at a very specific engine speed that the engine experiences during competition.

Some race engine builders prefer overbalancing by 1 or 2 percent for a high-revving engine and are convinced that this produces more power. In theory, overbalancing can serve to dampen valvetrain harmonics at a specific engine speed. To overbalance, instead of using 50 percent of reciprocating weight when making the bobweights, you might use 52 percent of reciprocating weight. If underbalancing is desired, the bobweight's reciprocating weight might be 48 percent. Again, under- or overbalancing is often a trial-and-error approach, unless an engine builder has developed a specific routine in his builds (valvetrain geometry, spring pressures, timing system, camshaft, etc.) where under- or overbalancing has proven to be successful.

External versus Internal Balancing

A crankshaft, depending on engine design, may be internally or externally balanced. Internal balance refers to a crankshaft where all balancing (removal or addition of weight) occurs on the crankshaft counterweights and requires the use of zero-balanced crank dampener and flywheel. Of course, this assumes that the pistons, rods, etc., are already weight matched. When an internally balanced crankshaft is placed on the crank balancing machine, there is no need to attach either a front dampener or flywheel, because an internally balanced crankshaft requires the use of a zero-balanced dampener and a zero-balanced flywheel.

An externally balanced crankshaft uses a weighted dampener and weighted flywheel (where each features a balancing weight or pad). In this case, the dampener and flywheel must be attached to the crankshaft during spin balancing of the crank.

With an internal balance, because the dampener and flywheel are zero balanced and do not affect crank balance, the dampener and/or flywheel may be replaced during servicing at any time without affecting crankshaft balance (provided you always install a zero-balanced dampener or flywheel).

Late-model engines commonly feature a toothed reluctor wheel that provides a crankshaft position reference for electronic engine management. If the wheel was removed for any reason or a new crank did not feature an already-installed wheel, make sure that the wheel is installed onto the crank prior to balancing. Adding a wheel after balancing could result in an imbalance condition. If the crank is designed to use a reluctor wheel, it must be in place before attempting to balance the crank.

Dampeners and Flywheels

If the crank is internally balanced, the crank dampener and the flywheel must be zero balanced. This can be done on the balancing machine with special arbor fixtures to secure the units separately. However, a convenient approach is to mount them to the crank, after the

ENGINE BALANCING

crankshaft has been balance corrected. If the dampener and/or flywheel aren't precisely zero balanced already, any imbalance is then discovered and corrected on the dampener and on the flywheel, without any further correction to the crank itself. If this approach is taken, the dampener and flywheel must be reinstalled in exactly the same clock positions used during balancing. If the crank snout is keyed, the dampener only installs in one location anyway (examples of exceptions are OEM LS engine crank dampeners that are not keyed). The flywheel may or may not be indexed to only bolt onto the crank in one location only. If not, place a permanent matchmark on the flywheel and crank flange.

If you purchase zero-balanced dampeners and flywheels from reputable makers, checking them probably isn't necessary, but if you really want to be picky and to verify balance, it's worth considering.

Viscous Dampeners

A viscous-type harmonic dampener is different than an OEM-type elastomer-dampened unit. And as such, you need to be aware of the following. A viscous dampener (ATI, Fluidampr, etc.) takes advantage of the centrifugal force created by a captive fluid inside the dampener ring. Although an elastomer-ring type dampener is designed to only cancel a crankshaft's harmonic vibrations at a predetermined frequency range, a viscous-type dampener is designed to cancel harmonic vibrations at any RPM.

As far as crankshaft balancing is concerned, here's what you need to know: if the engine is an internally balanced design (where all of the crankshaft balancing occurs at the counterweights and the dampener and flywheel are zero-balanced on their own), the viscous dampener itself is already balanced, so there's no need to perform any balancing work on the dampener at any time. If the engine is an externally balanced design (where the front dampener and the flywheel are integral components of crank balance), the viscous dampener consists of two parts: an outer dampener ring and a center hub. Disassemble the dampener to separate the ring from the hub. Mount only

If the crankshaft harmonic balancer features an offset weight pad, this clearly indicates that the crankshaft is to be externally balanced. Unlike an internally balanced crank where the front dampener and flywheel do not need to be installed to the crank during balancing, a weighted dampener must be installed to the crank. If the dampener is replaced down the road, the crank should be rebalanced with the new dampener in place.

A flywheel/flexplate that features welded-on weight was intended for an external balance. For example, if you purchased a rotating kit with crank, rods, pistons, rings, bearings, and flywheel, the weight on the flywheel was added to externally balance the crank. If you're performing an internal balance job, be sure to obtain a flywheel that is already zero balanced.

AUTOMOTIVE MACHINING: A GUIDE TO BORING, DECKING, HONING AND MORE 147

the hub to the crank snout (along with the flywheel at the rear crank flange) for crankshaft balancing. Do not attach the viscous dampener ring to the hub for balancing.

In short, never install a viscous-type dampener or dampener ring to a crank for spin-balancing because the centrifugal internal action of the dampener's fluid serves to absorb and mask some of the crank's harmonic disturbances and results in a false spin-balance reading.

Even if the crank is to be internally balanced, and even if you trust the dampener hub to be zero balanced, installing the dampener's hub to the crank during the balancing setup can't hurt, and you are able to compensate for any slight deviation of hub balance with the hub in place. If the hub is not keyed to the crank snout and relies only on an interference fit, be sure to place matchmarks on the hub and crank before removing the hub from the crank snout, so that the hub and dampener assembly is final-installed in the same clock position during final engine assembly.

Clutch pressure plates can be checked for balance by mounting the pressure plate to an already-zero-balanced flywheel on a balance arbor. Any weight correction is made by welding weight onto the pressure plate cover. Again, quality pressure plates should already be zero balanced from the factory, but checking, and correcting if necessary, eliminates a potential customer's complaint of vibration.

If a torque converter is to be checked or corrected for balance, the fluid must be drained first. If the converter does not feature a drain plug, you may drill and tap a hole and install a plug, but if you do that, you should install an identical plug 180 degrees from the first plug to negate the weight of the first plug. If fluid remains in the converter, your spin balance readings aren't repeatable as the fluid slings around inside. Quality torque converters should already be balanced, so you really shouldn't need to spend time trying to balance them.

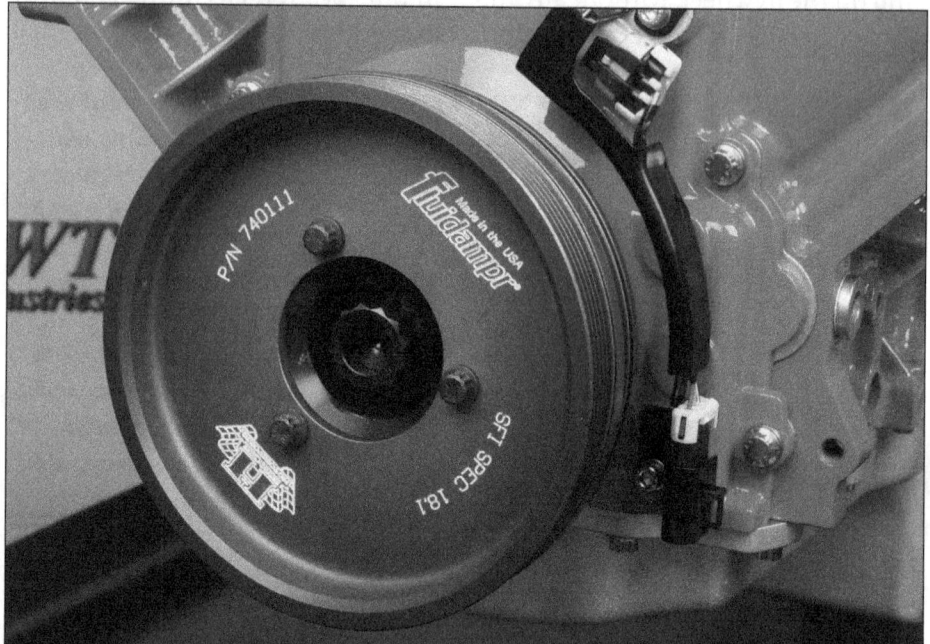

A viscous dampener features an internal cavity with a special silicone fluid that slings around inside and offsets harmonics. Never mount a viscous dampener onto the crankshaft during spin balancing, as this type of dampener may mask vibrational harmonics in the crank.

Equipment Required for Balancing

- A digital weight scale (to weigh reciprocating parts and to create bobweights)
- Bobweight sets (to create facsimiles of your reciprocating parts)
- Spin-balancer unit with computer control
- Drill press (for removing weight from crankshaft counterweights). This can be a separate unit, but it's much more efficient to purchase a built-on drill press as part of the spin balancer bench. This eliminates the time-consuming act of carrying the crank back and forth between the balancer and a stand-alone drill press.
- Flywheel adapter hub (to allow separate spin balancing of flywheel when zero-balancing of flywheel is required)
- Set of bobweight cards (to record all weights)
- If you plan to spin-balance items such as flywheels, impellers, boat propellers, fans, etc., make sure you purchase a balancer that offers a segment mode to allow single-plane balancing.

CHAPTER 13

CLEARANCE CHECKING

Never assume that the clearances are correct. Checking and verifying bearing, piston, ring, and retaining clearances are critical for both stock rebuilds and modifies engine builds.

Main Bearings

Using an outside micrometer, carefully measure the crankshaft's main journal diameters and record the measurements. Set up a bore gauge to this measurement and adjust the gauge dial to the zero mark.

Install the upper and lower main bearings and install the main caps; torque the main cap fasteners to specification. Insert the bore gauge into each installed main bearing. The difference from the gauge dial's zero mark indicates how much larger or smaller the main bearing is relative to the crank journal. For instance, if the gauge reads .002 inch greater than the crank journal diameter, you have an oil clearance of .002 inch.

If a check using standard-thickness bearings reveals an inadequate oil clearance, performance bearing makers offer bearings in "X" size, with the "X" indicating that the bearing shell is .001 inch thinner, which provides an additional .001-inch clearance. Builders often mix and match standard with X bearings to obtain the exact oil clearance desired. For instance, if you need to pick up an extra .001 inch, you could use one standard bearing and one X bearing on the same journal. Each bearing half in an X bearing set will provide .001-inch additional clearance. Generally, when mixing thicknesses, the thicker bearing insert is installed as the lower bearing (for example: standard insert as the upper and X insert as the lower). One example is that a standard bearing insert for a small-block Chevy measures .095 inch thick, while an X bearing measures .094 inch thick.

After a bore gauge is set up to match the crank main journal diameter, the gauge is inserted into the installed main bearing to determine the bearing I.D. relative to the crank main journal.

An upper H-series main bearing insert from MAHLE Clevite. Stamped "STD" to indicate standard thickness. This small-block Chevy upper bearing thickness measures .095 inch.

CHAPTER 13

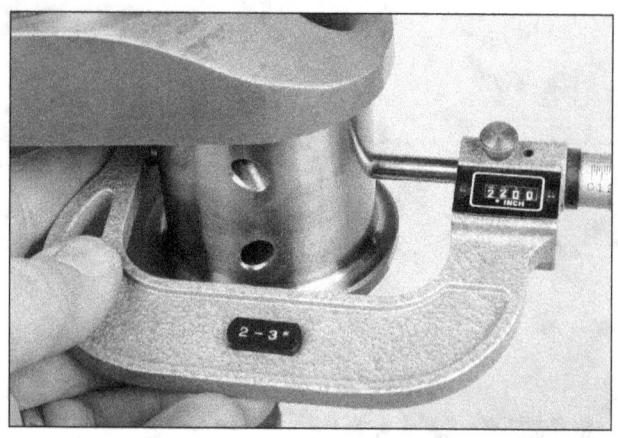

Measure crankshaft main journals with a calibrated micrometer. Make sure that the journal is clean before measuring, with no grease or oils present. Measure each rod journal as well. Make sure that the micrometer anvils are squared up and flush to the journal surfaces.

Rod Bearings

Using an outside micrometer, measure the crankshaft's rod journal diameters. Record this measurement. Remove the rod's cap and install the upper and lower rod bearings, and reinstall the rod cap; torque the rod bolts to specification. To stabilize the rod and to protect the rod from damage, place the rod big end into a dedicated rod vise while torquing the rod bolts. Set up a bore gauge to match the rod journal diameter, then zero the gauge dial. Insert the bore gauge into the rod big end bearing and note how the reading differs from the rod journal diameter. The difference indicates how much greater or lesser the bearing bore diameter is relative to the rod journal diameter. For instance, if the bearing measurement reads .0024 inch greater than the journal diameter, you have an oil clearance of .0024 inch. When using the bore gauge, gently rock the bore gauge back and forth to obtain an accurate reading. The point at which the gauge needle moves to maximum and then moves to minimum, the minimum point represents the true reading.

When measuring main or rod bearing inside diameters, keep the bore gauge anvil and plunger away from the bearing parting lines, because the area adjacent to the parting lines is slightly tapered to promote oil ramping. Also avoid contacting any oil holes or grooves in the bearings.

Cam Bearings

Generally, in an overhead-valve engine, cam bearings are installed and then the camshaft is test-fitted. If the cam rotates easily on its bearings, cam-to-bearing clearance is considered acceptable. However, if you want to know what the oil clearance actually is, use a micrometer to measure the camshaft's journals. Set up a bore gauge to match the journal diameter, then zero the gauge dial. Insert the bore gauge into the installed cam bearings and observe how the bearing inside diameter differs from the cam journal diameter. For example, if the bearing inside diameter reads .0018 inch greater than the cam journal diameter, you have an oil clearance of .0018 inch. As with main or rod bearings, be

When removing or installing rod caps on the workbench, it's best to use a dedicated rod vise to secure and protect the rod. These vises feature composite material on the jaws to prevent nicking or gouging the rod big ends.

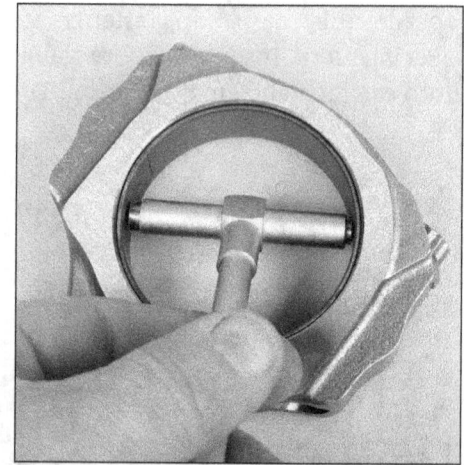

With rod bearings installed and the rod bolts fully tightened to spec, a snap gauge or bore gauge can be used to measure installed bearing I.D.

CLEARANCE CHECKING

When test fitting the camshaft, it must rotate freely by hand. If it's difficult to turn or if you feel resistance in one spot, the cam bearings likely require hand scraping using a sharp cam bearing scraper.

careful to avoid dropping the gauge anvil and plunger into the cam bearing oil hole.

If the camshaft shows resistance to rotating by hand, remove the cam and inspect each cam bearing. You should be able to see slight wear marks on the bearing(s). Using a sharp, dedicated cam bearing scraper tool, the area of the bearing that appears to be tight can be carefully relieved. Reinsert the cam and verify that you have smooth rotation.

Cam Thrust

A flat-tappet camshaft features slightly tapered lobes. A slight crown on the face of the flat-tappet lifters allows the lifters to rotate to prevent excess wear. The taper profile on the lobes, a slight offset of the lifters' bores relative to the cam lobes, and the action of the distributor gear all tend to "pull" the cam rearward, so cam endplay isn't as critical.

However, when you're dealing with a roller camshaft, the lobes are straight, with no taper. The roller lifters need to be maintained on-center with the lobes, so you need to avoid excessive cam walk, but you still need a bit of endplay to prevent a too-tight fore/aft fit. A retainer plate at the front of the block may be used, or the addition of a roller-bearing thrust button may be required to act as a positive stop between the cam nose and timing cover. The thrust button can be shimmed to adjust endplay. Comp Cams, for example, recommends roller cam endplay at .004 to .010 inch. Excessive endplay can cause roller lifters to run at the edges of the lobes, and if the cam features a distributor drive gear, too much endplay can result in premature gear wear and timing fluctuations.

For performance applications, some builders prefer to add a thrust button to reduce cam walk, even to a flat-tappet cam, to reduce timing fluctuations.

Piston-to-Wall Clearance

When reconditioning a block or when prepping a new block, cylinders are bored (if necessary) and final-honed to obtain the desired bore diameter and piston-to-wall clearance. The piston skirt must be measured with a micrometer, at the specific height specified by the piston maker. When piston skirt diameter is known, the cylinders are

If a flat-tappet cam is to be used, use a dial indicator to check cam thrust. In this example, you have cam thrust at .004 inch.

CHAPTER 13

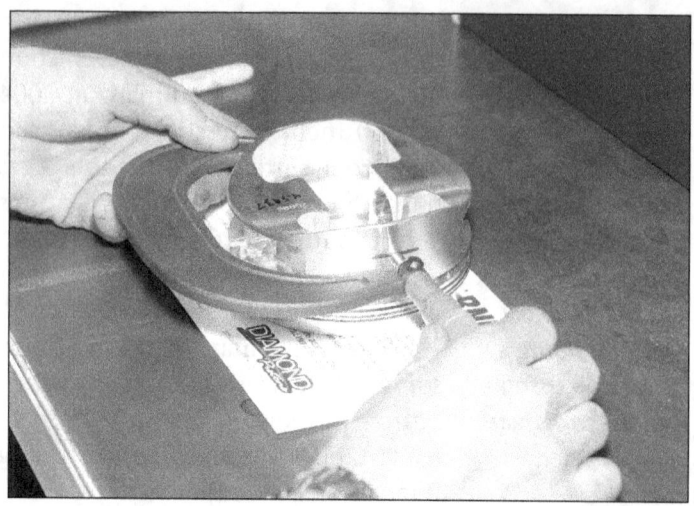

Prior to final honing the cylinder bores, measure the piston skirt using a micrometer. Measuring must be performed exactly at the skirt height specified by the piston maker.

With a pair of rods installed to a common crank rod journal, use a feeler gauge to determine rod sideplay.

honed to provide the needed wall clearance. Always refer to the piston maker's clearance recommendations, which is based not only on the piston design and material but the intended application as well. For instance, a street naturally aspirated application might call for .004-inch clearance, while a forced induction and/or nitrous application may call for slightly greater clearance. A cylinder bore gauge is carefully adjusted to the measured piston diameter and inserted into the cylinder bore to determine the difference, which indicates piston-to-wall clearance.

The type and construction of the piston affects the desired piston-to-wall clearance. For instance, high-silica hypereutectic pistons do not expand as much under operating temperature as forged pistons. As a result, hyper pistons usually require a tighter wall clearance when compared to forged pistons.

Generally speaking, a hypereutectic piston may require approximately .0015- to .0025-inch clearance, while a forged piston of the same diameter may require .004 inch or so for a naturally aspirated street application. If the application calls for forced induction or nitrous injection, an additional .001 to .002 inch or so of wall clearance may be required. As I've mentioned repeatedly, always refer to the piston maker's recommendations for wall clearance.

Rod Sideplay

Connecting rod sideplay refers to the distance that each rod big end can move front-to-rear on its journal. With the crankshaft installed in the block, insert the rod bearings and install the rods to the crank. Make sure that each rod is oriented properly on its journal, with the chamfered side of the big end facing the crank fillet. In an engine that features a pair of rods on a common journal, both rods must be installed to each journal. Using a feeler gauge, push the rod big ends away from each other by hand and insert a feeler gauge between the rod big ends. Refer to the engine specifications for rod sideplay, but it should generally be in the range of .010 to .019 inch.

Lifter Bore

Measure the O.D. of a lifter body. Using a bore gauge, measure the inside diameter of the lifter

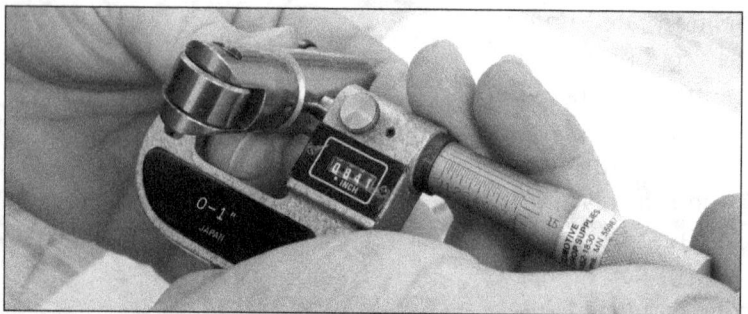

Before checking lifter bore clearance, make sure that the lifters are clean and free of any particles.

The lifter bores must be clean as well. Measure the lifter body diameter with a micrometer.

---

152 AUTOMOTIVE MACHINING: A GUIDE TO BORING, DECKING, HONING AND MORE

CLEARANCE CHECKING

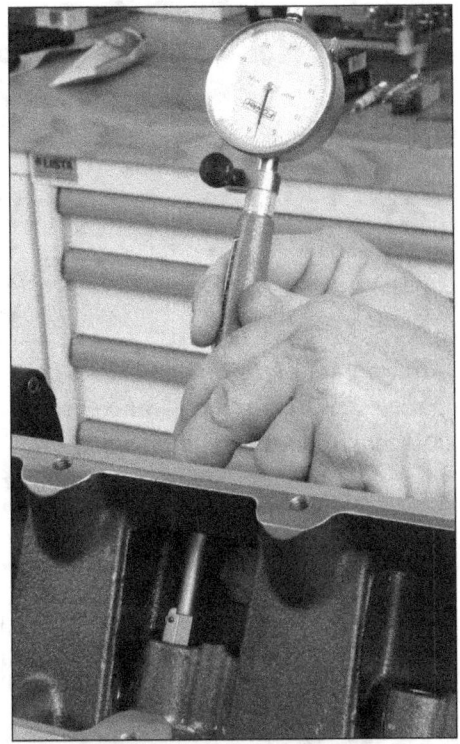

Adjust a lifter bore gauge to the lifter diameter and insert into the lifter bore to determine lifter-to-bore oil clearance.

bore. Always refer to the engine specifications for recommended oil clearance. Generally, lifter-to-lifter bore clearance is in the .0015-inch or slightly greater range. Regardless of the spec, each lifter should easily drop into its bore. If lifter bores must be enlarged, it can be done either by honing or machining with a cutter. In terms of obtaining the best surface finish for oil retention, some lifter makers may recommend honing or cutting.

With the block secured upside-down on a stand, lay the upper main bearings into their saddles and place the crankshaft. When checking only for crank counterweight clearance to the block, there's no need to install the main caps.

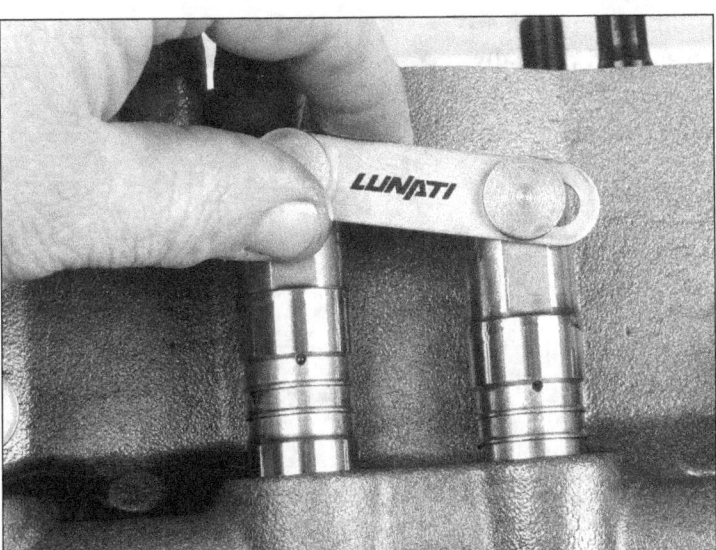

Lifters should drop into their bores easily. Any resistance indicates a too-tight lifter bore.

Crank-to-Block Clearance

When using a crankshaft that has an extended stroke, you must check crankshaft counterweight clearance to the block, primarily at the lower web and oil pan rail areas. With the block positioned upside-down on a stand, install the upper main bearings in the block bearing saddles. Apply a thin coat of oil or lube to the bearing faces. Lay the crankshaft onto the upper bearings. Carefully rotate the crankshaft, noting clearance between the counterweights and the block. To accommodate any dynamic and thermal expansion issues in the running engine, minimum clearance should be approximately .080 inch or more. Examine clearance at each counterweight as you rotate the crank a full 360 degrees. Mark the block with a marker pen at any tight clearance areas. If any clearance issues are found, remove the crank

CHAPTER 13

With the area of interference marked, a die grinder is used to create a relief by the estimated depth, which then must be rechecked with the crank and rod in place.

During test fitting of this engine, the rod big ends contacted the inner edge of the oil pan rails. Areas of concern were marked for grinding.

Aftermarket performance blocks commonly provide a rod clearance notch to accommodate common stroke increases. Depending on the stroke of the crank, this may or may not clear your combination.

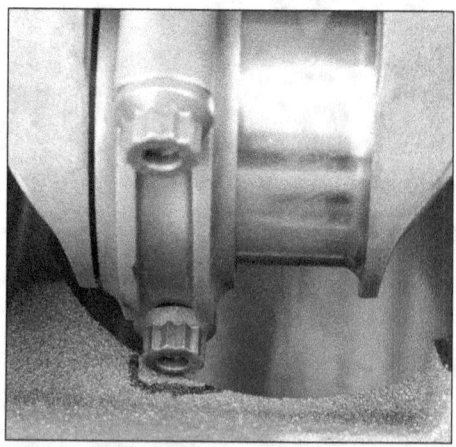

During test fitting, the rod bolts interfered with the block pan rail inboard area.

After grinding a relief, the fit was again checked to verify adequate rod bolt clearance.

and the upper bearings, and use a die grinder to relieve material in the appropriate areas. After cleaning the block, install the upper bearings and crankshaft and double-check to verify clearances.

Rod-to-Block Clearance

As with potential crankshaft-to-block issues, if you're using a stroker crank, you must check rod big-end-to-block clearances. With the block upside-down on a stand, install the upper main bearings and apply a thin coat of lube to the bearing faces. Install the crankshaft, install the lower main bearings to the main caps, lube the lower bearings, and install the main caps. Assuming the cylinder bores have already been bored and honed to size for your pistons, assemble rods to pistons and arrange the rods/pistons on a clean workbench. There's no need to install piston rings at this time. Remove the rod caps from each rod, keeping all rods and their caps organized. Install upper and lower rod bearings to the rods and caps and apply a thin coat of lube to the exposed bearing faces. Apply a thin coat of oil to the cylinder walls.

Perform this check one cylinder at a time. Cylinder by cylinder, starting with cylinder number-1, install a rod and piston assembly. Snug the rod bolts so that the cap is fully seated. There's no need to fully torque the rod bolts to spec at this time.

Carefully and slowly rotate the crank a full 360 degrees, closely watching the rod big end for clearance at the block webs and pan rails. If you find an obstruction or inadequate clearance, mark the block with a pen.

Remove that rod and piston and continue the process with remaining bore locations, marking any clearance issues as you go.

Minimum rod big end to the block should be at least .080 inch or more. If clearancing is required, disassemble to a bare block, grind clearance as needed, wash the block, and reinstall the crank and rods to verify your clearances.

CLEARANCE CHECKING

When using an increased-stroke crankshaft, check for possible rod big end clearance issues with the camshaft. This shot shows a rod shoulder that seems close to the cam tunnel, but further checking verified that clearance was not an issue. This is the reason that many aftermarket block makers offer block versions with raised cam tunnels.

If top and second piston rings must be filed to fit the cylinder bore, a small, flat, fine file may be used. A bench-mounted ring filer makes the job easier and quicker. Gently apply pressure to force the ring end into the diamond wheel, keeping the ring flat on the tool base and the end square to the abrasive wheel. File the same amount from each end of the ring's gap in small increments, checking installed gap as you go. Until you become accustomed to how much material is removed per stroke of the filer, plan on performing this task several times to creep up on the desired gap. After the ring has been filed to fit, use a small, flat, fine file to deburr the filed edges.

Piston Ring Gap

After the cylinders have been final-honed to size, check the piston ring end gaps in each cylinder. In some cases, you may be using file-to-fit rings. Organize the rings on a clean workbench, grouping all top rings and second rings. With the cylinder walls clean, carefully insert a top ring into the cylinder by hand. Using a ring-squaring tool, push the ring down into the cylinder. The ring must be "squared," meaning that it must be placed at the same depth around the entire circumference of the ring. The ring should be placed approximately 1/2 to 1 inch below deck.

Using a feeler gauge, measure the ring end gap. Refer to your piston spec sheet for recommended gap for top and second rings. If the ring has no gap, it must be filed to fit. Remove the ring and, using a fine file or a dedicated ring filer, file an equal amount from each end of the gap, clean the ring, and reinsert into the cylinder and measure the gap. Perform this in gradual steps to avoid removing too much ring material. After the ring is properly gapped, use a fine file to carefully remove any sharp edges and burrs from the filed ends. Clean the ring and place it on a clean workbench, marked for the specific cylinder where the check was performed. Continue this for all remaining top

When checking installed ring end gap, the ring must be squared in the bore at an equal depth along the entire circumference of the ring. A ring-squaring tool such as the one shown here makes this easy. Simply insert the ring, place the tool into the bore, and press down until the tool base is flush to the deck. This type of squaring tool is adjustable for bore diameter.

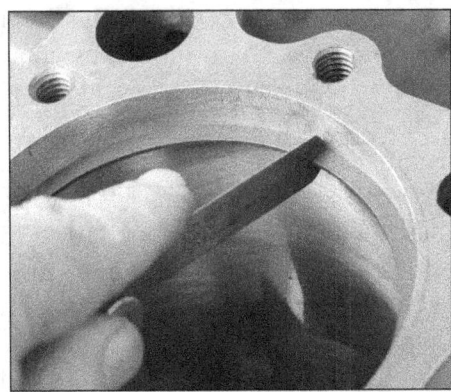

With the ring squared in the bore, use a feeler gauge to measure the ring end gap.

AUTOMOTIVE MACHINING: A GUIDE TO BORING, DECKING, HONING AND MORE

CHAPTER 13

With the dial indicator mounted rigidly, the gauge plunger is set with a slight preload of about .050 inch. The crank is pushed fully in one direction, and the dial is adjusted to the zero mark. As the crank is pushed in the opposite direction, the amount of endplay is revealed on the gauge. Repeat this check several times to verify an accurate measurement.

Here a dial indicator is set up to check crank endplay. If the block is aluminum, placing the magnetic base to the front of the main cap suffices.

rings, then repeat the process for all second rings. Keep all rings organized on a per-cylinder location basis.

Crank Thrust

Install the upper main bearings and apply a thin coat of lube to the bearing faces. Make sure that the crank is clean, with any residue or shipping surface grease cleaned from all journals. Install the crankshaft to the upper bearings. Install the lower main bearings to the main caps, apply lube to the bearing faces and install the main caps, fully tightening all main cap fasteners to specification. As you tighten the main caps in steps, start by tightening to about 10 to 15 ft-lbs, then rotate the crank and gently knock it forward and rearward with a plastic or rubber mallet. Continue tightening to about 30 to 35 ft-lbs and rotate again. Continue until all main caps are fully torqued to specification.

Place a magnetic-base dial indica-

If the block is cast-iron, the dial indicator's magnetic base may be placed against any convenient flat surface. Make sure that the magnetic base is rigid and does not rock or wiggle.

tor stand onto the face of the block, or to the face of the front main cap if you're dealing with an aluminum block. Adjust the stand so that the dial indicator gauge plunger contacts the front of the crank, at either the end of the snout or at the front of the first counterweight.

Using a clean pry tool such as a long straight-end screwdriver, pry the crank fully rearward, placing the pry tool between a counterweight and a cap; be careful not to contact any journal surface. With the crank moved fully rearward, adjust the dial indicator to place about .050 inch or so preload against the crank, then zero the gauge.

156   AUTOMOTIVE MACHINING: A GUIDE TO BORING, DECKING, HONING AND MORE

CLEARANCE CHECKING

Thrust bearings feature front and rear bearing shoulders to provide a bearing buffer that locates the crank's fore/aft clearance. If crank thrust is too tight, the thrust faces may be slightly relieved by laying the thrust surface against a clean sheet of emery cloth on a perfectly flat hard surface and rubbing the thrust surface against the abrasive.

Next, carefully pry the crank fully forward, and note how far the crank has moved on the dial indicator gauge. Repeat this measurement several times to make sure that you're obtaining an accurate and repeatable measurement. This movement distance represents the crank's endplay, or thrust movement. Refer to your engine's crank endplay specification. Generally, crank endplay should be in the range of .005 to .008 inch, but don't assume. Always refer to the specs. Depending on thrust bearing style, if endplay is too tight, you may be able to shave a bit of material from the thrust bearing thrust faces by laying a new sheet of emery cloth onto a flat, hard surface such as glass or granite and rubbing the thrust face against the emery cloth. If you do need to shave the thrust faces, measure the existing thrust face width with a caliper or micrometer and record the measurement. Constantly remeasure as you remove material to avoid removing too much. If crank endplay is excessive, again depending on the thrust bearing style, you may be able to order a thrust bearing with a thicker thrust wall.

Valve-to-Piston Clearance

As I discussed in Chapter 8, valve-to-piston clearance must be checked in both the vertical and radial planes. In the vertical plane, you're checking for the clearance between the valve face and the valve pocket. In the radial plane, you're checking for the radial clearance of the valve head to the radius of the valve pocket in the piston dome. Refer to Chapter 8 for the procedure in checking these clearances. One method involves clay checking, where modeling clay is applied to the piston dome and the crank is rotated to allow the cam, lifters, pushrods, rockers, and valves to run through a complete cycle, providing witness impressions that allow you to measure valve clearance by cutting a cross section of the clay and measuring its thickness. Another method involves using a dial indicator to measure valve movement relative to the piston dome.

A rule of thumb is to obtain approximately .080 to .090 inch of vertical intake valve-to-piston clearance and about .100 to .110 inch of vertical clearance for exhaust valves. A forced induction application generally calls for greater clearance, in the range of .125 inch for intake valves and .175 inch for exhaust valves.

Valve radial clearance should be in the range of .085 to .100 inch.

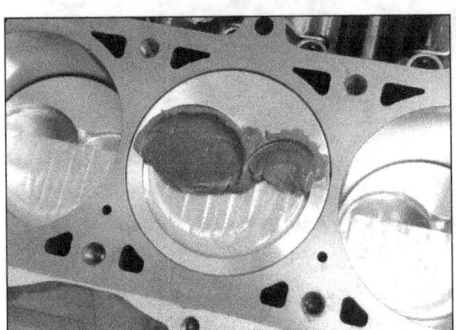

Applying clay to the piston requires cleaning the piston dome so that it's completely dry for the clay to stick. The valve faces need to be lightly oiled to prevent the clay from sticking to the valves.

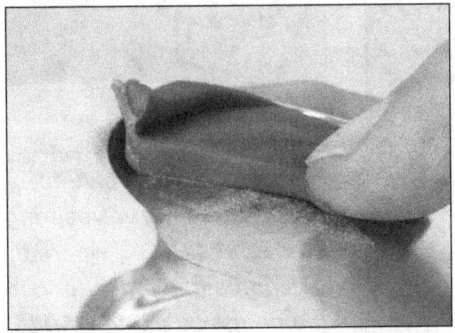

The clay is sectioned with a razor and measured for thickness. Using clay is helpful but may not be extremely accurate, considering potential springback of the compressed clay, but it gets you in the ballpark.

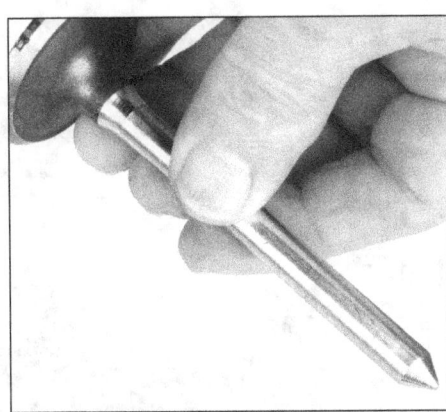

To create a witness mark onto the piston that indicates the valve's centerline, a spare valvestem tip is ground to a point.

AUTOMOTIVE MACHINING: A GUIDE TO BORING, DECKING, HONING AND MORE

CHAPTER 13

The valve head is measured for diameter.

A point-machined spare valve is inserted to place a reference center mark onto the piston.

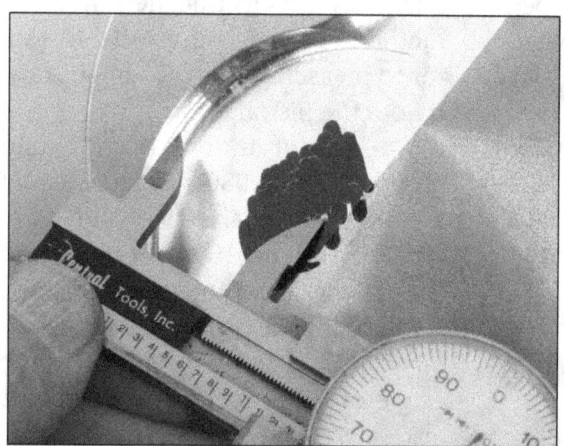
The radius measured from the valve's center point.

Here an exhaust valve-to-piston clearance is being checked. With a light checking valvespring installed, and with the piston moved to 10 degrees BTDC, where the valve should be closest to the piston, position a dial indicator contacting the top of the retainer. Preload the gauge by about .150 to .200 inch and zero the gauge.

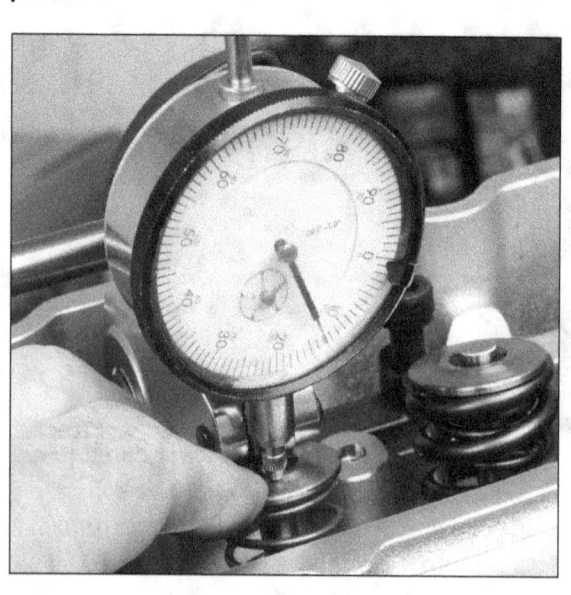
By pushing the retainer down until the valve touches the piston, note the sweep movement of the gauge needle. In this example, you note an exhaust valve clearance of .113 inch.

CHAPTER 14

FINAL ASSEMBLY

Provided here are generic tips involved in final engine assembly. Different engine designs have their own design differences and nuances. Because the majority of this book's audience is likely geared toward single-cam overhead-valve V-8 engines, this chapter focuses on popular V-8 engines. However, many of the same basic principles apply, regardless of engine design. If you're not familiar with your specific engine, be sure to read the appropriate service manual or engine assembly book that covers that specific engine.

Cleaning

Clean, clean, and clean again. Prior to final assembly, every component involved must be absolutely clean and free of any contaminants, including airborne dust (as much as possible). Clean all head bolt holes and main cap threaded holes using a dedicated chaser tap (not a common cutting tap), followed by solvent with a rifle brush, followed by blowing clean with compressed air. Wash the block using Dawn dishwashing liquid and hot water, scrubbing all cylinder walls, main bores, and cam bores using a cam bore brush. Clean all oil passages with bristle brushes and rinse thoroughly with hot water, flushing all bolt holes, inner and outer surfaces, oil passages, and coolant passages. Blow dry with compressed air. Immediately wipe the cylinder walls with a light oil or ATF. This helps clean the microscopic peaks and valleys of the honed surfaces.

If you're dealing with a cast-iron block, surface rust can occur quickly after it dries. At this point, it's not a bad idea to mask the block carefully and spray a light coat of an etching primer. This prevents surface rusting on the exterior and provides a base for paint application when you're ready to paint. Lightly wipe a thin oil to all internal machined surfaces.

With the block mounted to a rotating engine stand, cylinder bores must now be wiped clean using a fast-evaporating solvent and dried. Use white lint-free rags and wipe until you can wipe with no visible signs of contaminant on the rags. Then immediately coat the cylinder walls with clean engine oil.

Clean main bearing upper saddles and main caps. Do not apply any oil to the bearing saddles or bearing surfaces of the main caps. Clean the crankshaft thoroughly, including running a skinny rifle brush through

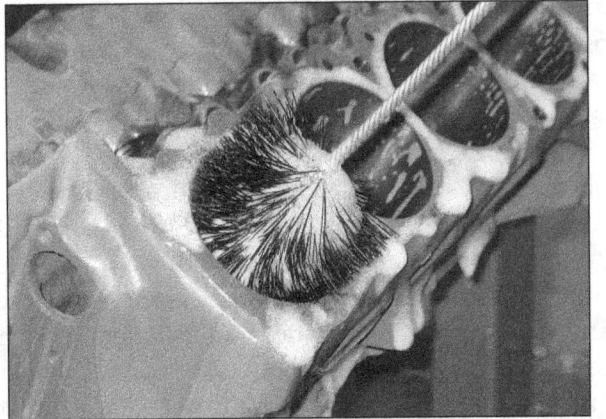

Thoroughly wash and clean the entire block using a quality detergent such as Dawn dishwashing liquid and hot water. Cam tunnels and oil passages may be cleaned using specific-sized, long-rod bristle brushes available from engine builder supply sources such as Goodson Tools.

Rinse the block thoroughly and blow-dry with compressed air, and immediately apply a thin coat of oil or ATF to cylinder walls.

AUTOMOTIVE MACHINING: A GUIDE TO BORING, DECKING, HONING AND MORE 159

CHAPTER 14

all of the crank's oil passages, and blow clean with compressed air. Lightly coat the main and rod journals with clean oil. Position the crank on a clean surface and cover with a new, clean plastic bag to prevent dust particles from contaminating the surfaces.

Install the camshaft bearings using a camshaft bearing installer tool. Some blocks require bearings of the same size from front to rear, while others require staggered-diameter bearings, with dedicated bearings for each bearing bore. Pay attention to the cam bearing package for instructions. When installing cam bearings, make sure that the oil hole in each bearing aligns with the oil feed hole in the cam bores.

When all cam bearings have been installed, carefully insert the clean camshaft to verify fit and ease of cam rotation. If the cam sticks or is not easily rotated, remove the cam and inspect each bearing for signs of rubbing. A sharp bearing scraper may be needed to remove any high spots. If you're not experienced with this procedure, let a skilled engine builder handle this for you.

Cam

Install the cam bearings to the block using a cam bearing installer tool. The tool is a long bar with an adjustable mandrel at the end that captures a single bearing. Install the rear cam bearing first, followed by working your way forward. Slip the bar and mandrel through the first four bearing bores, install the rear cam bearing onto the mandrel, and tighten the mandrel. Be sure to align the bearing's oil hole with the oil feed hole in the bearing bore. Using a brass hammer, tap the end of the

Depending on the engine, the camshaft bearings may be of identical sizes or they may be stepped in diameter and sized for each bearing bore. Pay attention to the cam bearing package instructions. Before installing cam bearings, obtain a reference for the location of the cam bore oil feed holes. The oil hole in the cam bearings must align with these holes.

bar to interference-fit the bearing. Recheck to make sure that the oil holes align. Repeat this for number-4, number-3, and number-2 cam bearings. Switch to the tool's short drive bar and install the front bearing. Some engines use the same bearing for all bore locations; others (LS, for example) require dedicated-per-bore bearings. Check the cam bearing box for instructions on bearing locations.

When dealing with a V-type engine, installing the cam at this point is easier with the crank out of the way. With cam bearings installed and having test-fit the cam in the block to check for clearance, coat the cam lobes and journals liberally with engine assembly lube. For flat-tappet solid or hydraulic cams, you must use the recommended extreme pressure lube on the lobes called for by

Using a cam bearing installer tool, install the rear cam bearing first, working your way toward the front of the engine with successive bearings. Verify oil hole alignment during each bearing installation.

Installing the front cam bearing requires a short mandrel driver, included with cam bearing tool kits. The bearing is captured on the expandable driver tool and is tapped into place with strikes from a brass hammer.

the cam maker. Next, coat the cam journals with engine assembly lube.

Because roller camshafts do not experience the same rubbing friction as do flat-tappet cams, there is no critical break-in frictional concern

FINAL ASSEMBLY

Prior to installing the camshaft, liberally lube all lobes and journals. Although journals may be coated with oil or assembly lube, the lobes must be coated with a high-pressure lubricant appropriate for the cam. If in doubt, always use the lube supplied or recommended by the camshaft maker. Smear the lube along the entire surface of each lobe. Using a camshaft installer tool helps in controlling and guiding the cam. Install the cam very carefully to avoid scratching or nicking any cam bearings.

The block's upper main bearing saddles and the upper main bearings are installed dry. Do not place anything between the bearing and its saddle. The exposed bearing surfaces are lubed prior to crank installation. Make sure that all upper main bearing oil holes align with the oil holes in the saddles.

between cam lobes and lifter bearings. However, these surfaces still require a quality lubricant. A quality engine assembly lube should be adequate, but as a failsafe, if the cam maker recommends and/or supplies a specific lubricant, it's always best to follow their recommendation.

When inserting the camshaft into any overhead-valve engine, use extreme care to avoid nicking or scratching the cam bearings, as this could easily result in lowered oil pressure. Take your time, and support the cam sufficiently to avoid dragging lobes across the bearings. A handy camshaft installation tool handle helps to control cam insertion.

When the cam is in place, check for rotation. It should easily rotate within its bearings.

Upper Main Bearings

Clean the bearing bore saddles. Install the upper main bearings to the block's bearing saddles. Upper and lower main bearings differ, so look closely at the backside of each bearing (marked UPPER or LOWER). The upper bearing shells feature an oil passage that must align with the oil hole in each saddle. Always install main bearings dry. Don't apply anything between the main bore saddle and the bearing. When the upper bearings are in place, apply a coat of

If the crankshaft requires a two-piece rear main seal, install the upper seal to the block with the seal lip facing to the front of the block. Seat the seal fully into its groove; then, if necessary, trim any excess from the exposed seal tips, leaving perhaps .020 to .030 inch exposed above the cap mating surface. Refer to the engine manual or to the seal maker's instructions regarding how much crush depth is required. After the seal halves are installed to the block and cap, apply a small dot of RTV to the seal ends immediately prior to cap installation. Rear seal materials differ. If the seal is made of PTFE, install the seal dry. Always refer to the appropriate service manual for specifics regarding your engine's rear main seal.

engine assembly lube to the exposed surfaces of each bearing, making sure to also lube the thrust bearing surfaces.

Crankshaft and Rear Seal

If your application requires a two-piece rear main seal, the upper seal must be installed prior to installing

CHAPTER 14

Prior to final assembly, make sure that the crank and main caps are absolutely clean. Take the time to organize the main caps and bearings on a clean work surface.

With the upper main bearings lubricated, carefully lay the crankshaft onto the upper bearings, being careful not to nick the crank journals in the process. Do not rotate the crank at this point.

bearings, being careful not to scratch or ding the journals. If you're dealing with a separate one-piece rear main seal, guide the seal along the crank flange to align it into the block's seal groove while positioning the crank.

Avoid rotating the crankshaft at this point; rotating it could push bearing lube out onto the main cap mating surfaces or potentially dislodge an upper bearing.

Main Caps and Lower Bearings

Your main caps should already be numbered for position. With caps and lower bearings clean and dry, install the lower bearings to all main caps. Apply engine assembly lube to the exposed bearing surfaces, including the thrust bearing surfaces.

If your block features main cap registering dowels, install the main caps by hand initially, using the dowels as locating guides. If no dowels are present, insert two opposing-side main cap bolts through the main cap to use as guides. Be sure to lube the bolt threads with the proper lube (oil or a specific fastener lube recommended by the bolt maker). Also apply the same lube to the underside of the bolt heads and to any washers.

If the crank features a one- or two-piece block-to-crank rear seal, you might want to wait to install the rear main cap at this point.

Hand-thread the bolts into the block. When the cap is aligned, gently tap the cap further to make full contact, using a clean plastic hammer. If you're using main cap studs, you can install the studs to the block first (threads lubed and hand-tight), using the studs as alignment guides. Apply lube to the exposed lower threads, washers, and nuts. After the

the crank. Install the upper half of the seal firmly into its groove, with an equal installed height of both seal ends. If the seal ends protrude above the rear main cap's mating surface, carefully trim the ends with a sharp razor, leaving about 1/16 inch or less above the mating surface. If the crank requires a one-piece real seal,

install the seal to the crank flange. On some engines (GM's LS platform, for example), the rear main seal is installed to the rear engine cover, which is installed after the crank is fully installed.

With the engine block secured in an upside-down position, carefully lay the crankshaft onto the upper

FINAL ASSEMBLY

After the main cap bearings are installed to the caps, apply assembly lube to the entire exposed bearing surface. Don't forget to coat the thrust bearing faces on the thrust bearing as well.

Place all main caps into position, paying attention to location and orientation. Initially snug the main cap fasteners to about 10 ft-lbs and check for ease of crank rotation. Finish tightening all main cap fasteners according to the sequence and values that apply to your engine.

caps are reasonably seated, begin to snug the bolts or nuts to approximately 10 ft-lbs or so, in the tightening pattern appropriate for that engine.

Even though you should have performed a crankshaft fit and bearing clearance check earlier during test fitting, at this point, gently rotate the crank to verify ease of rotation. Also at this time, use a plastic hammer to tap the crank forward and rearward while rotating. This can sometimes aid in ensuring cap alignment. When you're satisfied with crank fit, install the rear main cap.

If the crank requires a two-piece rear main seal, be sure to install the lower seal to the rear main cap, checking for seal fit and any excess seal crush depth. Apply a small dab of RTV to the exposed ends of the seal and then install the rear main cap.

Tighten all main cap fasteners to the specified value, always following the correct tightening pattern, in stages. Instead of fully tightening to value in one pass, tighten the fasteners in three steps. For example, if the recommended value is 70 ft-lbs, tighten initially to 25 ft-lbs, then to 45 ft-lbs, then to 70 ft-lbs. Follow the correct pattern in each stage. Verify crank rotation after each step (although you may feel a bit more resistance with the rear main seal in place).

If the rear seal is incorporated into a rear engine cover (for example, in an LS engine), install a new rear seal to the rear cover. New seals (or a new rear cover with seal already installed) include a white nylon guide disc at the inside diameter of the seal. This disc allows you to center the seal to the crank flange during installation and prevents the seal lips from folding rearward during installation. Carefully place the rear cover into position, allowing the nylon guide to center onto the crank flange. Gently but firmly push the cover fully toward the block. When the seal engages onto the crank flange, the nylon guide pops loose. Install the rear cover bolts only finger-tight at this point. Although the series of bolts locates the rear cover, bolt hole clearance is enough to allow a bit of wiggle room. Lay a straightedge along both the oil pan rail and rear cover, at each side, making sure that the rear cover is flush with the pan rail surface. Then, tighten the rear cover bolts to specification.

When installing any rear main seal made of PTFE, never apply oil or lube. Install the seal dry. Follow the instructions for the seal. Depending on seal material, oil may or may not be needed. Also, if using a two-piece rear seal, follow the seal maker's advice for seal half-installed crush depth (how far the seal should protrude above mating surfaces).

After the crank is fully installed, verify crankshaft fore/aft thrust movement. This reveals how much clearance you have at the thrust bearing surfaces. Mount a magnetic-base dial indicator stand onto the front of the block (or in the case of an aluminum block, you might be able to mount the magnetic base to the

When the crank is fully installed, use a dial indicator to check for crank thrust movement fore/aft.

AUTOMOTIVE MACHINING: A GUIDE TO BORING, DECKING, HONING AND MORE

front main bearing cap). Set up the dial indicator so that the plunger contacts the crank snout nose or the front face of the front counterweight. Using a long flat-tip screwdriver, carefully push the crank fully forward. Adjust the dial indicator with a bit of preload, to zero. Then push the crank fully rearward and note how far the crank moves. Repeat this in both directions. Again, always refer to your engine's specifications. Generally speaking, crank thrust should be in the .005- to .007-inch range.

Pistons and Rods

Place each connecting rod into a rod vise and secure the big end. Loosen both rod bolts using a hand wrench. Avoid using an impact wrench. Remove the rod from the vise and back the rod bolts out about halfway. While supporting the rod cap with one hand, lightly tap the rod bolts with a plastic hammer to dislodge the cap from the rod. Do this over a clean workbench, with the rod held over a padded towel. Remove the cap and bolts from the rod and place the rod, cap, and bolts on a clean workbench. Organize all rods and their respective caps and bolts in an organized row. Be careful not to mismatch rods and caps. Always keep each cap with its original rod.

One easy method to remove rod caps is by using a rod cap separator tool. It allows you to separate the cap from the rod smoothly without having to use a hammer.

Assemble each rod to its piston. If the design features a rod pin that is interference-fit to the rod small end, heat the rod small end in a rod heater unit, then place the piston onto the rod and slip the wrist pin into place, centered, with each end of the pin at the same distance at each side. Apply lube to the surfaces that will contact the piston before installing. Verify that the piston rotates smoothly on the wrist pin. If the design features a full-floating pin, where it is able to rotate on both the rod and piston, lube the wrist pin, and slip it into one side of the piston's pin bore. Place the rod small end between the piston pin bosses and slip the pin through to engage the opposite piston's pin boss. Because the pin is free to float, retaining clips must be installed in the outboard pin bosses to prevent the pin from walking out.

The two common types of pin clips are the spiral-lock style and the C-clip style. Each type requires its own unique installation method. The spiral-lock style is gently spread apart with your fingernails, far enough to expose the ends of the clip. Insert one end of the clip into the pin bore's clip groove, and "spiral" the clip into the groove by walking it into the groove with a small flat-tip screwdriver until the entire clip snaps into place. Tap the installed clip with the wrist pin to verify that it's fully seated. Install the opposite-side clip in the same manner. C-clip installation requires inserting one end of the clip into the pin bore groove and walking the remainder of the clip into the groove by applying pressure in a clockwise or counterclockwise direction. Installing either style of clip can be frustrating for inexperienced

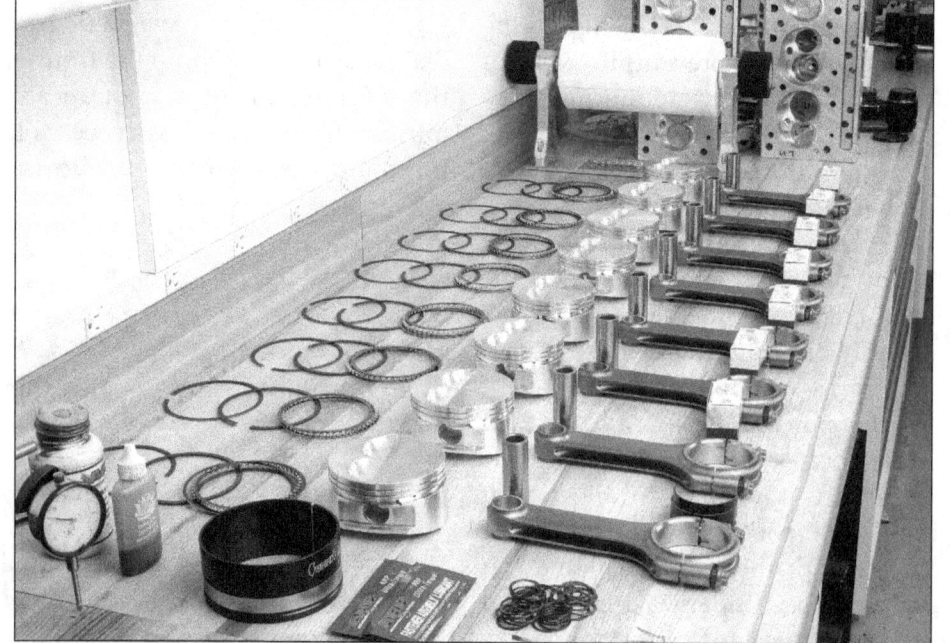

Organize all rods, pistons, bearings, rod bolts, and rings in order prior to assembly, on a clean work surface.

With the rod secured in a rod vise, loosen the rod bolts. Never place rods in an unpadded bench vise.

FINAL ASSEMBLY

installers, so patience is required. It's absolutely critical to verify that both clips are fully seated in their grooves. Specialty clip installation tools are available to aid in installation.

Some pistons require a single spiral-lock clip at each boss; others require two spiral locks at each end. Your new piston set includes pins and the appropriate locks.

When preparing to install pistons to rods, pay attention to piston orientation. For engines that have one intake and one exhaust valve per cylinder, valve reliefs must be positioned inboard, closer to the intake side of the head. Intake and exhaust valve pockets must be oriented to match the valve layout of the heads. Some pistons feature a mark on the dome that indicates which side of the piston must face toward the front of the engine.

Connecting rod big ends feature a larger chamfer on one side. The chamfered side must face the crank journal's fillet.

After the pistons have been installed to the rods, install the piston rings. If the piston has a short compression distance (where the oil ring groove intersects the wrist pin bore), the ring set includes a support rail for each piston. This rail provides oil ring support at the two void areas above the wrist pin bores. The

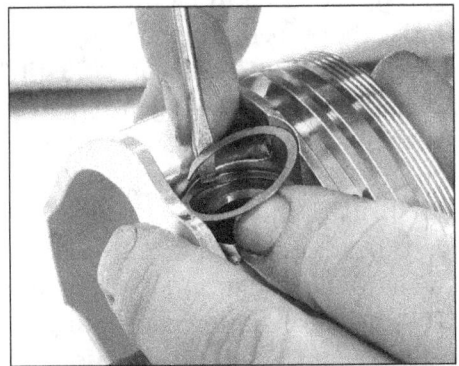

If the piston and rod is designed to use a free-floating wrist pin, lube the pin and insert the pin through the piston pin holes and rod small end bore, making sure that the piston is properly oriented to the rod, considering which cylinder bore the rod and piston will be installed. To prevent the wrist pin from sliding out of position, install retaining clips. If using spiral-lock–style clips, gently spread the clip apart with your fingernails, enter one end of the clip into the piston's pin bore groove, and walk the clip into the groove until it fully snaps into place. C-clips are installed in a similar manner by starting with one end into the groove and working the clip along its radius until it snaps into the groove.

If an oil ring support rail is required, install it to the floor of the oil ring groove and make sure that the rail's small male dimple faces downward and is centered over one of the open void areas above the wrist pin bore.

When installing the second and top compression rings, you must use a piston ring spreader tool. Spread the ring only far enough to slip over the piston. Do not overspread, bend, or twist these rings.

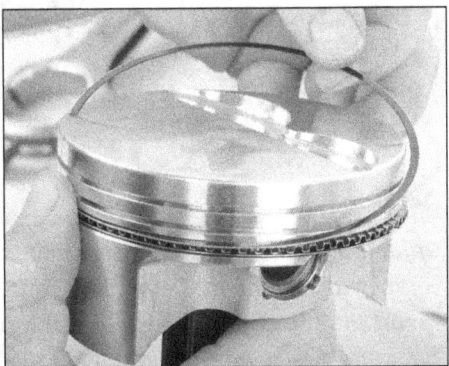

After installing the oil expansion ring, install the lower oil ring rail, capturing the lower lip of the expansion ring. Make sure that the expansion ring's ends have not overlapped. They must remain butted flush. Then install the upper oil ring rail, capturing the upper lip of the expansion ring. Oil ring rails may be installed by hand, spiraling them into place.

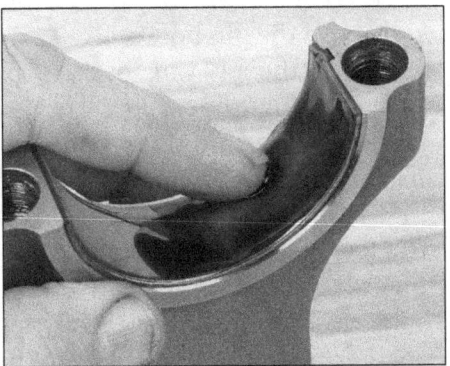

With the upper rod bearing and rod bearing saddle clean and dry, install the upper rod bearing with the bearing tang registered into the saddle's tang groove, and coat the exposed bearing surface with assembly lube. Pay attention to the rod bearing halves, as they are marked on the back for upper and lower locations. Bearings marked UPPER install to the rod saddle, while bearings marked LOWER install to the rod caps.

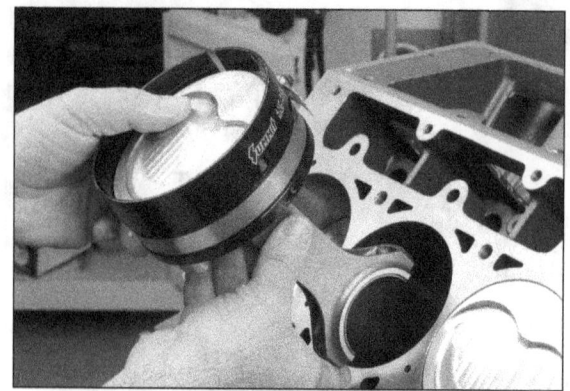

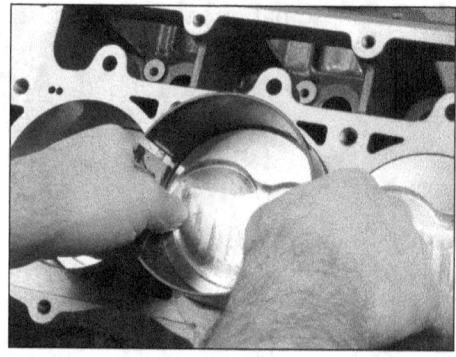

Rather than using an archaic piston ring compressor tool that is difficult to control, the best route is to use a one-piece machined ring compressor that is specifically sized for your cylinder bore diameter. An alternative is an adjustable compressor, which is very similar to a one-piece tool but is adjustable within a range of diameters. The inside of the compressor features a tapered surface that compresses the rings as the piston is pushed through. Insert the big end of the rod and the piston skirts into the tool until the ring package has been captured. With the crank's rod journal positioned at or near bottom dead center and the cylinder wall clean and oiled, carefully insert the assembly into the cylinder until the piston skirts enter the bore and the compressor tool bottom is flush with the block deck.

Holding the compressor tool down firmly, push the piston into the bore until the entire ring package has entered the bore.

support ring must be installed first. The support ring features a small male dimple, which must face downward, directly at the top of one of the pin bores. This small dot protrusion prevents the support ring from rotating, keeping its gap away from either void above the pin bores.

Install the oil ring package by first installing the support rail (if needed). Make sure the support rail sits flush at the bottom of the oil ring groove. Next, install the oil ring (the low-tempered wavy/convoluted ring) to the oil ring groove.

Next, install the lower oil ring rail, making sure that it locks into the lower lip of the oil ring and that the oil ring ends have not overlapped.

Next, install the upper oil ring rail. Follow the piston or ring maker's recommendations for orientation of the oil ring rail gaps.

Oil rings and rails can be installed by hand, by gently spiraling them onto the piston and into the groove. To install the second ring and the top compression ring, you must use a ring-spreader tool to gently spread the ring gap to slip onto the piston.

Do not bend or spiral the second or top rings; this may warp or break the rings. After installing each ring, check for free rotation of the ring within its groove. If a ring sticks, inspect closely for the cause of the obstruction and correct as needed. Again, follow piston or ring maker recommendations for orientation of all ring end gaps.

Because the above information involves final assembly, I did not address piston ring end-gap checking, which needs to be done during earlier test fitting. Always check the gap of each ring in its intended cylinder bore before installing rings to pistons. Some rings are "file-fit," requiring filing the gap ends as needed to obtain the correct installed end gap.

Install the upper connecting rod bearings to the rod saddles, with both saddle and bearing dry. Dry-install the lower rod bearings to the rod caps. Apply engine assembly lube to the exposed bearing faces. Apply a coat of engine oil to the cylinder wall. Some prefer to also apply

If you need assistance in continuing to push the piston down, use a special long-nose piston hammer. While guiding the rod big end and its bearing onto the crank journal, push or tap the piston gently until the rod's upper bearing seats against the journal.

FINAL ASSEMBLY

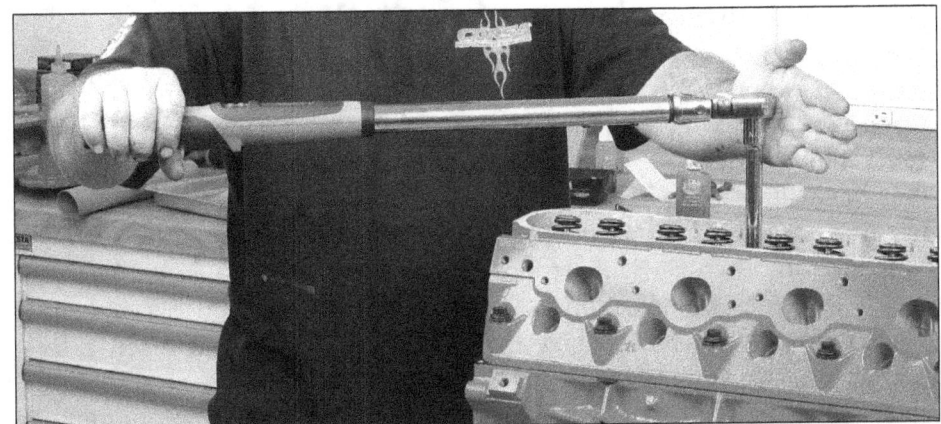

Torque each rod bolt according to recommended value.

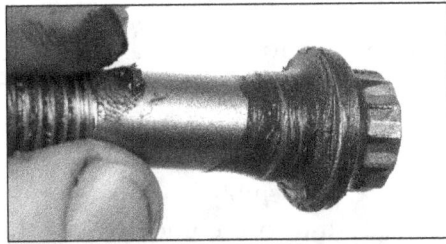

Always use the fastener lube that is recommended for your rod bolts, and follow the rod or rod bolt maker's specifications for bolt torque and/or stretch. Apply fastener lube to the bolt threads and to the underside of the bolt head.

oil to the rings. Orient the piston ring gaps in the clock positions recommended by the piston maker. The primary goal is to avoid a potential lineup of ring end gaps from one ring to another.

Rotate the crankshaft to place the intended rod journal at or near BDC to minimize the chance of nicking the journal during rod installation and to provide optimum access to the rod bolts.

Using a clean piston ring compressor tool, compress the entire ring package to allow the ring package to enter the bore. Various types of ring compressors are available. The safest and easiest to use are the types that feature a one-piece machined construction, with the inside diameter sized for a specific bore diameter; or an adjustable style that can be pre-adjusted for bore diameter. Both styles feature a slight inside taper that compresses the rings as the piston is pushed through the tool. These styles of ring compressors allow you to easily slip the piston and ring package into the bore with simple hand pressure. Install the ring compressor onto the piston, capturing all rings. Carefully insert the rod into the bore, followed by inserting the piston skirts into the bore. Seat the bottom of the ring compressor firmly against the block deck and begin to push the piston into the bore. The piston and rod must be oriented properly so that the rod big end bearing squarely engages the rod journal. If you feel a solid resistance while pushing the piston, stop. The big end of the rod may be contacting the crank counterweight or one of the rings may have slipped out from under the compressor tool and may be trapped against the block deck. Examine, determine the cause, correct, and then proceed.

After the top ring has entered the bore, remove the compressor tool. Using one hand to guide the rod big end onto the rod journal, continue to push the piston with the other hand until the rod's upper bearing gently seats onto the crank's rod journal. If you need assistance in moving the piston deep enough into the cylinder for rod bearing contact to the journal, a special long-nose plastic piston hammer is useful. Tap the piston lightly while guiding the rod onto the journal.

When the rod and upper bearing have contacted the journal, apply assembly lube onto the lower rod bearing's exposed surface and install the rod cap, making sure to properly align the cap to the rod in the

If monitoring bolt stretch, after applying torque, place the same stretch gauge, without disturbing the dial setting, onto the rod bolt and determine how far the bolt has stretched. Compare this to the specified stretch. In this example, maximum bolt stretch was listed at .0055 inch, and the reading on the gauge shows that the bolt has stretched .005 inch, safely within its spec.

correct orientation, with the etched numbers on rod and cap aligned, and with the chamfered side of the cap facing the journal fillet.

Clean the rod bolts, then apply fastener assembly lube to bolt threads and to the underside of the bolt heads. Hand-install and snug both rod bolts, and torque to the specified value according to the rod or rod bolt maker's specifications, or to OEM specifications if using new OEM rod bolts.

An alternative bolt tightening method favored by many builders is referred to as the bolt stretch method. When rod bolts are fully tightened, they begin to enter an elastic state to provide proper clamping load. By monitoring how far the bolt stretches as it is torqued, this provides a more accurate determination of clamping load. Aftermarket performance rod bolts feature a small dimple at each end to accommodate the stretch gauge anvils. Before installing a rod bolt, place the bolt onto a specialty rod bolt stretch gauge, with the pointed anvils contacting the bolt ends, under a slight preload. Zero the gauge by rotating the gauge dial. You now have a reference of bolt length in its relaxed state. Without disturbing the gauge dial, remove the bolt from the gauge and install the bolt. Torque the bolt just short of its specified torque value. For instance, if the torque spec is 65 ft-lbs, torque to 55 ft-lbs. Then carefully install the same stretch gauge onto the bolt and determine how far the bolt has stretched. For example, the rod maker may specify that stretch is not to exceed .005 inch. If the bolt has only stretched, say, .002 inch at this point, apply additional torque of 60 ft-lbs and recheck stretch. Usually, tightening to the specified torque value reveals proper stretch that does not exceed the maximum, but creeping up on stretch allows you to reach your goal without potentially overstretching the bolt. Each builder may have his or her own method, for instance, such as simply torqueing to full valve and then verifying stretch. Tightening rod bolts by monitoring stretch provides greater accuracy and consistency of clamping loads, rather than depending only on torque value, which may be affected by the friction encountered during tightening. This method is more time-consuming, as the gauge must be zeroed for each rod bolt prior to bolt installation and tightening.

Do not assume that all rod bolts are manufactured to exactly the same length. In even the best rod bolts, there are variances of a few thousandths of an inch. The gauge must be zeroed for each individual bolt in its relaxed state before installation.

Installing rod bolts by using the stretch method is not mandatory, but for those builders who are concerned with the details, it offers a higher degree of precision.

Instead of waiting until all pistons and rods have been installed, after fully installing each rod/piston assembly, rotate the crankshaft to verify smooth operation. If there's a

When all rod bolts are fully tightened, use a feeler gauge to measure rod end sideplay.

problem, you'll know which piston/rod assembly is the cause.

After each pair of rods has been installed to a common rod journal, check for rod sideplay. Again, this should have been checked during test fitting, but perform this check again during final assembly. Manually spread the rod big ends away from each other and insert a feeler gauge between the rods. Refer to your engine's specifications, but generally sideplay should be in the range of .010 to .018 inch or so.

Timing

Assuming the engine features a chain-driven camshaft gear, soak the new chain in clean 30W engine oil overnight. If not already installed, install the appropriate locating key into the crankshaft's keyway and install the crank gear. Depending on design, the gear may slip over the snout and engage the key by hand, or it may require a slight interference fit. If an interference fit is required, you may heat the gear in a conventional oven, which expands the gear enough to allow a hand installation, or you may use a soft aluminum or brass tube of the appropriate diameter to tap the gear into place. Either way, apply a thin coat of oil or assembly lube onto the crank snout before gear installation. Be sure to install the gear in the correct orientation, with the side that features a slight inner diameter chamfer facing the block and the timing dot indicator facing forward. Verify that the gear is seated fully onto the snout.

Rotate the crankshaft to place the number-1 piston at TDC. Lip the cam gear onto the cam and rotate the cam until the cam gear timing mark is at six o'clock. Remove the cam gear, install the timing chain to the cam gear, engage the chain onto the crank gear, and install the cam gear to the cam, making sure that the two timing dots are aligned. Pay attention to the timing set instructions for gear clock positions.

Commonly, the dot on the crank gear may be at twelve o'clock and the dot on the cam gear at six o'clock (dots facing each other). Rotate the crank two full revolutions and confirm that the timing dots remain aligned. This theoretically sets cam timing at zero. Although this is a good starting point, it's recommended to degree the cam to ensure correct cam timing. Refer to CarTech's *Modern Engine Blueprinting Techniques* for tips on cam degreeing.

Secure the cam gear to the cam with the appropriate bolt(s), applying a medium thread locker to the bolt threads and tightening to specified torque value.

Prior to installing the timing cover, if your camshaft is a roller type, a thrust button may be needed to adjust the amount of camshaft fore/aft movement. The thrust button installs to the center hole of the cam gear.

Depending on oil pump location and the length of its pickup tube, the pickup tube must be secured in the proper position. This short tube is secured via two mounting bolts and a support brace. An oil pump pickup with a long tube features a support bracket that attaches to one of the main cap fasteners. By the way, if the build features a windage tray, be sure to check for crank and rod big end clearance, especially if the crankshaft features a longer-than-stock stroke length. If interference is found, the tray may need to be trimmed or spaced farther away with spacer washers.

Oil Pump and Pickup

Avoid installing the oil pump and pickup tube before all pistons and rods have been installed, from an access standpoint. It's always a good idea to prime the pump before installation. This may be done by removing its cover plate and applying oil or assembly lube to the gears and reinstalling the cover. Depending on engine type, the oil pump may be installed to the bottom of the engine or it may be installed to the crank snout, as in GM's LS engine family), or, as in older Mopar applications, the pump may be externally mounted to the block. If the pump installs to the bottom of the engine, onto the rear main cap, for example, or at the front and features an intermediate drive shaft for the distributor, install a new drive shaft to the pump and install the pump using a new bolt and torque to specification. If the pump is directly driven by the crankshaft snout, it must be installed after installing the timing set.

After installing the pump, install its pickup tube and screen to the pump. Depending on the style and length of the pickup tube, the tube may require additional bracing by attaching its tube bracket (if featured)

Initially install the camshaft and crankshaft gears so that the timing marks align, with the cam gear mark at six o'clock and the crank gear mark at twelve o'clock. This provides a good starting point prior to degreeing the cam.

If the engine features a crank-driven oil pump, as shown in this LS example, the timing set must be installed prior to pump installation.

CHAPTER 14

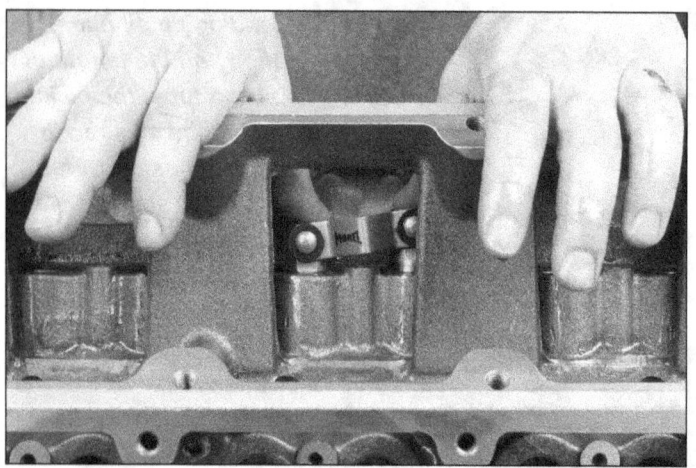

When roller lifters are featured, each pair must be registered together to keep the lifter roller bearings in plane with the cam lobes. Depending on engine design, various methods are available. These roller lifters are paired together with a "tie bar" that allows lifter travel and prevents lifter rotation. Lifters should easily slip into their bores with no resistance. Recommended clearance is likely around .0015 inch or so, depending on the engine.

to one of the main cap bolts. In this case, one of the main caps likely features a threaded stud tip to accept the pickup tube's bracket.

If you plan to install a windage tray, it should have been test-fitted earlier to verify that neither the crank counterweights nor rod big ends contact the tray. If you are installing a windage tray, verify again that you have adequate clearance by slowly rotating the crank while observing clearances.

Lifters

With lifter bores clean, lube the lifter bodies with oil or assembly lube. If you are using flat-tappet lifters coat the faces with the appropriate extreme-pressure lube using the same lube that was applied to the camshaft lobes. If using roller lifters, lube the roller bearings with assembly lube. Insert the lifters into their bores. Lifters should slip in easily. For flat-tappet lifters, also verify that they rotate within their bores easily. Roller lifters, by design, must not be allowed to rotate. Depending on design, roller lifters may be prevented from rotating with the use of "dogbone" guides, plastic lifter trays that guide a bank of four lifters (as in OEM LS engine designs) or by lifters that are paired together with pivoting "tie bars." Any of these approaches serve to keep the roller bearings in plane with the cam lobes.

Heads

With block and head decks perfectly clean and dry, install the appropriate locating dowel pins or sleeves to the block decks. Do not ignore this. Don't rely on only head bolt or stud locations to properly register the head to the block. Carefully install the head gaskets to the block decks, verifying gasket orientation. Many head gaskets are labeled "FRONT" to indicate orientation. If so labeled, the word "FRONT" should be located toward the front of the block, and the label should be visible after the gasket is installed. If installed improperly, you can easily block off critical water passages. Double-check gasket placement before installing the heads. If using MLS (multi-layer steel) cylinder head gaskets, make sure that both the gaskets and your hands are clean before installing. MLS head gaskets feature a special sealing coating. *Do not* wipe the gaskets with any solvent, to avoid damaging this sealant. Do not apply any additional sealing chemicals to either side of the gasket (although some exceptions may apply when dealing with certain vintage engines that require composite or copper gaskets).

Carefully position the cylinder head onto the block deck, making sure that it sits flush and has registered onto the locating dowels. Inspect carefully to make sure that the head

Prior to installing head gaskets, the decks must be absolutely clean and dry. Be sure to orient the head gaskets correctly to avoid blocking off critical water or oil passages. This MLS gasket is labeled "FRONT" at the forward upper corner. Also, if the cylinder bores have been oversized, verify that the gasket bores are correctly sized for the bore size.

is not held away from the gasket and deck before installing the fasteners.

Depending on the application, cylinder head clamping may involve OEM bolts or aftermarket bolts or studs, the choice of which dictates the tightening method.

Regardless of the type of fastener, always install new head fasteners. OEM torque-to-yield bolts must never be reused, as these have already been stretched to near their yield point and do not provide proper clamping load. Even if the bolts or studs are not torque-to-yield, the history of these fasteners may not be known from a standpoint of their strength status, so don't take a chance. Always use new fasteners.

Make sure that all female thread holes in the block decks are clean and that threads are in good condition. This should have been done previously, using a dedicated chaser tap to clean and restore the existing threads. Never use a common cutting tap; it can remove material and weaken the threads.

Lubricate the fastener threads with the appropriate lube. This may involve clean engine oil or a quality low-friction thread fastener lube. When using aftermarket performance fasteners, always follow the recommendation of the manufacturer (for example, when using ARP bolts or studs, use their Ultra-Torque fastener assembly lube only).

In some applications, one or more head bolt holes in the block may be open to water, in which case a specialty high-temperature thread sealant is needed (available from fastener makers such as ARP).

When using head bolts, apply the correct lube not only to the threads, but also to the underside of the bolt heads and to both sides of washers (if featured). This provides a more accurate torque application.

If head studs are to be used, lube the lower threads and install the studs only hand-tight. Do not apply excessive torque when threading the studs into the block. The clamping load is achieved by tightening the nuts.

Gasket makers and some high-performance piston makers provide orientation markings. This Mahle MLS gasket front is labeled, and the JE piston features an arrow that indicates which side of the piston needs to face forward. If head studs are to be installed, some builders prefer to preinstall them to serve as additional guides during head placement.

Carefully install the cylinder head, making sure that it fully seats against the gasket and deck. If studs have been installed, be very careful not to nick the head deck by bumping it into the stud tips.

CHAPTER 14

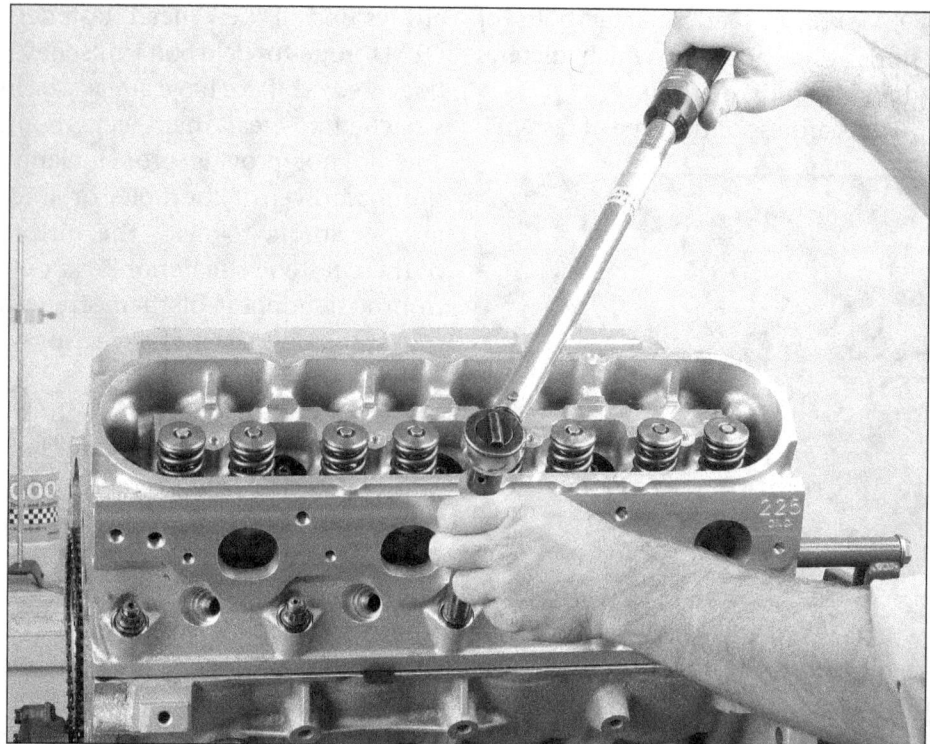

Tighten all head fasteners in the correct pattern and at the correct torque values, both specified by the head maker. If using OEM torque-angle bolts, you need to adhere to the published torque and additional angle rotation. For any high-performance application, the use of high-performance aftermarket head bolts or studs is highly recommended, from a standpoint of strength, durability, and simplicity of tightening.

Apply the proper lube to the stud upper threads and to the underside of the nuts and to both sides of washers.

When using head studs, perform a stud fitment check to the block deck before installing the gasket and head. With a stud hand-tight, check to see if the stud's lower threads disappear into the threaded hole. If the unthread shank portion of the stud digs into the hole, this could potentially create a stress area that could result in cracking the block deck.

Tighten all head fasteners in the proper pattern to evenly spread the clamping load. Tightening methods vary depending on the type of fasteners being used. If the bolts are new OEM "torque-plus-angle" type, tighten to the specified torque value, followed by additional rotation of the bolt heads to the specified number of degrees. The angle tightening procedure can be performed in several ways. You can apply a small paint dot onto each bolt head, which provides a reference in terms of angle rotation, or you can use an inexpensive angle gauge that fits onto your socket wrench. The easiest and most accurate approach is to use a combination torque/angle wrench. Adjust the torque setting, tighten to the specified torque, then switch to the tool's angle mode, set the desired angle, and continue to tighten until that angle has been reached.

However, if using new high-performance aftermarket bolts (or studs), you only need to adhere to a specified torque value. When tightening, apply slow and smooth effort to the torque wrench. Avoid quick jerks, which can result in inaccurate loads.

Pushrods and Rocker Arms

At the point of final assembly, your pushrod lengths have already been determined (at least they should have been by now). Apply a high-pressure engine assembly lube to each tip of the pushrods. Carefully insert all pushrods, making sure that the lower tips engage into the respective lifter cups.

Prelubricate the rocker arms (and rocker shafts, if so equipped), at all pivot and friction points prior to installation. Avoid tightening rockers against excessive valve-spring pressure. At each location, the camshaft lobe should be placed on its base circle. Tighten the rocker arm bolts to the specified torque value. Some intake rocker arm bolt holes may be open to intake runners (for example, with the LS engine). In those applications, be sure to apply a thread sealer to the intake rocker bolt threads.

Although rocker arm to valve-stem tips should have been checked during test fitting, verify that all rocker arm tips are reasonably centered to each respective valve tip.

If the application requires pushrod guideplates, install these prior to the rockers, and pay attention to location as you tighten the bolts to prevent pushrod-to-plate rubbing.

If using adjustable rocker arms, adjust valve lash at each rocker arm location with the respective cam lobe on its base circle. Adjust the amount of valve lash following the specifications for your engine.

FINAL ASSEMBLY

Lube both pushrod tips prior to installation. With the rocker installed, verify that the rocker is properly centered over the valve tip and that rocker tip sweep across the valve tip is acceptable. Some rockers are nonadjustable and are simply tightened to a torque value, in which case pushrod length is critical. If rockers are adjustable, secure the retaining nut with a wrench while adjusting valve lash.

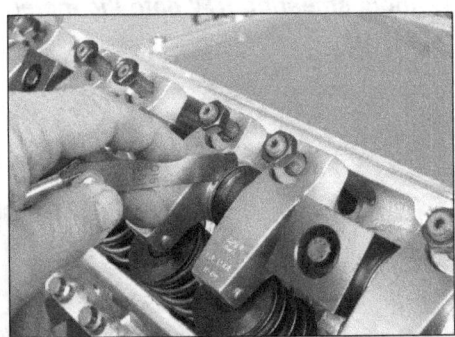

Shaft-mounted rocker arm assemblies must be adjusted to center rocker tips at the valves and to provide the specified clearance between rockers and spacers.

Intake Manifold

Depending on engine design, the intake manifold may require sealing both at the port locations and at the front and rear rails. An LS engine, for example, only requires port sealing, while an early generation small-block Chevy also requires a seal at the front and rear rails where the manifold meets the block. Some engines, such as early Chrysler or Pontiac engines, for example, may feature a valley plate that seals the lifter valley.

Depending on the engine and the builder's preference, OEM-style gaskets may be used to seal the front and rear block rail areas, while some prefer to apply a bead of RTV instead of using rail gaskets. Early generation Chevy engines specify rubber or cork/rubber end-rail seals, which commonly posed leakage issues as they often moved under compression. Many builders prefer to apply a bead of RTV on the rails to obtain a seal between the intake manifold and block rails instead of using the OEM-style rail seals.

Again, depending on the particular engine, port sealing may involve a one-piece gasket at each bank or individual O-ring seals at each port. If a one-piece gasket is required, you may apply a thin coating of RTV around each port, which aids in holding the gasket in place during assembly and will provide additional sealing to compensate for any minor voids or pits in the mating surfaces. If each port requires an O-ring, lightly lubricate the O-rings with a nonharmful

If the intake manifold will be sealed with a pair of one-piece gaskets, secure the gaskets to the heads for proper port and bolt hole position. Depending on design, the gaskets might register to the heads via built-in locating pins or may require a thin application of RTV. However, some manifolds feature machined grooves around the intake ports that are sealed with O-rings.

lube such as Vaseline or white lithium grease. This helps to keep the O-rings in place during installation and allows the O-ring surfaces to slide a bit to prevent damage in case you move the manifold around a bit during alignment.

Always tighten any intake manifold to the specified torque value, in a crisscross pattern, to evenly spread the clamping load and to prevent potential manifold warpage.

Depending on engine design, some intake manifold bolt holes may be open to oil, requiring a thread sealant on the bolts. Regardless of the design, however, it's a good idea to apply some type of thread lubricant to the bolt threads to achieve accurate torque values. If using aftermarket bolts, follow the recommendation provided by the bolt maker. If stainless steel bolts are being used, always lightly coat the threads with the proper lube to avoid potential thread galling.

Regardless of whether or not the intake manifold accepts a carburetor or a fuel injection throttle body, be sure to seal the plenum opening with tape (preferably body shop tape) to

Tighten intake manifold bolts to the torque value listed by the manufacturer, and always follow the recommended tightening sequence to avoid warpage and leaks.

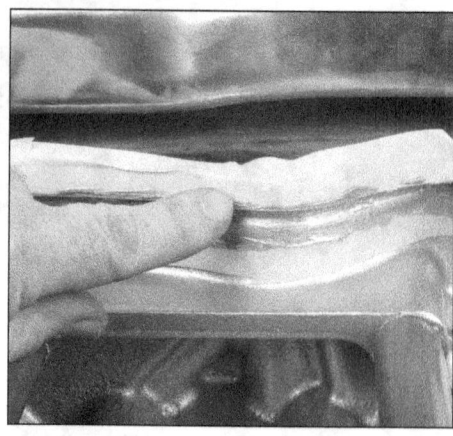

For intake manifold applications where the front and rear of the manifold must seal to the engine block, the use of a quality RTV is often preferred to rubber or cork/rubber rail seals. If applying RTV, one trick is to first mask off the manifold and block edges. After the manifold is fully tightened, any excess RTV can be wiped off without smearing RTV onto the metal surfaces.

This Holley intake manifold features machined grooves around each port, to be sealed with supplied O-rings. This provides good sealing while eliminating the need for a sometimes-ugly one-piece gasket.

prevent foreign objects from entering until the carb or throttle body is installed. If the intake manifold features bung holes for fuel injectors, install the injectors now or tape off the holes.

Distributor

If the engine uses a distributor, lubricate the distributor driven gear with engine assembly lube. Remember to install the distributor's seal where the distributor housing contacts the mounting area. Using a long flat-tip screwdriver, gently rotate the drive shaft to align to the distributor's shaft. With the number-1 piston at TDC on its firing stroke, install the distributor so that the rotor tip approaches alignment with the number-1 spark plug location of the distributor cap. Depending on engine design, the rotor may rotate clockwise or counterclockwise. The distributor's shaft tip engages to the oil pump's intermediate drive shaft. Check the overlap engagement of the oil pump driveshaft to the driven tang in the distributor nose, which should be about 1/4 inch. Never force the distributor's gear engagement. If aligned properly, it should slip into place easily. Do not tighten the distributor hold-down bolt fully because you need to adjust timing during initial firing. Carefully follow the firing order and route plug wires accordingly.

Be sure to use the correct distributor gear material that is compatible with your camshaft's gear. Using the wrong distributor gear can result in severe tooth damage to the distributor gear and/or the camshaft's gear teeth.

Four types of distributor gears are available: composite, bronze, cast-iron, and hardened steel. If your cam is cast-iron, use a cast-iron or composite distributor gear. If the cam

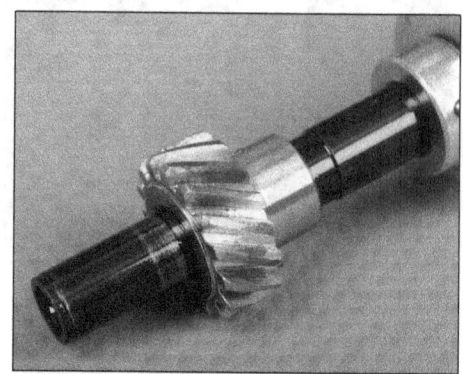

The distributor driven gear material must be compatible with the camshaft material to avoid damage. Distributor gears are available in composite, bronze, cast-iron, or hardened steel materials. A bronze gear is pictured here, which is compatible with a steel billet camshaft. Selecting the wrong distributor gear can lead to quick and severe damage to the distributor gear, cam gear, or both. Here, a brass gear was used with a billet cam. Note the severe tooth damage, which required a complete engine teardown.

FINAL ASSEMBLY

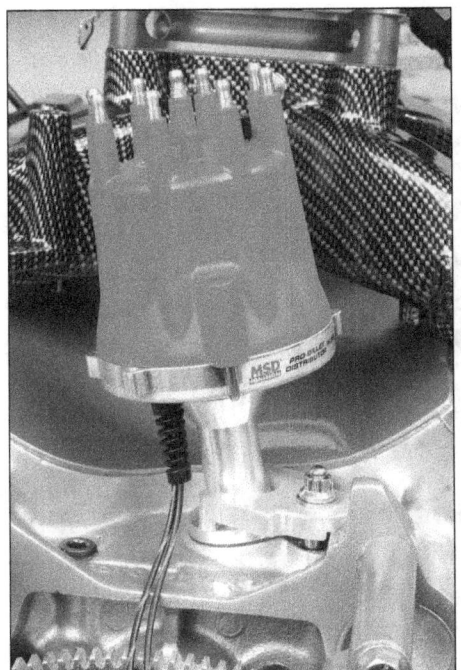

Rotate the oil pump intermediate shaft to allow proper alignment of the distributor's rotor to the distributor cap contacts. Remember to install the required gasket to the underside of the distributor shaft mounting boss.

Before installing the timing cover, apply a bit of oil to the front seal lips, unless the seal is PTFE, in which case it should be installed dry. In the majority of cases, the timing cover must be installed prior to the oil pan.

For engine designs that feature a front and/or rear cover that mates to the oil pan, consider laying a straightedge across the block pan rail and bottom face of the cover as you tighten the cover bolts to ensure even gasket sealing.

If using an increased stroke crankshaft, make sure to check for oil pan clearance before installing the pan. With the engine upside-down on the stand and the pan simply placed in position, check for any potential interference. In areas where the oil and timing cover meet at the corners, apply a dab of RTV at these intersecting points.

is ductile iron, use a hardened steel or composite distributor gear. If the cam is machined from steel billet, use a bronze or composite distributor gear. If in doubt, use a composite gear; this type of gear is safe to use with all camshaft materials.

Timing Cover, Rear Cover, Oil Pan and Valvecovers

The order in which you install the front timing cover, rear cover (if used), and oil pan can vary depending on engine design. In many cases, the timing cover must be in place prior to mounting the oil pan. If the front cover and/or rear cover share the oil pan gasket at their respective locations, in addition to installing the proper gaskets, apply a small dab of RTV where the oil pan and cover meet at each corner of the block. In most cases, two small-diameter locating dowel pins are at the front of the block to properly locate the timing cover. Don't forget to install these pins if needed. If you're dealing with an LS engine, don't forget to install the plastic O-ringed oil restrictor "barbell" plug at the rear of the block prior to installing the rear cover. Always use the gaskets recommended for the engine and torque all bolts to the specified value. If you are using aftermarket rocker arms that are larger than stock, make sure that your valvecovers provide adequate rocker arm clearance. In some cases, taller valvecovers are needed.

If your block is equipped with a mechanical fuel pump mounting boss but you plan to run an electric pump, don't forget to install a block-off plate at the mounting boss. Coat a new fuel pump gasket lightly with RTV and install the gasket and plate. Follow OEM specs for the mounting bolts.

If you have changed to a different oil pan and pickup tube, or if you plan to run an aftermarket engine oil

CHAPTER 14

Certain engines, such as older Ford and Chrysler V-8s, feature a separate water pump mounting base that is sandwiched between the block and pump. Be sure to seal both with the appropriate gaskets.

dipstick, add the amount of oil specified for your oil pan sump. Then insert the dipstick and determine if you need a different length.

Water Pump

Whether installing a belt-driven or electric water pump, install with new gaskets. Depending on the application, water pump gaskets may be composite or aluminum that feature a printed bead seal. If composite gaskets are to be used, apply a thin coat of RTV or Indian Head gasket shellac to both sides of each gasket. If the gaskets have metal cores with printed sealing beads, install these dry. Don't guess at bolt tightness. Follow the recommended torque value and tighten using a calibrated torque wrench, in a crisscross pattern (alternating from top left to lower right, etc.) to evenly spread the clamping load. If a gasket sealer was applied to the gaskets, allow it to cure for at least 24 hours before firing the engine. If you plan to run the engine on an engine dynamometer, be sure to remove the thermostat; the dyno system provides a regulated water flow, and the thermostat will be in the way.

Electric water pumps, such as the Meziere unit shown here, are extremely efficient and eliminate parasitic belt drag horsepower loss. The pump shown here on an LS build also features a free wheeling idler pulley that accommodates an OEM serpentine belt drive for other accessories.

Crankshaft Balancer

Apply engine oil to the timing cover's front seal before attempting to install the balancer/dampener. Also apply a light coat of oil or anti-seize to the crank snout surface. Many balancers feature an interference fit onto the crankshaft snout. Never force a balancer onto the snout by hitting it with a hammer. The balancer must be drawn into place smoothly and evenly, using a dedicated balancer installation tool. These tool kits include threaded mandrels in popular thread sizes that engage into the crank snout's threaded hole. An installation plate, large nuts, and a bearing ride on the threaded mandrel. Hold the end of the mandrel's hex stationary with one wrench and turn the larger nut with another wrench; this allows you to draw the balancer onto the snout. If you don't own a balancer installation tool, you need to buy, borrow, or rent one. This is the only acceptable way to install an interference-fit balancer. Tighten the large nut until the rear-most surface of the balancer makes full contact and stops.

Remove the installation tool and install a new crankshaft balancer bolt, torqueing either to OEM specification if using an OEM bolt, or to the specification recommended by the aftermarket bolt maker.

A crankshaft balancer must be drawn onto the crank snout smoothly. Never try to force a balancer on by striking it. Always use the appropriate dampener installer tool as shown here. Hold the hex at the rear end of the threaded mandrel steady while tightening the large nut. A bearing is located between the nut and adapter plate.

www.ingramcontent.com/pod-product-compliance
Lightning Source LLC
Chambersburg PA
CBHW081446070526
44586CB00019B/2254